Adulting

Adulting

HOW TO BECOME A GROWN-UP
IN 468 EASY(ISH) STEPS

Kelly Williams Brown

GRAND CENTRAL
PUBLISHING

NEW YORK   BOSTON

All line drawings by the author.

Grand Central Publishing
Hachette Book Group
1290 Avenue of the Americas
New York, NY 10104

www.HachetteBookGroup.com

Printed in the United States of America

RRD-C

First Edition: May 2013
20 19 18 17 16 15 14 13 12

Grand Central Publishing is a division of Hachette Book Group, Inc. The Grand Central Publishing name and logo is a trademark of Hachette Book Group, Inc.

The Hachette Speakers Bureau provides a wide range of authors for speaking events. To find out more, go to www.hachettespeakersbureau.com or call (866) 376-6591.

The publisher is not responsible for websites (or their content) that are not owned by the publisher.

Library of Congress Cataloging-in-Publication Data
Brown, Kelly Williams.
    Adulting: how to become a grown-up in 468 easy(ish) steps / Kelly Williams Brown. — 1st ed.
        p. cm.
    Includes index.
    ISBN 978-1-4555-1690-2   1. Young adults—Humor.   2. Adulthood—Humor.   I. Title.
    PN6231.A26B76 2013
    818'.602—dc23

                                                            2012033589

To Barbara, Joel, and Barbara

Contents

Adulting

Introduction

What's that you say? You're a colossal sham who will never have your life in order? One who eats microwave taquitos in lieu of breakfast? One who has many dead bugs trapped between the windowpanes in your bedroom, which doesn't make sense, because *how did they even get there?* One whose actions do not reflect the fact that, chronologically, you are absolutely, completely, and undeniably an adult?

Yes. Of course you think that. Everyone does. There is not one adult on this earth who has not felt the deep, unsettling feeling that their life is wobbly and unmanageable, no matter how diligently they sort the recycling and iron their sensible slacks. This is supported by the popular, though incorrect, perception that you're surrounded by people who have it together while you flop around like a fish who can't remember to pay her water bill.

I swear I paid this.

We look jealously around at others, noting their lack of grubby visible bra straps or crusty under-eye mascara sprinkles, and it's hard not to be resentful. *Why you and not me?* you think, squinting angrily at this person who probably has a beautiful apartment and an actual career and a boyfriend who never uses a skateboard to go from place to place.

But perhaps he has $12.37 in

↑ Fig. I
Mascara
Sprinkles
(aka failure flakes)

his checking account, or she has no idea how to cook anything, or he slowly lets his car rot from inside rather than pony up the thirty bucks to get the oil changed. Chances are good that person is looking at you the same way.

We all sense our own dysfunction so clearly. And because we can't do that one thing—whether it be keeping a clean house, not feeling shy and awkward at work, or having a credit score of 750—we assign it a high priority on our own personal Things That You Must Be Good At If You Wish To Be A Functional Adult list. We don't remember the fourteen things we do reasonably well; we remember our one arena of miserable failure.

There are certain parts of being a grown-up that come easily to us, and some that...don't. When I asked people what advice they have, they'd say, "Well, this probably seems really obvious, but [thing that was not at all obvious but afterward *did*, in fact, seem obvious and a little embarrassing that someone had to tell a twenty-seven-year-old]."

For example, I am really, really bad at keeping my house clean. I am good at lots of things, but noticing dirt in crevices is not one of them. In fact, I do not even see the crevice itself. It *may as well not exist.* So while I don't need to worry about, say, honing my thank-you-note-writing skills, I do need to figure out how to see the crevices that others do. Then I have to remind myself of those crevices, at least once a week.

It is these small discoveries and decisions that, in the end, allow you to behave like an adult. It's developing those good habits; it's having toast with peanut butter instead of cigarettes for breakfast. It's not always, or even usually, fun. But it has perks—personal pride, financial security, and the feeling of accomplishment and control that comes when you just swap in a new toilet paper roll rather than resorting to fast-food napkins.

You can't control the economy, or whether you're single, or when your cat decides to vomit neon orange tummy contents onto your white rug. *What is she even eating that is that color?* But there are lots of things you can control, and lots of decisions are up to you.

It feels like there are all these things that People Should Know, and if you don't know them, it means you're stupid. You're not. Not knowing how to sew on a button isn't the end of the world. Just figure out *how* to sew it on rather than obsessing about *why* you don't know, then tumbling down into the Why Am I Like This Canyon. Fill that gap, and then not only will you know how to sew on that button, but you will feel all grown-up and powerful. So go forth, perform these steps (if you want!), check them all off, and feel smug at your newfound adult skills.

Here is what I'm trying to tell you: *Adult* isn't a noun, it's a verb. It's the act of making correctly those small decisions that fill our day. It is one that you can practice, and that can be done in concrete steps. And if you slip up and have Diet Coke for breakfast, no one busts in and snatches away your Adult card. Just move forward and have milk tomorrow.

QUESTIONS...AND *ANSWERS*

Q: **What is adulting? Does it have anything to do with adultery?**

A: It does not. The word *adulting* is taking a noun, *adult*, and making it a verb. Actually, this strategy works with many nouns (sandwiching, Nashvilling, bridesmaiding, et cetera). But point being, adult isn't something you are, it's something you do. You are a grown-ass man, or grown-ass woman, and you can act like it even if you don't feel like it on the inside.

Q: **Who are you to tell anyone how to be a grown-up?**

A: I'm Kelly. I'm a reporter for a newspaper in my late twenties who has red hair. You should know this important thing about me: I'm not a super-great grown-up. I'm *okay* at it, and improving steadily, but I'm in no way a model of what adulthood looks like. I am not the Martha Stewart of basic human competence. Lots of times, Comcast has to call and ask nicely, then not-nicely, for me to pay my cable bill. Or my sink is full of gross dishes, which languish as a tomato-sauce-encrusted monument to my shortcomings.

A while ago, I was talking to my beloved friend Ruth, who suggested I write an advice book, perhaps as a way of extricating herself from the bossy advice monologue I was in the middle of. My mind flashed to the dishes, and my disorganization, and all the things that make me fall into I'm-not-a-grown-up anguish, and I felt I was in no position to tell people how to conduct their lives.

But I decided, since I am a reporter whose job is to go find people who are smart and ask them about things and distill what they tell me into something readable, maybe I could treat this as a reporting project.

This is the result. I definitely threw in things I've learned in my six years of being on my own, but most of this is from others. Lots of times, I've identified them by name and quoted them; others just wanted to share their ideas without their names getting in print. Sometimes, it was just someone saying something really smart to me in a bar. I included those tips, too, even though I didn't know their names. Wise random strangers at bars are modern-day Oracles of Delphi, except drunk and sometimes leaving abruptly when it's their turn for karaoke.

Q: Do I have to do all these steps? At once? They're a lot. It's kind of overwhelming.

A: Nope. You do not have to do a single one of them, ever. It's not a moral judgment—you're not a better or worse person if you have a soup ladle, for example. If you don't want to do a step in this book, if it doesn't make sense in your life, then don't— none of the steps is of "Don't commit genocide!" importance.

Nor should you feel like all these things can or should happen overnight. There are lots of steps you've already done, and some you will never do. The point of this book is not to induce guilt about things you can't do or haven't done. Give yourself credit for the things you do, fix the small things you can, accept that some things won't come easy, or may never come. The point of this book is that even though things seem—and are—complicated and difficult, we have control over ourselves. Someone is a grown-up by virtue of acting like one. And no matter who you are, you can be a grown-up.

A SPECIAL NOTE TO MALE READERS

Hello! I am so glad you're here. I'm a big, big fan of your gender. Most of the stuff in this book is for everyone. But watch out! Some specific advice is more geared toward the ladies. If you read some-thing and think, *Huh, I don't think* I *need prenatal vitamins*, then you're probably right. I don't want you to feel left out. There are lots and lots and lots of things written about and for you, including maybe 85 percent of this book. So if you get to a step that doesn't apply, go ahead and skip it, maybe doodling a masculine doodle of a race car or a wizard over the text. Or be transgressive and read it for super-secret insights into us ladyfolk (spoiler alert: *urinary tract infections!*).

DISCUSSION QUESTIONS

1. Which is a better name for mascara sprinkles: Satan's Pepper or Failure Flakes?
2. What is something that other people notice and you never do, even when it's pointed out to you, at which point you act like you knew that all along even though it still isn't totally clear?
3. What is your biggest adult failure to date? Be honest. Did it involve coconut-flavored rum? It did, didn't it? Oh, coconut rum.

1. Get Your Mind Right

The vast majority of this book is full of practical, interacting-with-the-world sorts of steps—wiping your counters or breaking up with your surly boyfriend or whatever. Most of being an adult is not up in your head, it's in your actions. In fact, let's get this out of the way now: Intentions are nice, but ultimately intentions don't really matter because they only exist inside you. Meaning to send a thank-you note but then not doing it is exactly the same as never thinking to send one—that person is still receiving zero thank-you notes.

So, yes. Actions are greater than intentions. But before we get to those actions, there are just a few things you should know.

Step 1: Accept that you are not that special

This is the most difficult and important thing to accept if you wish to be a grown-up: You are not a Special Snowflake.

Step 2: Appreciate those who disagree with step 1

Well, you are to some people. Your parents, presumably, love you very much and think you are perhaps the most adorable, talented thing ever to prance upon this earth. Your friends agree with them, as do your favorite teachers, as does your significant other. When there is a You Parade, these people will be the flag bearers, the drum majors and

also, you know, I would be remiss not to mention my internship, which...

The Specialest Snowflake of all

majorettes, so make sure you are always flag bearing and drum majoring for them, too. These people who think so highly of us are very special and precious, and we must treasure them. Because here is the truth: Most of the world doesn't give a flying fuck about you.

Step 3: Don't get hurt when the world doesn't care about you

It's not as depressing as it sounds. It's not as though the world *hates* you—it just has no idea who you are. It is, at best, indifferent to your wants and needs, your preferences, your pet peeves, and so on. When you walk into a new office, new city, new country, whatever, you are starting from scratch and cannot call upon that loving capital that your friends and family have for you. You sometimes find patches of immediately friendly people, but that won't be the rule. It is now up to you to find and surround yourself with people for whom you feel affection and respect.

People will come to care about you, but only if you give them a valid reason. Don't assume they'll give you love like your parents, emotional support like your best friend, and cheerful feedback like a soccer coach for seven-year-olds. Because they won't, unless you give them good reason to. And even then, they still probably won't.

Step 4: Accept that right now, you are small-time

Before you go out into the world to seek your fortune, you make a lot of assumptions about how easy things will be or how quickly you'll rocket to the top. You might hit this wall, hard, when *The New York Times* doesn't beat a path to your door, but instead it is time for you to go be a reporter in rural Mississippi. Or you graduate law school with glorious visions of the important work you'll do for the Southern Poverty Law Center, but find yourself photocopying briefs in Shreveport. Whatever happens immediately post-graduation, chances are good that it will be at least a little disappointing.

So for right now, being a small-time whatever is your position. It's not shameful and it doesn't mean you're a failure. It means you're embarking on adulthood and starting from the beginning, just like every other person in the world must do. When you begin at the beginning, any progress you make is yours. From now on, it doesn't matter who your parents are or how much money they make. It's time to make your own money. You are the captain of your own destiny, even if it isn't all that glamorous or fabulous at the moment.

Step 5: Set reasonable goals for yourself

There will never be a time when every item in my house is meticulously organized in cute storage solutions. It will just never, ever happen. So looking at a bunch of organization blogs and despairing that my living space doesn't look like theirs is not a healthy thing for me to do.

A big part of being a well-adjusted person is accepting that you can't be good at everything. Some things will always be hard. Decide what you *can* do in those arenas, without making yourself crazy or setting unreasonably high expectations, then feel proud when you do it.

Step 6: Stop enjoying things ironically. Just enjoy them

Know what? I love Britney Spears and Forever 21. And I could pretend like it's this whole meta thing where I'm not actually enjoying it but rather just making this esoteric statement on lowbrow culture, but (*insert handjob motion here*).

The truth is that I love trashy dance pop and the garments that are its clothing equivalent. You don't need to make your tastes a self-conscious statement about who you are. Just unapologetically like the things you like.

Hey! Guess what!?! I'm back! With some new perspective on that terrible thing you did!

The Shame Boomerang

Step 7: Avoid shame boomerangs

I'm just going with *shame* because it would be too cumbersome to call them "Shame, Anxiety, Remorse, Dread, and Any Number of Ugly Emotions Boomerangs."

Here's how that process works:

Inciting shame incident → bad feelings → forgetting and/or getting distracted for a little while → shame boomerang returns → bad feelings *the sequel*, et cetera, *all damn day*

This is the excellent strategy put forth by Internet friend Emily:

Step 1. Acknowledge the problem, and take any possible steps to correct it.

Step 2. Figure out how you will avoid making this same mistake again.

Step 3. Decide on a coping mechanism mantra that you will repeat when the shame boomerang returns ("It's done, and I won't do it again") and then play a diverting mental game, like thinking up what you would name a trio of Siamese kittens.

She didn't put this in, so I will:

Step 4. Really try not to make the mistake again. If the mistake happens again and again, then take a hard look at what you are doing and why.

Step 8: Remember your circle of concern versus your circle of action

Grief counselor Susan Gelberg was the one who told me about this, and said it's helpful for people who are experiencing anxiety and anguish.

There is a big circle, one that contains all of your concerns, ranging from the super mundane ("Why can I never get the stupid wispy sides of my bangs straight? What if they're somehow made of a lost colony of pubic hair?") to the overwhelming ("Global warming! *Fuck!*"). But there's a smaller circle inside that circle, which is your circle of action.

Inside that circle are the things you can actually effect change on. Work on those things. Those are the things that will help you feel as in control as any one person has the ability to be.

Step 9: Begin to separate, in your mind, things that are a Valid Long-Term Plan versus Not A Valid Long-Term Plan

Lots of things are NAVLTP. That is a fun word to try to pronounce out loud, but a bad thing to have in our lives. Common NAVLTPs include:

• Boyfriends you really love but know you don't want to spend your life with.
• Smoking.

• Jobs with little to no possibility for advancement. Not that you need to be the ruthless climbing-the-ladder type, but most people want, eventually, to have a job that is slightly more challenging and lucrative than their current position.

• If you have a drinking problem, you need to deal with that sooner rather than later. One caveat here is that many people who drink a lot in their early twenties do, in fact, kind of naturally taper off as time goes on and hangovers become tougher to deal with. This will happen almost overnight, and it is God's way of preventing thirty-five-year-olds from drinking until 3 AM and making bad life choices. But if you find yourself drinking more, not less, as you age, that is something to consider.

Step 10: Be okay with being alone

Lunch, the bus stop, shopping, parties—all these situations and more, you should feel fine being alone in. Here is what *you* think others are thinking when they look at you:

Oh my God, that girl has no friends and no significant other. Wow. How has she made it through life this far without finding a single solitary person to care about her?

Here is what they are actually thinking:

I wonder if I remembered to turn off my hair straightener, where is Laura? She was supposed to be here by now, ugh, I hate PT Cruisers so much; how do people not understand that those cars look like giant ugly eggplants? . . . [other thoughts completely unrelated to you because no one notices or cares that you're by yourself] . . .

You, meanwhile, will be with yourself for the rest of your life, so you'd best learn to enjoy your own company.

Look comfortable alone. You are not itchy, you are not fidgety, you are not looking around desperately for whoever will rescue you from the terrible fate of not being engaged in boring small talk. You're *fine*.

Step 11: Recognize six-month problems

When you get really upset about something, ask yourself if this is something you will remember in six months. Most things aren't. Most things are six-day problems, or six-minute problems. If the answer is *No, I will not remember this*, then you need to try to do your best to move on. If the answer's yes, you *also* need to do your best to move on, but at least a *no* answer puts you in the proper frame of mind.

Step 12: Distinguish between horses and zebras

I am constantly seeing medical dangers and significance everywhere. I don't have a head cold, I have meningococcal meningitis! And will soon die! I start thinking about how tragic this will be for everyone I know; how sad they will be when they hear how this bright young life was snuffed out so needlessly. What will they say at my funeral? Et cetera... and then I get over whatever extremely minor ailment it is, and forget all the dreadful predictions I made. Until the next time I get sick, and it isn't a headache, *it's brain cancer!* Or maybe *a tapeworm has gotten in my head!*

Once, I had a mosquito bite on my arm, and it was infected, so obviously it was the same antibiotic-resistant flesh-eating bacteria I saw a story on CNN about. I called my godfather (who is also a doctor) to confirm my suspicions that I should head to the emergency room.

Luckily, my brilliant godmother (and intermediary to my godfather) answered, and gave me the best quote ever. She was saying it in the context of medical maladies, but I believe it can apply to many other things, too:

"If it's making a galloping noise, it's probably a horse, not a zebra."

In other words, the simplest explanation is probably—not always, but probably—the correct one.

So when you are unreasonably fretting about something and coming up with zebra explanations ("My boss is quiet this morning, so I'll bet she's going to fire me!"), try to steer yourself back toward horse-thinking ("She's probably tired or busy").

Step 13: Pay attention to natural consequences, then learn to anticipate them

Natural consequences is actually a parenting concept, but one I use on myself, because sometimes my ability to thoughtfully reflect on a difficult situation is in line with a four-year-old's.

A natural consequence is, essentially, a situation where a parent doesn't have to punish a child for wrongdoing because the universe sort of takes care of that. A natural consequence of splurging when you don't have the money to do it is that you can't go out with friends. A natural consequence of hooking up with someone at work is that you then get to remember it in all its Technicolor, bodily-fluids glory every time you sit across from them in a meeting. And so on.

I have taken to whispering, to myself, *Natural consequenceeeeessssss!* when I am experiencing one, to give myself a little Pavlovian incentive not to do it next time.

Step 14: Remember that, for better or for worse, you are in control of your physical self and surroundings

You can make your bed (see step 33) or not make your bed. You can buy paper towels or not buy paper towels. Neither makes you a better or worse person, but you should accept that if you want your bed to be made, there is but one person in the world who is going to do it and that person is you. Extrapolate this principle to many, many other things, because more often than not, it applies.

Step 15: When necessary, look at yourself in the mirror and give yourself some Real Talk

Are you familiar with the concept of Real Talk as popularized by R. Kelly? It means just what it sounds like. We all need a little Real Talk in our lives, but there is only one R. Kelly and so many of us, so you'll need to give it to yourself.

This sounds a little crazy, but looking yourself in the eye in the mirror and saying something aloud is oddly effective. It makes whatever you are trying so hard to mentally avoid into something that exists in the real world. It reminds you that the lies, or truths, you tell yourself are as significant as the lies and truths you tell others.

"This relationship is over, and you need to end it."

"Right now is not the right time to be crying at work. You are a grown-ass woman, and you're going to splash cold water on your face, take a minute to compose yourself, and then go slay it out there."

"Your needs are not more important than other people's needs."

Please note: There is a big, big difference between berating yourself and Real-Talk-ing yourself.

Step 16: When something bad happens to you, do not rush immediately to figure out why it wasn't your fault

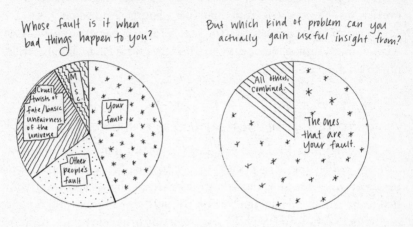

Whose fault is it when bad things happen to you?

But which kind of problem can you actually gain useful insight from?

MISC.

Cruel twists of fate/basic unfairness of the universe

Your fault

Other people's fault

All others, combined

The ones that are your fault.

Point being: before you rush, internally, to deflect blame, figure out what lesson you could/should be learning here.

Step 17: Get used to giving more than you get

A natural transition, as we go from being kids to adults, is to go from being self-oriented to other-oriented. When we're little, all this love flows to us, and none is expected back. That ratio has now changed, and if you don't acknowledge it, you will not be a pleasant person to be around.

ADULTING DISCUSSION QUESTIONS

1. What is your worst-ever shame boomerang?
2. Who is the least-special Special Snowflake you know?
3. If you had a pet zebra, what would you name him? Here's a few to get you started: Edwin Brewster, Señor Stripes, Karen, Pickles, Trotters.

2. Domesticity

One of the most jolting days of adulthood comes the first time you run out of toilet paper. Toilet paper, up until this point, always just *existed*. And now it's a finite resource, constantly in danger of extinction, that must be carefully tracked and monitored, like pandas?

It's not just the toilet paper. There are so many endless tiny details to attend to. Food does not spontaneously manifest itself in the fridge. Surfaces become increasingly sticky and dust-covered if not wiped. Disgusting things, like overflowing toilets and dead squirrels your cat leaves on the bedroom floor, are on your shoulders. No one else will remove that spider biding its time in the shower until it can lay eggs in your ears. No friendly stranger will knock on your door to ask if any ketchup has spilled in your fridge and hardened into indelible red paste, then offer to scrape it up. Half-empty beer cans will release foul, regret-scented gases until you empty and recycle them.

But now, the good news: Billions and billions of people around the world manage to live in a home without directly killing themselves or others via their irresponsibility, and chances are very good you are one of them. There is a 98.5 percent chance that you will manage to keep toilet paper stocked regularly, especially if you...

Step 18: Buy toilet paper in bulk

Sure, this is a specific rather than general step, but it can be extrapolated to this whole chapter. You see, toilet paper is something that you will always, always need. Let's look at this graph illustrating that very principle:

Because toilet paper is non-perishable (thank God, because that would be disgusting), you may as well go ahead and buy a whole bunch of it at once. It saves you money, cuts down on future toilet-paper-purchase expeditions, and guarantees you will never, ever have to leave your house at 5 AM with a digestive system that is on the march. It's not as though the grocery store clerk will look at this large purchase and assume you poop a lot, so just go ahead and do it.

All right. Now that the most important step is out of the way, let's start with searching for a place to call your own, then on to decorating, cleaning, and showing off your domesticity.

Step 19: Find the right place for you

People who live in Manhattan or San Francisco may as well skip this step, since you'll be lucky to find someone willing to rent you a closet without putting down first and last years' rent. But for those with a little more choice in their real estate, here are some great things to look for in an apartment:

• **Hot water:** Go turn on the shower and make sure there is sufficient water pressure and it's nice and strong and not, as my mom once memorably said of my shower, like having an eighty-three-year-old man pee on you. Also, does the water get hot? Is it the either-scalding-or-frigid kind of shower? That's nice to know.

• **Safety:** Come back by the area at night, during the day, on the weekend, and so on. Make sure you feel reasonably safe at all these times.

• **Volume:** Consider whether there is something very loud nearby, like a fire station or train tracks or a high school with a substandard but enthusiastic marching band. Will this make you crazy?

• **Management:** Does the landlord seem at least semi-reasonable? Landlords are tightly wound people, generally speaking, so you have to give them a little leniency, but make sure they set off no Insanity Bells (see step 123). It's okay to ask to chat with another tenant and see what kind of person you are entering into a long-term legal contract with. Because chances are that if you are in a conflict with them, they will win. They have money and lawyers. They're businesspeople. Make sure they're the kind you want to be in business with.

• **Electricity:** Be sure to check all the light switches and, if you can, the electrical outlets, perhaps by taking along your cell phone charger. Otherwise, you could end up like my friend who had fourteen decorative outlets and two that actually powered things. It's also useful to check on how many and how well placed they are. If you like to blow-dry your hair, look for an outlet in the bathroom. It's nice to have several in your bedroom so you're not constantly tripping over your bedside lamp's cord that must stretch taut through the air. And so on.

• **Closets and storage:** Do they exist? Some old houses had bedrooms without closets. Having at least one big non-bedroom closet is a lifesaver, so long as you do not follow my example and allow it to become a dangerous and unstable mess, like a tiny Baghdad right there in your apartment.

• **Appliances:** Is there a dishwasher, or a washer-dryer? These things are luxurious, but if there is nothing you hate in the world more than hand-washing dishes, then you might make that a condition of your search. Also, if there are washer-dryer hookups, do not kid yourself into thinking you're actually going to buy a washer-dryer unless you are so grown-up as to be way beyond this book.

• **Accessibility:** Can your furniture logically get up the stairs and into the apartment? It's a good plan, if you have really large and/or awkwardly shaped things, to measure them in advance, then take a tape measure along with you.

• **Pets:** If you have a pet, can they live here with you? The lure of a nice apartment is not justification for dropping your pet off at the shelter.

• **Paint:** Can you paint the walls? What if you agree to paint them back to the original, sanitarium white when you leave?

Normally, you can expect to pay first and last months' rent, plus a deposit. Be sure to first read carefully and then keep copies of everything you sign, and find out what the policy is to give notice when you're ready to move out. Most require thirty days' written notice, and no, calling them thirty days ahead of time will not cut it.

Step 20: Be a good tenant

Ninety percent of this is paying your rent on time, but also be sure to alert landlords right away when there is a problem, particularly if it has to do with mold, plumbing, or other issues that could seriously ruin their property. It is their property, even if you pay dearly to use it, and you need to respect it as such.

This also means being gentle with hardwood floors, and knowing how to patch any nail holes you might put in the walls. So a couple quick strategies to make sure you can eventually get your deposit back:

Step 21: Learn how to patch nail holes

This is surprisingly easy, although it's for use on drywall, not plaster. If you have plaster then for God's sake be careful because it is *complicated*. YouTube is your friend. But for drywall: Go to a hardware store and get a putty knife, sandpaper, and some spackle (for smaller jobs) or joint compound (also known as drywall mud). Put a little bit of the compound into a ziplock bag, then cut a corner out so you have a way to pipe it into the hole. Use the putty knife to smooth it out and get off the excess. Wait for it to dry per the instructions, then sand it so it's smooth. A little paint, and it's like the hole was never there.

Step 22: If you need to match paint, chip off a paint sample

This should happen in a discreet area, but take a screwdriver and get a little paint chip off the wall. Then, when you take it to the home-improvement store, they can scan it and match the shade perfectly.

DECORATING

So now you have a place. A big, empty place.

I spent my first few months of living on my own with a decoration scheme that would befit a very casual junkie (casual about home decor, not casual about heroin use). I eschewed traditions like dressers, instead opting to leave my clothes in piles on the floor that in a pinch could double as a couch, since I didn't have an actual couch. If you closed your eyes and also were on heroin, I imagine it would have been like sitting on a very flat beanbag chair.

Needless to say, this setup made me feel batshit insane and like a complete failure at life. So soon enough, I bribed a co-worker who had a pickup truck with a six-pack of beer and got a bunch of Goodwill furniture. It is embarrassing, now, to recall how proud I was when someone came over and I was able to offer the luxury of sitting on an *actual couch*.

Here is what I'd consider the bare minimum, furniture-wise:

- **Kitchen:** A small table and at least two chairs
- **Living room:** A couch, a bookcase or shelving, and a coffee table
- **Bedroom:** A bed, a nightstand, a dresser

Here are some things that can be nice to acquire once you are no longer offering sweater piles for your guests to sit on:

- **Living room:** A desk, a love seat or occasional chair, side tables, something to set your TV upon that isn't the box it came in
- **Bedroom:** An additional dresser, if necessary; a vanity

- **Bathroom:** A storage option of some sort if your bathroom doesn't have any

Step 23: Find furniture on the cheap

Goodwill, Craigslist, garage sales, and your parents' friends are all your friends, although you should make sure ahead of time that you have some way to get your inherited goods and purchases home. IKEA, of course, is the poor twenty-something's wonderland, so long as you don't mind having the same dresser as all your friends, which I most certainly do not.

A couple notes of caution: When looking for old furniture, quality counts. Be sure to jiggle it to make sure it's sturdy. Particleboard is no good, at least not used. The heavier, the better, if it's made of wood. Use your measuring tape to make sure whatever item this is can fit through your door, and won't look ridiculously large in your space. Also, if you live in a bedbug-prone area, just skip secondhand uphol-stered stuff. It's not worth the risk.

How to decorate

If you have absolutely no idea of what you want your house to look like, look in your closet. My friend Carol, who has the most beauti-ful home of anyone I know, said she thinks that people should sort of match their houses. So do you like to wear a lot of bold, primary colors? Are you more a neutral person? Is your stuff old-fashioned and ornately detailed, or minimalist? Chances are if you like it on your person, you'll like it in home decor.

Another good first step can be to start with a single object that you just really, really like. My little sister found an antique water-mister, the kind that an eccentric old lady would use to spritz her orchids in the 1950s, and whenever she wanted to add something to her room, she made sure it would match the spritzer.

Painting walls does make a huge difference. If you don't want to commit to painting the whole apartment, painting just one wall can do a lot, even if it's one of the very short ones.

It's worth it to get a couple samples of the paint and test on your wall first, to confirm you actually like them and make sure they look the same in your apartment as they do on the tiny swatch. When you go to buy paint, describe the wall surface to the paint store people—they can tell you if you need primer or not.

Before you begin, put masking tape along the edges of the wall and over anything that shouldn't be painted, like baseboards and trim. Unscrew light switch and outlet covers, then cover the floor with a tarp or a *lot* of newspaper. Go crazy on that last step and be extra, extra cautious so you don't drip paint everywhere. You'll also need a paint pan, a smaller brush, and a roller for covering larger areas.

Step 24: Frames, not posters

Oh, college. There are so many reasons we are all nostalgic for you, but interior decor isn't one of them. Frames don't have to be expensive, either—every time I go to Goodwill, I see thousands of frames for fifty cents or a dollar apiece. If you want to be all Rockefeller about it, IKEA has them for five to thirty dollars.

Art is something else that you can slowly but surely acquire. It doesn't have to be insanely expensive—prints from local artists, small bits of wall art, and stuff from especially talented friends and family members are all wonderful. But treat 'em right, and get 'em framed.

Step 25: You can be poor and still have a really cute apartment

It just takes extra effort and creativity. My friend Ariella had the amazing idea of putting pages from vintage children's books up on her wall, an idea I promptly stole. White spray paint goes a long, long way toward making clunky ugly wooden things into something rustic and cute looking. Most knickknacks and decor items you find at Goodwill are hideous, but some are adorable and cost fifty cents.

Step 26: Get a nice, actual bed

Once you turn twenty-three, there is a steep drop-off on the acceptability level of a mattress on the floor. But do not let external judgment be the thing that steers you to an actual bed. No. You owe it to yourself.

If you're like most people, your bed is the physical object in the world that you will touch the most. You spend a third of your life with that thing! It should be comfy. If you can scrape together five hundred dollars—maybe, say, from a tax return, or maybe put away forty dollars each month—you can sleep like a king for years and you will never, ever regret it.

> **Step 1.** A nice mattress. Go to several mattress stores. Try all the different ones out, and don't feel uncomfortable about rolling around, getting your significant other to come along and lie down with you, and so on.
>
> **Step 2.** Know that mattress stores are weirdly into haggling, so start by really lowballing them, then go from there. What are they going to do, kick you out of the mattress store?
>
> **Step 3.** Figure out what this nice mattress will sit upon. Box springs aren't totally necessary, especially if you plan on a platform bed. On the other hand, the very cheapest bed solution (and the one I use) is a Hollywood bed frame, which does require a box spring. These can almost always be found at Goodwill or garage sales. If you do this, you may also want to buy a bed skirt.

Step 27: Create a correspondence drawer

This can be done for twenty-five dollars or less. Pick a drawer—hopefully that flat, long one in the middle of your desk—and put the following things in it:

- One book of stamps, to be replaced as needed
- A checkbook
- Business envelopes
- Two nice-ish pens, one blue and one black
- Plain card stock and envelopes that you can then doodle something on before sending as a thank-you note or a just-because letter
- Address labels, if for some reason some company has sent them to you
- If you're advanced, a little address book

Then, on the rare occasion when you do need to send a letter (or, um, a rent check), it'll be smooth, capable, responsible sailing.

Step 28: Buy tools. Five should be sufficient, for now

If you don't already have a big toolbox of tools, chances are you are not the kind of person who needs a big toolbox of tools. But really, for a person of negligible-to-average handiness, these five things suggested by Ben, the handiest dude ever, will take you far:

1. **Hammer:** For the hammerin'. You'll also probably want to get an assortment of nails—home improvement and hardware stores sell small boxes that contain several different types.

2. **Adjustable screwdriver set:** It's a single screwdriver handle with different-size bits you can pop in and out. "It's much cheaper and handier than a full screwdriver set," Ben said, "and while it's not optimal for major projects, it's more than enough for small projects."

3. **Crescent wrench:** A crescent wrench can be adjusted to any size by using the little dial to increase or shrink the width of the teeth to match the bolt you're tightening/loosening.

4. **Tape measure:** Good for so many things: measuring distance to center a portrait on the wall, placing furniture, figuring out whether your furniture will even fit up the stairs, and so on. Also, as Ben noted, it's fun to push the button and suck the tape back into the device, no matter how old you get.

5. **Cordless drill:** "Hanging drapes? Hanging a heavy mirror? Without a cordless drill, these will be a huge pain in the ass," Ben said. "Manually turning a screwdriver into the wall so you can hang your drapes is torture." Plus, unlike your screwdriver set but like your tape measure, a cordless drill is sort of fun.

Step 29: Get a stepstool (and use it to check your smoke detector)

Another non-fun, non-glamorous, but super-useful purchase. You know when you're guaranteed to use it? When you check the batteries in your smoke detector once a month, as grown-ups who do not wish to perish in a fire should make a habit of doing. It's nice to do this on the day you send your rent check in (or that it's withdrawn from your bank account).

Step 30: Make two copies of your keys, then give one to a friend, and hide one somewhere near your house

Sooner or later, you will lock yourself out of your house. It's just unavoidable.

So make and give a copy of your key to a friend. Ideally, this friend lives very close to your apartment, and super ideally, they are your awesome neighbor who will come over and pet-sit when necessary. Anyway, give them a copy pretty much as soon as you move in, then hide another copy (unlabeled!) within a couple blocks of your house.

CLEANING

Full disclosure: Cleanliness is my Everest.

Even when my house is clean—say, if company is coming over, which is pretty much the only time my house is really, really clean— it's still obviously a recent and temporary effort, like a five-year-old dressed up in a tiny ill-fitting blazer.

But while my house will never be one that gleams with tidiness, I can still keep it from falling into the unlivable hellhole territory that it was in for much of my early twenties.

Step 31: If you are really terrible at cleaning, it may be worth it to hire a cleaner, and ask if they can tutor you while they clean

Ask in advance, since of course what most housekeepers are signing up for is cleaning, not teaching the terribly incompetent how to wipe. But I did this and found Karen, whose wonderful advice is peppered throughout this chapter. She, without judgment, did everything from changing my hand-washing routine to explaining what spring cleaning is all about. Plus, I find it much easier to maintain cleanliness than to get it to that state in the first place.

Which brings me to cleaning schedules.

Step 32: Do some cleaning daily

Here's a list of things that should take you no more than fifteen minutes, but if you do them each day, your habitat will never sink into unbearable filth.

- Do the dishes (for more on this, see the Cooking chapter).
- Take the time to put things away where they go. Hang up your clothes, put the others in the laundry, put away any new purchases, and so on.

See? You can do that. You can even sing yourself a happy little cleaning song of your own invention when you do it.

Step 33: Make your bed, every morning

People go back and forth about whether making your bed is a colossal waste of your rare and precious minutes. But to me, it's worth it, because then no matter what, there is a small, tiny space in the world that I know is orderly, which is more than worth the forty-five seconds it takes me to get it into that condition.

As soon as I get out of bed, I tuck the top sheet back in, smooth out the blanket, and fluff the pillows a tiny bit. Then there is this nice clean plane that I can lay an outfit out on, plus the whole room looks neater (fact: It's impossible for a room to look clean with an unmade bed). Each night, when you come home tired and ready to relax, you'll walk in and your bed will be made, a small testament to control over your universe.

Plus, it's way nicer to get into a made bed. Not like when all the sheets are bunched up and you get tangled in them and feel more like a complete failure at life than the situation really warrants.

The longest sheets should go without washing is two weeks; wash them in warm water by themselves, using half the usual amount of your detergent. Try to have at least three sets of sheets. For more on laundry, see steps 243–258 in the Maintenance chapter.

Step 34: Get in the habit of mindlessly tidying

Some excellent times to tidy:

- While you are on the phone, wander around straightening things up.
- If you've just put something in the microwave or under the broiler, spend those three minutes wiping counters or doing dishes.
- While waiting for the bath to fill or the shower water to heat, wipe down the sink and the outside of the toilet.

Step 35: Do not leave to crust for tomorrow what may be wiped up today

Here is something that I am so, so embarrassed that I had to be told not six months ago, as I somehow had never absorbed it in childhood: When there are little spills or splatters, wipe them up right then.

For years, this was my mental process for spills:

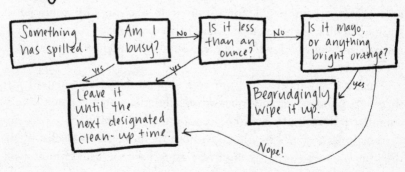

My Spill-assessment process:

But here's how actual adults do it:

Correct spill-assessment process:

Seriously! It will never be easier to wipe up something than right when it is fresh. It is less likely to stain, dry, crust, et cetera, and you will have to wipe it up eventually. Just do it now.

Step 36: Be mindful about your garbage

This means getting decent trash cans, making sure you have liners and/or leftover plastic grocery bags for them (do *not* neglect this step or your garbage can will grow tiny, smelly civilizations in the bottom by this afternoon), and figuring out what the recycling process is in your neighborhood.

If you live in a place with curbside recycling, learn the rules. It'll be run through either the city or the county, so just Google "[my city name] recycling." If you don't have a bin, call and ask for one.

Remember that leftover, crusty food is not made into anything except compost. (And if you want to do that, *congratulations*, because you are super functional and caring.) You will never buy a sketchbook made of Post-Consumer Dried Pizza Cheese. So generally speaking, items that are contaminated by food in a way that can't be washed (think porous things, like cardboard) should just be thrown away, and items that can be washed (glass, plastic, waxed cardboard) should be recycled.

If your curbside recycling doesn't take glass, then figure out where to take it to recycle. Or just accept that you're going to throw it away. Whatever you do, do not allow an army of white wine bottles to amass under your kitchen sink, like those terra-cotta soldiers, except made of shame.

A bucket list

So this is not a bucket list as popularized by the 2007 Morgan Freeman–Jack Nicholson movie of the same name, but rather a list that contains a bucket, which I did not own for my first three years of solo living.

Some basic cleaning supplies that everyone should own:

• Dawn dish soap. It is truly astounding what some dish soap in warm water will clean, but more on that later.
• A broom and dustpan.
• A mop.
• A bucket.
• Paper towels.
• Rags. **Note:** It's best to have old towels and some (unused, obviously) cloth diapers. The towels are great because they attract dirt, while the cloth diapers won't scratch your mirror or windows.
• A scrubber.
• A toothbrush, for little crevices (think between the faucet and back of the sink).
• Bleach. (More on this later, but in the meantime, remember that anytime you're working with bleach, you should have gloves on.)
• Cheap white vinegar; a solution of one part vinegar to two parts hot water is a wonderful glass cleaner.
• Spray bleach solution. This can be used on many things, including mold, floors, painted surfaces, and so on.
• Knee pads, which make scrubbing a billion times less painful and Cinderella-like.
• Latex cleaning gloves.
• Pledge for wood.
• Goo Gone, which does wonders on weird sticky messes.
• A duster, although you can certainly use the rags for this.

Step 37: Get a toilet plunger

Toilets are actually pretty easy to fix, but not without a plunger. First, if it's overflowing, turn off the water using the little knob shaped like a football that is probably somewhere around the base. A quick how-to: Plunger goes in the bowl over the drainage opening. Make sure there is a nice seal (visually, obviously), then plunge four or five times. Remove plunger, try to flush the toilet, and if that doesn't work, give it another go. Wash off the plunger using household cleaners and a good spray of Lysol.

Step 38: Master other basic toilet repairs

Happily, toilets are fairly simple creatures, and most things that ail them are easily fixed. Nearly all home-improvement stores sell toilet repair kits that have blessedly simple instructions. If it's anything that you can't immediately diagnose when you take the top off the tank (for example: That little chain is broken! It should be replaced with a *non*-broken chain), then go ahead and ask your landlord.

Weekly cleaning

It's best to pick a two-hour window in which, every week, you do your weekly cleaning. Saturday mornings are perfect if you are not liable to be hung over; then you have a pretty clean house to enjoy all weekend. Per Karen's suggestions, here are the weekly chores:

- Clean your bathroom—that means the shower, tub, toilet, and sink.
- Do your laundry, including your bed linens.
- Sweep and then mop any non-carpet surfaces.
- Check corners for cobwebs.
- Wipe down surfaces that wouldn't be cleaned regularly, like the coffee table, desk, chairs, and so on.

Again, do-able.

The miracle of soapy water

A bucket of dish-soapy water feels very Cinderella-ish, which it most certainly is. But it's also an extremely useful go-to solution for cleaning most surfaces in your home. You can effectively use it to mop, clean counters, gently clean hardwood floors, clean sinks, wipe off many non-wood furniture items, and more.

One really effective strategy is to have two rags, a wet one and a dry one. Use the wet rag to wipe down (really use that elbow grease), and then use the dry one to clean up and wipe away any remaining flecks and dust.

Whenever either rag is getting dingy, wash it, wring it out, hang it up to dry, and grab another rag. Also, this sounds obvious, but rags can be laundered, albeit not with your other laundry. It's gotta be a rag-only load, unless you are cool with your clothes being washed in all that detritus you removed from your countertops.

Step 39: Tackle glass, mirrors, and windows

Of course, you'll want a glass cleaner for this. Karen said she found the most effective cleaning implement to be a cloth diaper, which doesn't leave behind lint or streaks. Spray down the surface thoroughly, then use one rag to wipe, and a dry one to polish. Windows should be cleaned every six months.

Step 40: Sweep slowly, and think about vacuuming if you have a pet

One mistake lots of people make when they sweep, Karen said, is that they try to do it fast, which just ends up kicking the dirt and dust into the air. Use slow, deliberate strokes. Sweep three-by-three-foot areas, only moving on to the next one after you are sure the current one is totally clear. Also, because I have a cat, I vacuum my hardwood floors, which seems to get them much, much cleaner than sweeping.

Step 41: Master bathroom cleaning

A clean bathroom, more than anyplace else, demands that bleach spray I mentioned earlier. A toilet gets wiped down pretty much all over—everywhere from the top of the tank to the grimy base part that seems like a disgusting magnet for hair and unspeakable filth. You'll want to clean the inside of the bowl using a toilet bowl cleaner and toilet bowl scrubbing brush, which gets washed afterward.

Step 42: Find a tub cleaner that works for you

Karen strongly recommends Soft Scrub with Bleach. Of course, you're welcome to branch out, but be sure to read the directions—lots of bathroom cleaners want to be left on for several minutes before you scrub with a scrubber.

Step 43: Every so often, bleach your sink, tub, and toilet

This assumes you have the usual surfaces (the white porcelain kind of sink and tub) and not some exotic, expensive material. Fill them with hot water, add perhaps half a cup of bleach to a tub or between an eighth and a quarter cup to a sink, then let it sit for twenty minutes. After you've drained and rinsed, any remaining grime is super easy to get off—and the sink or tub will be so, so white.

Step 44: Do at least a little spring cleaning

Wipe down all the surfaces in your home (doors, baseboards, windows) and tackle at least one big organization project; I always end up tackling what I refer to as Chernobyl Closet, which is wild and unknowable and always reverting to chaos. Get rid of stuff. You should also do this in the fall and winter. Why not?

Step 45: Do not keep things in your house that make you feel sad or bad

The world is full of things that make us feel sad and bad. There is no need to allow any of them in the one small corner of the world you can control.

If, every time you see an item in your home, it makes you cringe, then *throw that shit out*. If for whatever reason it's something that pains you to part with (like old love letters), ask a friend to store it at their house for the time being. Give the smaller clothing to a smaller friend.

If the item in question belongs to a roommate, and you really hate it as opposed to just finding it unattractive, ask in your sweetest, most non-confrontational voice if they'd consider moving it out of the common area.

Step 46: Think about strategies other than keeping every single item that may have a scrap of sentiment attached to it

This is hard for me, as I am the sort of person who keeps receipts from memorable manicures. I always have to remind myself that the vast majority of this emotional detritus never gets looked at. Some questions to think about when you consider saving something:

- Could you take a picture of it, or scan it/otherwise make it a file?
- Will you ever look at this again? Why?
- Do you have other, more significant items that speak to this memory/person?

Step 47: Replace things when they become disgusting

Here I am thinking of bath mats. Bath mats are like hamsters in that they have a very defined and short life span, although unlike hamsters they are sometimes kept around for years after their natural passing.

Shower curtains, hand towels, the little metal dish that goes around the heating element on an electric stove—these things, too, have a beginning and an end. If you ask yourself, "Hm, should I replace this [perishable item]?" the answer is almost always yes.

MOVING

If you've ever moved anywhere, which obviously you have, you know that moving is the second worst process in the world (ethnic cleansing is the first). After I moved my stuff across the country, I swore that I would never move again, that I would die in that little apartment by the railroad tracks.

But sometimes it's necessary. And you can do it.

Step 48: Get a big five-subject notebook, one with pockets to hold pieces of paper, one large enough to hold back the tide of moving insanity

Moving involves about 137 interconnecting processes, every single one of which is a huge pain in the ass. There's getting out of your old lease, getting the old apartment clean, finding a new apartment, forwarding your mail, squaring away pet stuff (one of the most amazing moments of my life was when a customer service lady for a major airline who didn't speak the best English asked what a "cat" is), getting rid of stuff, saying good-bye to people, and of course the question of how your things will get from one place to another.

Your patron saint of this process is a big notebook. Saint Notebook of Office Depot. It will have at least four sections: OLD APARTMENT, NEW APARTMENT, PACKING/MOVING, and MISC. In it, you will obsessively make and cross off lists. You will write down phone numbers and estimates of U-Haul trucks versus U-Pack. You will doodle a palm tree and dream of the carefree days before you foolishly decided to move. Any scrap of paper, no matter how inconsequential it seems, will be embraced by Saint Notebook's loving pockets.

Step 49: Give a bunch of stuff away

Moving provides the ultimate opportunity to decide how you *really* feel about each of the ten thousand items you own. Particularly if you are paying a huge amount to go cross-country. Ask yourself: If I left this somewhere while on vacation, would I pay the hotel to ship it back to me? Or is it easily replaced? *Would I even care it was gone?* Because when you pack something, you commit to it. You commit to carefully wrap it, carry it downstairs, put it in a truck with expensive and limited space, go days or weeks without it, carry it up the stairs, tenderly unwrap it, and find a place for it in your new home. If all this sounds reasonable, take it. If not, leave it.

Step 50: Get some decent boxes

Free grocery and liquor store boxes are good for two things:

1. Moves of less than ten miles, where they will travel exclusively via car
2. Books and other ultra-heavy things that should not go in big boxes because they would quickly get way, way too heavy.

They just cannot be your everything, box-wise. You need to get some real, larger, sturdy ones, and chances are you'll have to pay for them. Yes. This sucks. They should be free. Trusty boxes should be like rain. But they're not.

The money you spend here is emotional pain you save when all of them make it intact, rather than sharing their contents with the gutter at 2 AM when all you want to do is go to bed. While you're acquiring the boxes, get two rolls of packing tape, a sharp pair of scissors, and a couple of Sharpies.

Step 51: Things that live in the same room can and should go in boxes together

The box, of course, will be labeled with that Sharpie you just bought—LIVING ROOM! BATHROOM! OPIUM DEN!

Now. Obviously the caveat here is that big, sturdy things cannot travel with little breakable things, because they will unintentionally kill them. They don't mean to. But it's the inanimate version of Lennie and the puppy from *Of Mice and Men*.

Other good ways to organize is by how quickly you need this item to re-enter your life. Toiletries, hair dryers, underwear, anything that you'll need immediately should be labeled as such: OPEN ME NOW!!!! ☺ Put smiley faces on your boxes. It reminds you that you actually like your possessions, that they are not just hundreds of pounds of dog poop that you have to transport across state lines.

Step 52: Wrap fragile items thoroughly

Your first move is to acquire a giant pile of newspapers. More than you think you could ever, ever use. Then, every fragile item gets a lot of newsprint wrapped around it—again, more than seems reasonable—sealed with a little bit of tape.

After your items have been properly cushioned, find a sturdy vessel they can fit snugly within. Pots are especially serious about their work as protectors of the fragile; just make sure they're stuffed with newspaper so nothing can move around.

Step 53: If an item holds something in your apartment, it should hold something during the move

The idea here is to minimize empty space, so this is especially crucial for non-collapsible things. Baskets can hold pillowcases or towels. Tote bags can hold other tote bags. Pots hold other pots, plus bundles of silverware held together with strips of packing tape. Oh, packing tape. You're my only friend. You and Saint Notebook.

Step 54: If a larger item needs a smaller item to function, tape them to each other

TV remotes get taped on to the TV. (Not the screen. You know.) Once you have disassembled your IKEA furniture, the screws should get taped to the underside. Really, these items are going through enough stress already. No need to separate them from each other and add to it.

Step 55: Soft things go in big garbage bags

This includes non-delicate clothing, bedding, towels, cushions, and curtains if you have them. These things get casually tossed into a giant Glad bag, which you then kneel on to compress all the air out of. You're left with a dense yet soft nugget that can be placed between furniture items in the truck to keep them from knocking into one another. Or thrown at people in an affectionate but still semi-destructive way. We all need to blow off steam when moving.

Step 56: Precious things that could be ruined by water get wrapped in plastic and put in big Tupperware bins

You can't waterproof all non-waterproof possessions prior to a move. But some things are not merely things. Photo albums, love letters, your grandmother's sketchbook, and so on should be wrapped in plastic, then put in sealable containers. And really, unless you want them out on display, it's nice to leave them there once you're in your new place. You can still take them out and love them, just put them back when you're done.

Step 57: If your friends help you move, you owe them pizza and beer

You don't *have* to give them pizza and beer, but any decent person would. No one wants to help you move, but they will, because they love you. Nourish them, body and soul, with pizza and nice beer.

On the flip side, when your friend is moving, offer to help without their asking. This is great, great karma, and lets them off the hook for asking you something that they know you want to say no to. And hey, free pizza.

Step 58: Breathe, because it will eventually be over

Moving can make you crazy like a breakup makes you sad, which is to say, more than you ever thought possible. But be that as it may, eventually, it will be over. Slowly, the pain of moving will recede into a vague memory of hard times, as happens to women with childbirth. You can start your new life, decorate your new apartment, and swear to never, ever, ever move again. Thus, the cycle of domesticity begins anew.

DISCUSSION QUESTIONS AND ACTIVITIES

1. Name one thing that you overlooked before you signed a lease for an apartment that you really, really wish you hadn't.
2. What is the very, very worst chore that exists in the whole world?
3. Make a diorama of your house when it was its very messiest, then share with the group. How did revisiting this scene make you feel?

3. Cooking

Unless you aspire to a lifetime of going broke on takeout, followed by Lunchables and Top Ramen, you need to figure out how to make tasty and sustaining things for yourself.

Yes, yes: technically, sometimes it's cheaper for people who live alone to purchase pre-made food, but if you do this, you are cheating yourself out of something very human. For tens of thousands of years, we've prepared food and eaten together—it's sort of our species's thing. Even if you're just doing it for yourself (for now), there is something to be said for taking the time and care to make something delicious. Plus, nearly everything that you create in your kitchen will be healthier, less chemical-y, and less likely to make you fat than things that go directly from your freezer to your microwave.

To achieve these lofty goals, you'll need to stock a kitchen, figure out what you like and what ingredients it requires, learn a little about basic cooking techniques, and so on. You will get about 10 percent of that in these coming pages, since there are entire television channels and sections of bookstores dedicated to explaining the advanced ways of the kitchen. But if the word *sauté* makes you feel nervous, then angry at yourself for feeling nervous, then too apathetic to Google what sautéing actually entails, read on.

Step 59: Find an apartment you can cook in, at least a little

Per always, New York and San Francisco residents are excused, but everyone else: Do your best to find a spot with at least a decent kitchen. It won't be anything magnificent, but a few extra feet of counter space go a long, long way. Ditto a full-size stove and, if you can pull it off, a dishwasher.

Step 60: Start to put together your kitchen

First stop on the Putting Together Your Kitchen Train: pans!

My friend Sarah, who is the best home cook I know, had the following advice for poor would-be home cooks:

"Get a medium-size saucepan, a large saucepan, a large frying pan, and a griddle," she said. "If you're on a budget, check out thrift stores or garage sales. Look for signs of quality, like copper bottoms, cast iron, or stainless steel. Someone with limited money would do far better buying used than buying cheap stuff from Walmart. If you are determined to buy new, check out places like T.J.Maxx, the HomeGoods store, Ross—anywhere that's likely to have top-quality items for low prices."

As for knives, you really should spend some cash, although on the upside, you only really need one right at first. Get a chef's knife, and a sharpener, which you should acquaint yourself with. A chef's knife can do almost anything, if it's of good quality. Once, I dated a chef, and he had exactly three knives at home, two of which were chef's knives. You will also eventually need a paring knife and a bread knife and so on, but in a pinch, Sarah said, the chef's knife can do most of those things.

Step 61: Get you some plates, bowls, and so on

It doesn't have to be a ton—six place settings is good; eight is better. If you're just starting out and are quite poor, go with this: six big plates, six little plates, six bowls, six glasses, six forks, six butter knives, six spoons, six pint glasses, and six of something you can drink booze out of—perhaps stemless wineglasses.

These things can be had very, very cheaply at IKEA or Walmart, and unlike pots and knives, quality does not really count. Or be quirky and get a bunch of charmingly mismatched ones at Goodwill.

Step 62: Get the most basic implements

Price-wise, you can scrimp on these things without serious consequence, but you should certainly have at your disposal:

- A can opener
- A spatula
- A ladle
- A couple of wooden spoons
- Salt and pepper shakers (or, better yet, grinders)
- A whisk
- Measuring cups and spoons
- A colander
- A corkscrew (unless you never drink)
- A vegetable peeler
- A box grater

Step 63: Get some baking supplies

First thing: a roasting pan. You don't need a big one; nine inches by nine inches should be fine. If you're only going to have one, go ahead and get glass, because it's hard to ruin glass.

You'll need two cookie sheets—one will be for baking cookies and such, and the other one for non-baking (roasting potatoes or broccoli, say), because if anything besides straight-up baking gets on a cookie sheet designed for such things, it will ruin the non-stickness. If you are doing things besides baking on it, line it with aluminum foil first. Finally, I find cookie sheets with a lip on them way easier than their flat counterparts, because then if you're, say, heating tater tots up in the oven, you can just open the oven and give it a good shake so they'll turn over and brown evenly, rather than rolling right off the edge and down to the charred oven floor.

Get a covered Pyrex casserole dish, in which you can bake everything from homemade mac and cheese to a deep-dish cobbler to . . . a casserole.

Advanced purchase: An enameled cast-iron Dutch oven is a remarkably versatile thing. Use it on the stovetop for soups; use it in the oven for braising. You cannot make a delicious pot roast without first having a good pot at your disposal.

Step 64: Get the basic appliances

A toaster oven does an amazing variety of things (and works great if you only have something little to bake). Some sort of small food processor will make most recipes a lot easier; spring for a big model if you plan on cooking regularly. Finally, while a stand mixer is great, a handheld electric mixer will do much of what you require, mixing-wise.

Step 65: If you have the cash, these things make kitchen life easier

- A handheld juicer, to get every drop out of that lemon
- A rolling pin, which works better than a heavy round jar
- A little handheld grater

Step 66: Know where things are in your kitchen, and label when necessary

Make sure your kitchen has some sort of organizational system that makes sense, at least to you. If things do not come with labels, masking tape and Sharpie go a long way.

PROCURING FOOD SO YOU DON'T DIE

Cooking is wonderful, eating is great. But you know what most do not find pleasurable? That crucial first step of grocery shopping. Here is an adult person's grocery list:

- Eggs
- Milk
- Bread
- Chicken breast

...and so on. Here is my shopping list:

- 14 ingredients for whatever weird dish I am hungry for *at that moment*, like lamb-and-raisin empanadas
- ½ pound of sour strawberry belts, all of which will be eaten in the car

But so far as I can tell, there are in fact people who have the things for a delicious and sustaining weeknight meal right there in their homes. I asked Sarah what staples she likes to have on hand. Here is an abbreviated list (none of y'all are on the hook for, say, more than one kind of flour). But it's a great list, and you'll find on it most of the things you need for basic recipes.

Grains, legumes, and pasta:

- Black and pinto beans (these can be canned)
- Brown and white rice
- Lentils
- Oatmeal
- A couple types of pasta—maybe spaghetti and penne
- Cereal of choice (I like to have one responsible choice and one "I'm a seven-year-old" choice: say, Grape-Nuts and Cinnamon Toast Crunch)
- A good loaf of whole wheat bread

Fats:

- Olive oil
- Butter
- Bacon fat (seriously, pour this in a little jar after you cook bacon, then stick that jar in your fridge; it doesn't have that many more calories than butter, and it makes every vegetable in the world delicious when you sauté them in it)

Baking:

- Flour
- Sugar

- Honey
- Vanilla extract
- Baking powder
- Baking soda
- Dried cranberries (these are also key for salads)

Spices and condiments:

- Balsamic vinegar
- White wine vinegar
- Parsley
- Onions
- Garlic
- Ketchup
- Mustard
- Mayo
- Hot sauce
- Soy sauce
- Thyme
- Dill
- Oregano
- Basil

Perishables and produce:

- Milk (always reach behind the cartons in front and find one with the latest possible expiration date)
- Eggs
- Potatoes
- Onions
- Apples
- Salad greens
- Fruits and veggies of choice for snacking

No reason not to have a lot of your protein of choice frozen in individual portions—this could be chicken breast, or ground beef, or fish fillets. When you get it at the counter, ask the butcher to cut it into half-pound or pound portions and wrap them individually.

Step 67: Get in the zone while grocery shopping

This tip came courtesy of my friend April. She always gets bottled water and a PowerBar before she shops, then puts in her headphones and listens to music while she goes down the list. The PowerBar helps her avoid my sour strawberry belts mistake.

I suggest you use whatever songs inspire you to get on your grind and get it, as Young Jeezy would say. It's hard to go wrong with Florence + the Machine's "Drumming Song," or Kanye West's "Stronger." If it is an especially grueling trip, you may need to up the ante with Reba McEntire's "Fancy."

Step 68: Have a slated grocery shopping time that includes prep time built in for afterward

After you've made a list that includes replenishing any staples that are running low, includes any special items from recipes you'd like to try, and does not include more than two items that obviously have no redeeming value (I favor Hot Pockets)—and after you've successfully navigated the rocky aisles of Safeway—your job is still not quite done.

Christina, a truly gifted grocery shopper, weighed in with some tips.

"It helps if you set aside a few hours each week to prep. While this sounds hard, it just means that you make assembling meals as easy as possible for yourself later in the week, when you are tired and your feet hurt and every part of your body is screaming to order Chinese takeout," she said.

She recommends you go ahead and wash the greens and herbs, then makes the adorable observation that storing a glass of herbs in water is like "a bouquet of flowers for your fridge."

You could also take this time to mince onions and such, then perhaps go ahead and make a big batch of food that ages well for later in the week if you're tired and don't feel like cooking—think a bunch of roasted veggies, or grilled pork loin, or a pot of soup.

Step 69: Do put produce in the crisper drawer

It really does make a difference. But do not forget about it once it's out of sight and allow it to rot into a foul-smelling vegetal slurry that will coat the bottom of your fridge. That is something real and true and horrible.

Step 70: Store and freeze things properly

Always remember: Air is the enemy when it comes to storing or freezing leftovers. Get all possible air out before it goes in the freezer.

Yes, you can go the rinsed-out-yogurt-container route, but it's probably worth investing in some Tupperware or, even better, glass containers with Tupperware-style tops. Freezer bags and mason jars also work well.

Meat should be put in the freezer within two days, except for bacon, which seems to keep longer. Also remember that once things are frozen, it's really difficult to separate out individual portions, which is why you asked your butcher to separate things out, and also why, if you're freezing soup or something, you should dole it out into the amount you want for any given meal. Things in a freezer should be eaten within six months, and that is a maximum. Shoot for three.

COOKING

So what will you do with all these ingredients? Cook them, obviously. But how? As stated earlier, about a million books and two television channels are dedicated to answering that question, so I'll skip the in-depth recipes (except for a few that everyone should know) and instead talk about basic techniques and how not to hurt yourself in the kitchen.

Ways to cook things

Cooking things, of course, involves heat, which can be either moist heat involving water (think boiling) or dry heat (think baking). Here are the basics:

• **Baking:** This happens, obviously, in an oven, or even a toaster oven for your smaller jobs. Warm, dry heat rises from the bottom. Used on everything from cakes to roast chicken. Generally dry heat.

• **Boiling:** Submerging an item in water (or stock) that is boiling. The gentler forms of this are poaching (which happens in hot but not super-hot water; bubbles shouldn't be showing) and simmering (tiny bubbles are forming continuously on the bottom). **Quick note:** A rolling boil is different from a boil. A rolling boil involves the whole surface of the water moving as one—it's pretty violent looking, and throws off splashes with big bubbles. A boil is calmer, and involves constant bubbles perhaps the size of the tip of your pinkie.

• **Braising:** Some of the most delicious meat you will ever have is braised—think pot roasts, say, or lamb shanks. Essentially, braising involves partially covering the item with liquid (in the case of pot roast, maybe beef stock and red wine), then putting a lid on the pot so it is sort of both poached and steamed. This usually happens in an oven, and takes several hours, but seriously, it's worth it.

• **Broiling:** The top element in an oven gets very, very hot. This is a wonderful way to melt cheese or finish off meat for a delicious crust, but you *must* stay in the kitchen while this is happening, because it rarely takes more than two or three minutes. Use the minutes it takes to tidy up something in your kitchen, which is also a good plan when microwaving anything. Also, when you're broiling, be sure to move the oven rack so it is close to the top—you want the food only inches away from the broiler.

• **Frying:** Enough fat is put in a pan to cover the bottom, then the item is placed in the hot fat. This will nearly always take the form of pan-frying, assuming you don't have a deep-fryer at home. This is a great way to start meat that will be baked, as it gives it that crispy delicious exterior. But don't put too much of anything in at once when you're frying. When things are fried, they're generally giving off moisture. And if there are too many other things close by that are also giving off moisture, you'll end up with mushy steamed food instead of delicious fried food.

• **Sautéing:** This happens in a pan on the stove over medium-high heat. Turn the element on, then add some fat (oil, butter, whatever) and let it spread out. Then add your ingredient and use a wooden spoon to stir frequently. As with frying, be careful not to put too much in the pan at once.

• **Steaming:** You use a little steamer basket to raise food above water boiling down below. The rising steam cooks the food. So, like boiling, it adds no calories, but unlike boiling, it's much gentler on the food.

Step 71: Until you are a good cook, follow recipes

Recipes nearly always work, but you must follow them. Especially baking. No one is allowed to go out on a limb while baking unless they are a professional baker, because there is a huge difference between a quarter tablespoon and quarter teaspoon of baking powder, and things will be ruined.

With non-baking, there is a little more flexibility, but until you learn your way around the spice rack, it's a good idea to go with what recipes suggest, then if necessary add more salt or whatever when everything is done. It's obvious but bears saying: You can never add less salt (although you can water down soups, if need be), so it's worth going slowly and tasting frequently.

But if the recipe says a sauce should be thick enough to coat the back of a spoon, then cook it until the sauce coats the back of a spoon.

Step 72: Buy The Joy of Cooking

It has recipes for everything and, more important, tells you how to do things like sift flour and store mushrooms.

Step 73: Figure out how to make the breakfasts you like

This means mastering at least one style of egg cooking (Scrambled? Fried? Over easy? *The choice is yours!*) and perhaps frying bacon.

Happily, both these things are pretty easy. The eggs I'll leave up to you, but here's how to make bacon:

Put bacon in pan and fry over medium heat until crispy but not browned, turning when necessary to avoid burning. If you are frying a lot at one time, pour off the fat halfway through. Set bacon strips on a paper towel to drain.

If you want brown sugar bacon, which is great for salads and desserts, dip both sides of the bacon strips in brown sugar, then put a baking rack in a cookie sheet and lay the bacon on it. Put it in the oven and bake at 400 degrees for 17 to 20 minutes.

Step 74: Master oatmeal

It is hard to convince people of this, but oatmeal truly is miraculous. It gives you an amazing amount of energy, like cocaine, if cocaine were really good for your digestion and didn't ruin lives. Get some rolled oats, follow the very easy directions, and then add any of the following:

- Brown sugar and a little butter
- Raisins and almond butter
- Dried fruit of any kind
- Peanut butter and dried cranberries
- Honey and fruit
- Yogurt and walnuts

and...I can't attest to this last one but Sarah swears it is amazing and she never lies about these kinds of things:

"Make it, put it in square Tupperware, let it set, slice it, salt it, fry it, eat it with fried eggs," she said, then anticipated every single one of your reactions. "Yes, do it. Do it now."

Step 75: Learn to make soup

Soup is so easy and satisfying, and it really does get better with age. A couple of quick soup pointers: It's not hard to make stock (just boil savory veggies, like onion and celery and garlic, and optionally, animal bones, over low heat for several hours) but I've gotten great results by simmering store-bought chicken broth with garlic and onions and some herbs as a base, then adding my ingredients.

In general, you'll want to sauté veggies in fat before you add them, or they will become sad and limp. It's also a good idea to sear your meat. (That means cooking it, not all the way through, in a little bit of oil or butter in a very hot pan until a tasty brown crust forms. Be sure to leave it in place until the crust is really formed. No stirring.) Potatoes, rice, and pasta are all great to add bulk.

Remember that some veggies—potatoes, carrots, and other hard ones—take a lot longer to cook than, say, spinach. If something is delicate or quickly cooked, add it toward the end. Finally, be seasoning and tasting as you go—you want the flavors to meld.

HOMEMADE CHICKEN NOODLE SOUP THAT WILL MAKE YOU FEEL MUCH BETTER WHEN YOU ARE SICK

Chop up half of an onion, one carrot, and a stalk of celery into roughly equal-size pieces. Melt a tablespoon of butter in a pot, then sauté the veggies until they're soft, probably about 7 minutes. Add 4 cups of chicken broth (or 4 cups of water and enough condensed bouillon until it tastes right; I prefer Better Than Bouillon), 1 chopped cooked chicken breast, and a giant handful of noodles (egg noodles are traditional but I actually like Israeli couscous, which is these teeny little balls that do a great job of spreading themselves out and being spoon-able). Add some salt, pepper, thyme, basil, and oregano (adding the spices slowly, then tasting the broth), bring the whole thing to a boil, then reduce the heat and simmer for 20 minutes.

Step 76: Make good sandwiches

There is a reason that every culture has its version of the sandwich: You pick any of the four things you love most in the world, then get to eat them all at once and can even walk around while you do it, through the magic of carbohydrates.

Sandwiches are not rocket science. Generally speaking, one meat, one cheese, and an assortment of veggies will do you proud. Bread counts, though, so skip the Wonder Bread and get something decent. Toast it so it doesn't get soggy. Mayo, to me, is non-negotiable, but smushed avocado, mustard, or a thin spread of soft cheese can easily play the same role. The classic combinations are BLTA (bacon, lettuce, tomato, and avocado); salami and provolone; roast beef and cheddar; turkey and Swiss; and ham plus pretty much any cheese.

When making grilled cheese: Remember to butter the outside of your bread, and that a lot of cheese will soak into the bread. Put in more cheese than you think you need—maybe a layer that is half the width of a slice of bread—then a small sprinkle of salt over. Grill on a griddle over medium heat. Put a lid on the top for the first half, but leave it off after you flip the sandwich.

Step 77: Master the art of the meal salad

This is actually a great way to dip your toe into the waters of entertaining, because lunchtime is a great way to have people over and give them food without having to go full-dinner-party on them.

Sarah makes glorious salads, and here are her guidelines.

"What you need for a really good salad is greens, a fruit or vegetable, a nut or meat, and cheese," she told me, then suggested choosing at least one each from the following categories:

• **Greens:** Mixed greens, spinach, thinly sliced chard, mustard greens, watercress, and lettuce.
• **Fruit or vegetable:** Apple, pear, asparagus, cucumber, steamed broccoli, avocado, tomato, carrot—go for two or three of these.
• **Nut or meat:** Bacon, chicken breast, most nuts (as long as they are toasted).
• **Cheese:** Anything. There's almost no cheese in the whole world that won't be nice on your salad.

HOW TO MAKE DRESSING:

Most of the time, it's easier just to buy nice salad dressing, but every now and again a person gets a wild hair and wants to tackle the process head-on. Here's one of Sarah's easiest salad dressing recipes:

BALSAMIC VINAIGRETTE

¼ cup balsamic vinegar

½ cup olive oil

2 tablespoons mustard

Pinch of salt

Smaller pinch of pepper

Combine all the ingredients in a bowl and whisk, or put them all in a jar and shake it right before dressing the salad. Remember that it's easy to overdress salads, so a good strategy is dressing your leaves: When your leaves are in the bowl, begin slowly pouring the dressing and mixing, then taste a leaf and decide whether you need more. Add the rest of the salad ingredients later.

Step 78: Make non-bullshit potatoes

Here, I am thinking of instant mashed potatoes, which are just awful, especially since real mashed potatoes are among the easiest and most wonderful things on the planet. Eating delicious, non-gruel food is one of the prime advantages of being a human being in the twenty-first century, you know.

Here is how you make the real thing:

1. Cut some waxy-skinned potatoes (red, white, or yellow) into quarters or eighths. Peel them first if you feel it necessary, which I do not.

2. Put some water on to boil, and add salt until it is less salty than seawater, but still noticeably salty to the taste. Put the potatoes in the water while it's cold.

3. Boil until the potatoes are done, maybe 16 minutes or so. You'll know because you can poke them with a fork and encounter no resistance.

4. Drain the potatoes, then put the pot back on the burner for 30 seconds to evaporate excess water. Add a couple splashes of milk, 2 or 3 tablespoons of butter, and black pepper. Mash it up with a potato masher or a fork.

5. MASHED POTATOES.

Some optional but delicious things to add are dill, grated cheese of any stripe, sour cream, crumbled bacon and some of the grease that came with it, a little bit of ranch dressing powder, and roasted garlic.

BONUS ROASTED GARLIC RECIPE

Cut the top off a whole head of garlic, then set it on a sheet of aluminum foil. Drizzle olive oil on it, wrap it up in the aluminum foil, then set it in a muffin tin. Bake at 400 degrees for 35 minutes; when the garlic squishes easily, you are done. When adding this to the mashed potatoes, I just squish out the individual cloves and use most of the head, because more roasted garlic is better than less roasted garlic. You can also smear this on bread, or add it to pastas, or anything. It's fucking roasted garlic.

BAKED POTATOES

Get a russet potato. You will know it by its dry, brown skin and the fact that it looks like every other baked potato you've ever eaten. Turn your oven on to 375 degrees. Wash the potato and get all the dirt off, then rub the outside lightly with vegetable oil. Any oil, really.

You now have two options: You can either poke it all over with a fork *or* you can get a long, clean nail and insert it lengthwise through the middle, then skip the poking. Wrap it in aluminum foil, then bake for about an hour. You'll know it's done when you can (gently and carefully while wearing an oven mitt) squeeze it.

Cut it down the middle, then top with whatever your heart desires.

Step 79: Cook your chicken thoroughly

Here is how to make some delicious, simple, salmonella-free chicken for yourself.

1. Go to the store and get some chicken thighs. They are the best part of the chicken, anyway. If you're a boring person, go ahead and get boneless breasts instead, although if you can't handle bones you don't deserve to eat meat.

2. Turn your oven on to 400 degrees.

3. Put the chicken on a cutting board and rub olive oil all over, then salt and pepper it generously (as in, way more than you'd think), and add lemon or rosemary if you want. *Or* pour some soy sauce, chopped ginger, and garlic into a dish and turn the chicken over in it a few times so it's completely coated.

4. Put the chicken in a *roasting pan*. If you don't have one, go to Target and get one. If you are really poor, they have them at Goodwill, too.

5. Remember that it doesn't matter how raw-chicken-y your hands get during this process, but don't touch anything until you wash them, which you should do now. Any part of the counter that may have been contaminated with chicken should have a bleach-based cleaner sprayed on it.

6. Put the chicken in the oven, and watch a 30-minute sitcom or drama of your choice. Then turn the oven down to 350 degrees. Now you have between 10 and 30 minutes of cooking time left. Probably closer to the 10-minute side of things.

7. But here is how you'll know for sure that you've emerged from the salmonella valley: Poke the chicken with something sharp. The juice will always, cooked or not, be translucent, but if it's undercooked it'll have a red or pink tinge to it. If so, back in the oven! But if it's clear and colorless, your chicken is ready.

8. Enjoy not having salmonella.

If you want more chicken, or to impress someone, this is my strategy, which is adapted from Ina Garten's amazing and aptly named Perfect Roast. Also, go buy one of her cookbooks because every single one of her recipes turns out perfect.

CHICKEN

1 (5–6 pound) roasting chicken
Kosher salt
1 large bunch fresh thyme, plus 20 sprigs
1 lemon, halved
1 head garlic, cut in half crosswise

2 tablespoons (¼ stick) butter, melted
Freshly ground black pepper
1 large yellow onion, thickly sliced
4 carrots, cut into 2-inch chunks
8 small red potatoes, cut in half
Olive oil

The night before, do a dry-brining, which sounds complicated but is not and will ensure juicy, perfectly seasoned chicken. For every 5 pounds of chicken, use 1 tablespoon of kosher salt. Put your chicken in a pan, then reach inside the cavity and get out the giblets. (You are so brave and so strong! You are not afraid of a tiny chicken liver, even if you have to touch it with your fingers! Throw it away, and never think of it again!) Rub the salt evenly all over the bird. Cover loosely with Saran Wrap and put in the fridge overnight. At first, the chicken will give off a lot of water, but then it will all be re-absorbed and the skin will be taut and dry.

Turn your oven on to 425 degrees. Stuff the cavity with the bunch of thyme, both halves of lemon, and all the garlic. Brush the outside of the chicken with the butter and sprinkle with pepper. Place the onion, carrots, and potatoes in the roasting pan. Toss with salt, pepper, 20 sprigs of thyme, and olive oil. Spread around the bottom of the pan and be sure the chicken is breast-side up.

Roast the chicken for 1½ hours, or until the juices run clear when you cut between a leg and thigh. Remove the chicken and vegetables to a platter and cover with aluminum foil for about 20 minutes.

This is perfect for a dinner party, because it's impressive looking and delicious and you'll have at least ninety minutes of downtime after you put the chicken in. Remember that one 5-pound chicken serves about four people.

Step 80: Make a decent steak

This can be done beautifully in a cast-iron pan, or semi-beautifully in any heavy-bottomed skillet. I suggest a rib eye, which tends to hit the sweet spot between flavor and tenderness. In general, the less tender cuts (skirt, flank) have more delicious beef flavor, while the more tender steaks (filet mignon) have less.

I love using Allegro Marinade, which I was first introduced to in

Mississippi, where people understand how meat should taste. If you're a purist, you can certainly also just use salt and pepper. Take your steak out of the fridge about 30 minutes before you cook it, then either marinate it or generously salt and pepper it.

Get a pan very hot, then add just a little bit of oil (butter, ideally). If you're using cast iron, you can put the steak right in. Sear it for at least 3 minutes on each side.

Here's how to tell if your steak is ready, using nothing but your own hand and the magic of human touch. It involves the fleshy ball of your palm directly under the thumb, which you will touch while holding the rest of your hand in various positions. The result is how the steak will feel at various cooking points. The way it feels when your hand is relaxed is raw. If you touch your thumb to your pointer finger, then that little space feels rare. Your middle finger is medium-rare; ring finger is medium-well, and pinkie finger is well-done.

Once you take your steak off, it needs to rest. Let it sit on a cutting board, loosely covered in aluminum foil, for maybe 10 minutes.

Step 81: Get a Crock-Pot (or generic slow cooker, either way)

Crock-Pots are an astonishing invention, especially for anyone who lives somewhere even slightly cold. Toss a bunch of raw meat and sauce in your Crock-Pot in the morning, set it on low, and return 10 hours later to fork-tender pulled pork. Crock-Pots make your whole house smell like delicious meat, and then you come home and feel all domestic and satisfied and have a big pile of slow-cooked meat. Seriously. Crock-Pots.

Step 82: Throw a dinner party

...or an after-dinner party. Or a lunch party. If you're freaked out by the concept, it can be nice to ease yourself into it by a trial run where you're not on the hook for a full meal. Having people over for desserts, coffee, and drinks at eight is a wonderful way to do this, as is having people over for a big delicious lunch salad (see step 77). If you add bread and cheese to the mix, it's an inarguably complete meal.

Then, when you're ready, you can make the leap. First, let people know well ahead of time that you're having a dinner party and want them to come, and get a firm guest list. Four people is a fine number; eight is somewhat ambitious but do-able. Six is a sweet spot, especially since you have your six place settings.

Cook things you know how to cook, because it's a bad time to experiment. Also, consider what your afternoon beforehand will look like. One reason it's great to cook something that will take a long time in the oven is that you have plenty of downtime for preparing the other components.

Serve an appetizer of some kind that people can snack on while you put the finishing touches on dinner. Plan on forty-five minutes between the time people walk in the door and the moment dinner is served; it's great to invite close friends from whom you can get help if necessary.

Go ahead and set your table ahead of time, so you don't have to worry about it. If you want to be really fancy, here's how the multiple-fork-and-knife thing works. You'll have one implement per course (so if you serve a salad ahead of the entrée, that's a separate course). The implement you use first goes on the outside, and you work your way toward the inside.

Usually, people anticipate a meat, a starch, and a vegetable with dinner; something like roast chicken and vegetables with a salad is perfect. You don't need bread if you're serving potatoes, pasta, or rice with the meal. A dessert is nice but strictly optional; and when people ask what they can bring, you can and should say dessert or alcohol.

Step 83: Make a dope cheese plate

If you don't want to go the puff pastry route (see below), then a cheese plate is an easy alternative. Here are the components:

- One soft cheese (Brie, Camembert, Roquefort, Muenster)
- One hard cheese (pecorino, Manchego, Emmentaler)
- One orange cheese (cheddar, Cotswold, Gouda)
- Bread or crackers (one for two cheeses, two for three cheeses)
- One accent (strawberries, olives, pickled asparagus, sautéed mushrooms, artichoke hearts, et cetera)

Set the chunks of cheese on a board along with cheese spreaders (or butter knives, which work just fine). It's nice to cut the bread into elongated rounds; make diagonal cuts down the length of the bread.

Step 84: Do not fear the puff pastry

Mediocre cooks everywhere have a tremendous ace up their sleeve that they do not even realize. Puff pastry can transform almost anything dull and lame into something that looks intimidatingly hard and tastes delicious, thanks to all that butter. Every person in the world feels a little bit happier when they are eating a puff-pastry-based appetizer, and as such it's perfect for a dinner party.

Here's Sarah's take on the subject:

"The best way to thaw puff pastry is to put it in the fridge the night before you want to use it," she said. "If this isn't possible, put the puff pastry in its package on the counter and leave it for about an hour. *No longer,* because then it will get too warm and stick to itself and then you're completely fucked.

"After the hour, remove it from the box, take off the plastic, and lay one sheet on a cutting board, covered with a piece of plastic wrap or towel, then lay down the other piece and cover with another piece of plastic wrap or towel. Wait a little longer (about 20 minutes), then use as directed. Make sure that you use lots of flour with puff pastry, but not too much. It should not make the puff pastry white."

It usually comes in a square, so a good way to handle it is to cut it into nine little squares for small turnovers.

So now that your puff pastry is ready and willing, what to do with it? You could put any number of things in it, then bake according to directions! Like sautéed sausage and diced apples, or minced sautéed mushrooms with salt, pepper, and thyme, or even berries mixed with a little sugar. You can also bake it on its own with sugar on top, then put fresh fruit and whipped cream on. The world is yours!

BONUS WHIPPED CREAM RECIPE

Homemade whipped cream is . . . I wish I could come up with the right metaphor, but I can't, because it's beyond description, especially when set next to its fake, sad counterpart. When He feels so happy He could burst, God probably cries real whipped cream.

Here's how you make it: Put your mixer blades in the fridge for at least 20 minutes, or until they are cold. Put some heavy whipping cream in a bowl, then beat with an electric mixer until soft peaks form (when you pull your mixer out, the cream will sort of rise up in anticipation of getting eaten, then collapse back down on itself in disappointment). Add about a tablespoon of sugar per cup of cream, then beat a little more until it holds its shape. You can absolutely add dashes of things like vanilla extract, spices like cinnamon or nutmeg, and even essential oils, like lavender. Try hard not to take a spoon to it.

Step 85: Have some snacks and non-alcoholic beverages on hand for when company comes

One time, someone will unexpectedly drop by, and innocently ask if they could have a snack, or a glass of water. When you are forced to offer them leftover Chinese food and tap water, you will decide to always have around some crackers and cheese, or grapes. It's also a nice idea to have some chilled water, either in a pitcher or from a Brita filter, depending on how tasty your local municipal supply may be.

Step 86: Hand-wash dishes properly

Even if you have a dishwasher, there will still be times when it's necessary to hand-wash things, especially anything wood (think cutting boards and steak knives), anything cast iron, anything especially delicate like those terrifying giant wineglasses, and anything really nice (china or silver).

Here's how to wash things besides cast iron and wood: Fill a clean kitchen sink with nice, hot water and add some squirts of Dawn, then a splash of bleach. Let your dirty dishes sit in this for twenty minutes, then put on your latex gloves. One by one, take the items out of the water, scrub with a Dobie sponge, then rinse thoroughly in hot water. Put them in a drying rack, remembering that anything that can hold liquid (cups, bowls, plates with a lip) should be placed in a way that drains all the water out—either upside down or tilted that way.

Wood shouldn't soak in water because it gets warped easily, so just clean it thoroughly using your soapy, bleachy water.

Cast iron should never, ever go in water because it rusts so, so easily. To clean it, rinse with hot water and use a scrubber, but not steel wool, to get all the food off. Put it on the stove over low heat to evaporate all the water, then put a small amount of vegetable oil on a paper towel and carefully spread a very, very thin layer around the inside of the pan.

DISCUSSION QUESTIONS

1. Why does cast iron feel fine about being so impossibly high-maintenance, and *who are those people* who are like, "Oh, cast iron is sooooo easy!"?
2. Does it weird you out that your hand is made of meat, just like steak?
3. What could make a sandwich unacceptable? Give examples, and show your work.

4. Fake It Till You Make It

Now that interior elements of your life are in order, it is time to work on your fake adult veneer.

"But wait," you say in a concerned, alert voice. "Wait. Isn't faking wrong?"

No. Faking is terrifically underrated. Remember that thing about intentions versus actions back in chapter 1? If you spend your time now faking pleasantness and tidiness, during that process you actually *are* pleasant and tidy.

Besides, a little bit of faking is necessary to keep us all sane. If we were all our most real and raw selves every moment of the day, things would be just awful. The world would be full of man-size toddlers.

But how does one go about developing a smart, clever, socially adept, and charming veneer? By actually behaving in a smart, clever, socially adept, and charming fashion. And it's easier than it seems.

Step 87: Remember that the outside world only sees your outermost layer

This is easy to forget, since we spend all day sloshing around in our own inner monologues, but it's true. No one hears your thoughts except you. No one sees what you were like in high school, or how red your face looks after you've been crying, or even where you were this morning or ten minutes ago. They can only see whatever is on your outside *at this very moment*. Thus, it is easier than it might initially seem to fake it until you make it, which, not so coincidentally, is the title of this chapter. See what I did there?

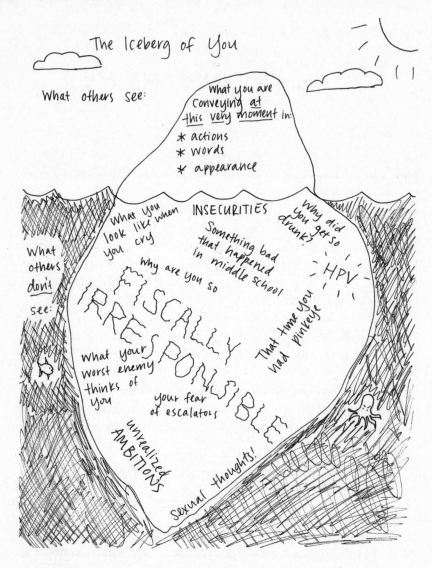

The Iceberg of You

What others see:

What you are Conveying at this very moment in:
* actions
* words
* appearance

What others don't see:

INSECURITIES

What you look like when you cry

Why did you get so drunk?

Something bad that happened in middle school

HPV

Why are you so

IRRASCALLY IRRESPONSIBLE

That time you had pinkeye

What your worst enemy thinks of you

your fear of escalators

unrealized AMBITIONS

Sexual thoughts!

Step 88: Watch ya mouth

You know that terrible feeling where you have put your foot all the way in your mouth, and saying sorry will not smooth things over? It's awful, right? And it gives you archival mental footage for when you're reviewing your own personal worst moments, to be sandwiched between that terrible day in eighth-grade gym class and the time you begged that guy to take you back. I do it all the damn time—mouthing off, at least. I am always, always, always saying something I shouldn't, but as I've gotten older I've learned it doesn't have to be this way.

There's an incredible Tupac song that does not mince words in its hook: "Motherfucker, watch ya mouth." Granted, Tupac is issuing threats to associates of a mid-1990s hip-hop label, but these are still powerful words to take with you wherever you go. Just because there is an idea bouncing around in your head does *not* mean it needs to be sent out into the universe. And if you follow these steps, you'll greatly reduce your chances of having to explore your toes with your tongue (metaphorically speaking).

Step 89: Be aware of local, national, and world events

You don't need to have your finger on the pulse of, say, parliamentary elections in Estonia, but grown-ups know who the prime minister of Germany is, what *NATO* stands for, how a bill becomes a law, and why they vote Democrat or Republican. They know who their president, senators, representatives, and local officials are, and the broad gist of what they do. They are registered to vote.

Just because something isn't happening in your direct orbit doesn't mean it's not important. I'm a frivolous person, and I like to discuss frivolous things, like what political parties various animal species would belong to (cats are monarchists; Labrador retrievers are Democrats; raccoons are anarchists). I don't cram every interaction with Important Heavy Facts about what's going on in Africa. But just because it isn't my favorite topic of conversation does not excuse me from the responsibility of knowing what's going on in places besides my head.

Surely everyone wants to stay informed for information's sake and needs no additional motivation. But just in case...staying abreast of current events will help you be interesting (see step 113) and minimize your chances of saying dumb things. Like the time I asked someone from Puerto Rico how they were enjoying their visit to the United States. (Puerto Rico, as everyone involved in the conversation immediately pointed out, is *in* the United States.)

Learn your national and local leadership and, um, geography. Try to stay aware of world events.

Step 90: Spend ten minutes a day gathering news, at least

One lovely habit to get into is putting on either NPR or C-SPAN while you get ready. Why just straighten your hair when you can straighten your hair *and* quietly absorb the fact that there is unrest in Liberia?

Step 91: Develop your own opinions

There is a group of people who dedicate themselves full-time to telling you what you should think about news, politics, and other information. They are called pundits, or commentators, or analysts, or columnists. Make sure that you don't confuse them with journalists, because they aren't the same thing. Developing your own opinion is great, but it can only be properly done when you've taken in all the facts, digested them, and then weighed them according to your values in your own mind.

This should be your method:

Take in facts → process/analyze according to your own personal value set and belief system → form opinion

This should not be your method:

Take in opinion from media, parent, or significant other → regurgitate opinion from media, parent, or significant other to anyone who will listen, then sloppily defend it to the bitter end

When you watch a news channel, you should be able to discern what is actually news versus what is an opinion-yelling party. The latter make you stupider every time you watch them. So don't.

Step 92: Revise your perception of partying

Partying as a college student and partying as an adult are two very different things. Yes, there are house parties hosted by non-professional friends, which are a blast. But there will also be more and more parties where getting drunk and hooking up are not the goal.

Bonnie is a family friend who has unfair amounts of graciousness to her name—she is a pro champion at entertaining and at making others feel at ease; best of all, she has that intangible quality that makes you feel like an equally elegant person when you're in her company. She was willing to weigh in on conversation, dos and don'ts in social gatherings, how to get in to the best parties, and what to wear once you are invited.

Step 93: Do not RSVP "maybe"

When someone asks you to do something, you have three options:

- **Option A:** Say yes.
- **Option B:** Say no.
- **Option C:** Say "Gosh, that sounds wonderful, but please let me check my schedule," then get back to them within twenty-four hours with Option A or Option B.

You'll notice there was no Option D: Say maybe. Because *maybe* says many things, none of them flattering:

- "Perhaps I'll go if nothing better comes up between now and then."
- "Your invitation isn't important enough for me to decide one way or another, until the day of."
- "I am a flake who can't even commit to an afternoon of something."

I am really terrible about RSVP'ing, because I feel guilty saying no to invitations, then I tell myself that not replying at all is better than saying no. It isn't. If you say no, maybe it's slightly disappointing (because honestly, your presence isn't going to make or break anyone's afternoon). If you don't say anything, you are compounding the slight disappointment of your non-presence with rudeness and flakiness.

As Bonnie noted, the trouble your host or hostess is going to is very large compared with the smallness of just saying yes or no. It's inexcusable not to choose.

Obviously, there's a much higher expectation level with, say, a wedding than a house party. Here are some considerations:

- Is this person going to spend money and/or plan ahead based on my presence? (Think weddings and dinner parties.)
- Are more than fifteen people invited? Your non-presence will be felt in a gathering of less than fifteen, and should be noted accordingly.
- Is this your last chance to see someone for a while? Going-away parties, even if they are large, should be RSVP'd to.
- If you wonder, *Should I RSVP to this?* the answer is yes. Remember, if everyone assumes it's not that important to RSVP, then the host really has no idea how many people will come. And that is the worst. So do unto others and RSVP.

Step 94: Err on the side of attending events even if maybe you don't totally feel like it

Do you know how hard it is to organize a party? Especially an elaborate, grown-up one? It's a huge pain in the ass. But this person is making that effort, and they want you to be there with them. It's only a few hours of your time. If you are being really, really good and doing something you hate, then do what my friend Sarah does and make a deal with yourself: *If I go to this baby shower, I will get myself a pedicure afterward.* Or, *I only have to stay long enough to talk to three people, and then I can leave.* And on that note...

Step 95: Learn how to make an appearance then bounce

So you've sucked it up and are going to something you don't totally want to. Yay! Pat yourself on the back for the consideration you are showing others...and console yourself with the fact that you don't have to stay forever, assuming it's not a formal sit-down dinner or what have you.

This is what you do: Show up right on time, which gives the host a feeling of relief that someone has shown up to their party and gives you social karma points. Hang out for a while—thirty minutes, minimum—and chat with at least three different groups of people. Then kind of casually drop the chestnut that you Cannot Stay. This should come in a voice of deep regret, one that conveys you wish you could stay right here, with them, forever and ever. Don't qualify your Not Being Able To Stay-ness with elaborate reasons why. Just, "I can't stay, but this has been *such* a great party."

Hot adulting tip: In general, the more you labor over explanations, the flimsier they seem. Don't explain why you have to leave and what you're going to do and that you wish you didn't have to do that and could stay here but (super-pained, elaborate explanation redacted). Just say you're so sorry you have to go. Period.

If they ask why—which would be strange—just say that you have a prior commitment. They don't need to know that your prior commitment is a promise to yourself that you wouldn't stay somewhere you didn't want to be for too long.

Step 96: Do not be intimidated by glamorous people

Every now and again, you will find yourself somewhere that is way above your normal schmancy-ness level. Maybe you got an unexpected free ticket to a ball, or maybe a friend of a friend is dating a quasi-celebrity. Get excited, because you are going to have a *blast*.

And you're not going to feel intimidated by your fellow guests. Glamorous people, in real life, are not all that glamorous, generally speaking. And it likely makes them uncomfortable being stared at or treated as such.

By the same token, don't underestimate yourself, or assume you shouldn't be there, even if it's not your normal crowd. As Bonnie put it, "You all arrived on the same guest list."

Step 97: Act like you've been there before

These are Bonnie's words verbatim, and I've found the advice valuable across many arenas in life. Whatever the event or situation, act as though you've been there before, not like a small and excitable country mouse. If you act like you belong, people will think you most certainly do.

Step 98: If you show up at a party and don't know anyone, don't flip out

I'm not sure why it's so hard for us to be alone for even three minutes at a bar or party, but...it is. You assume everyone is looking at you, feeling many things: pity that you clearly have no friends, loneliness from your lack of companionship, and disgust about whatever personality qualities you possess that leave you void of human company.

In actuality, people are probably not noticing that you're by yourself, or really noticing you at all (see step 10). But to alleviate your feelings of anxiety, just head to a place in the party where you stand in line with others—the bathroom, buffet, or bar, for instance—then give a neutral, amusing opening comment to someone. You already have lots in common: You are at the same party, waiting for the same thing. Go from there. If your target is not the chatty type, then get whatever you came for and head to another line.

Step 99: If you forget someone's name, try to trick them into saying it

Some people (me) are wretchedly bad with names. Every time I hear someone say their name, it's like a wispy cloud that passes quickly through my head, evaporating in the morning sun. This is really, really awful of me, because there is nothing worse than when people can't remember your name. And you never hear people mention with admiration someone's ability to never remember a soul.

This is fairly transparent, but if you absolutely cannot remember someone's name and there's no sign of them saying it, wait until someone new whose name you do know joins the conversation, then say to Nameless Person, "Oh! Do you know So-and-So?" Now let So-and-So do the heavy lifting for you.

You could also ask for their number and, when you get your phone out, ask how to spell it. Finally, if all else fails, starting a conversation about names in general ("I've always wondered if life would be different if I were an Esmerelda instead of a Kelly") will usually prompt Nameless to tell you theirs.

Step 100: Listen more than you talk

People will love you for it. Everyone is really dying to answer questions about themselves. If you treat every person like the most interesting person you've ever met, they will be. Every single person on this planet has fascinating things to say; they have a moment where they were happiest, or saddest; they know things you do not but would like to. Think of them as crabs, and your job is to extract all their delicious (if sometimes hard-to-reach) information meat.

Step 101: Ask good questions that take the speaker's answers into account

The secret to interviewing is not being so in love with your own questions that you don't listen to the answers given. Each question (so long as it's not a yes-or-no question) will open itself to an array of follow-ups. Even if the initial answer is short, you can draw shy or quiet people out on the second go-round.

Q: So where are you from?
A: Houston.

Possible follow-ups: Are they a Texans fan? Have they been to (Texas city you've been to)? Do they have any secrets to tolerating the humidity? How long have they lived there? What's Houston like? Is it anything like (city that you are in right now)?

Step 102: Do not talk about your deep, passionately held beliefs

This goes for Jesus, the Green Party, Judaism, numerology, the importance of never dating Scorpios, whatever. If you believe in it passionately but know the rest of the world doesn't, keep it to yourself unless other people ask you specifically. Even then, keep your answers brief unless this person really, really wants to hear about it.

Either they agree with you, which is sort of nice and makes for a superficial bonding moment, or they will be bored and/or offended. Since *boring* and *offensive* are among the worst adjectives that can be applied to a conversation (others being *spittle-flecked* and *grope-y*), better not to roll the dice and just steer clear.

"You shouldn't discuss something you feel intensely about, because your side of the conversation will probably sound like a lecture," Bonnie said. "Interests are great to share; passions, people need to be careful about."

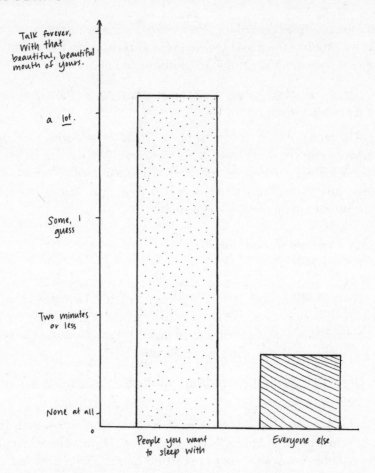

Talk forever,
with that
beautiful, beautiful
mouth of yours.

a _lot._

Some, I
guess

Two minutes
or less

None at all

0

People you want
to sleep with

Everyone else

Amount you wish to hear about people's deep,
passionately held beliefs.

Step 103: Curb your instinct to comment on other people's bodies aloud

This should be obvious, but it's not. People's bodies are not good conversational grist. Do not notice that they are pregnant, or sunburned, or look really tired unless they say it first. Because there is always that chance that they are actually just large and round, or have reddish skin, or feel at the peak of their vim and vigor but are naturally quite haggard looking. Women you encounter are not pregnant *unless they say so or are actively in labor.* Pregnant women usually refer to their pregnancies every ten seconds anyway, so it shouldn't remain a mystery for long.

Even if this person has a really, really obvious affliction, like a cast on their arm, still don't say anything. Chances are that this cast on their arm, being their one distinguishing characteristic, is all that anyone has talked to them about for weeks. They are probably tired of relaying that they were walking through a Safeway parking lot (or, as I call it now, "UnSafeway"), tripped over their own feet, broke their elbow, and were totally not drunk even though everyone assumed they were. For eight weeks, this is all I said to anyone, and it got very, very old.

If your conversation is with the kind of person who loves discussing their injuries (even though they shouldn't; see step 106), then they will find a way to weave these into the conversation.

Step 104: Don't comment on things people are; comment on things people do

The simplest example of this is not telling a tall person that they're tall.

So much in our lives is shaped by weird rolls of the genetic dice, or fate, or God, or however you choose to interpret that particular mystery. Whether someone is short or tall or originally from Canada or gay or Asian or born to rich parents or redheaded or whatever— that's not something they chose or cultivated in themselves, and it's not something they work for.

What makes someone good and valuable is not these traits. It's the choices they make and the things they do. I'd always rather someone tell me I'm a good writer than that my red hair is pretty, because one of those things is something I work my ass off at, and another is some protein encoding. Both are sweet things to say; one means a lot more to me.

It's not that you can't be proud of/pleased by these intrinsic things, but don't forget that the things you (and others) deserve credit for are the things you have control over.

Step 105: Don't emotionally rubberneck

If someone reveals a detail about themselves to you that suggests they went through something heavy, do not ask them about it. If they say their mother died, don't ask how. Don't ask people who say they are from New Orleans about Hurricane Katrina; don't ask people from New York City about where they were on 9/11. Revealing a biographical detail during small talk is not an invitation for you to ask anyone to rehash something that could be terribly painful. If they want to offer this information to you, they will.

If you're on the flip side of this and someone asks about something similar, you can absolutely say, "You know, it was very difficult and I don't generally talk about it in light situations." Yes, this is a tiny reprimand, but probably a good reminder for this nosy person.

Step 106: Quit talking about your own body

Remember that time someone told you in loving detail every single medical thing they've been experiencing lately (even the poop-related problems) and it was incredibly fascinating and not at all disgusting? No? That's probably because someone talking about their own body almost never makes people feel anything but uncomfortable. So apply this principle to yourself, even though it's hard, and realize that although the fact that you are valiantly soldiering through strep throat is very interesting to you, others don't care, and discussion should be limited to a need-to-know basis. What could they even add to that? They have no idea what your throat feels like.

Now. If someone who is dear to you is in bad health, of course they're welcome to talk to you about what they're going through—and if you're in that situation, you are welcome to do the same. There are mild and temporary inconveniences and then there are life-changing illnesses that warrant emotional support. But before telling your tale of tendinitis woe to co-workers, passersby, the checkout lady at UnSafeway, whomever, just realize that your body isn't good small talk.

Should you mention how tired you are?

Start!

Are you feeling tired? — No → Great! :)

Yes

Wow! How fascinating, and rare! others will definitely wish to hear about this!

→ Don't mention how tired you are.

Step 107: Don't tell strangers about your problems

So boring. So drab.

Step 108: If a stranger tells you something inappropriately intimate, be sympathetic and graceful

"If they're opening up like that, it could be poor training or it could be a call for help," Bonnie said. "In your mind, you must distinguish whether they simply don't know they shouldn't be talking about this, or if they're in actual need of assistance."

Step 109: Rescue a conversation from the brink of disaster

This is a great, characteristically brilliant Miss Manners trick for situations when someone has said something so egregious that the conversation has come to a halt. And there you all are, stuck in the agonizing awkward place this person just created with their words.

Pause, and take a beat to kind of reinforce the utter wrongheadedness of what they just said, thereby distancing yourself from that particular thought or sentiment. Then, say this in a slightly sympathetic voice:

"I'm sure you didn't mean that the way it sounded." And then change the topic *stat*.

For example:

"I'm sure you didn't mean that the way it came out. Anyway, oh! You guys! I forgot to tell you, [good news about your life]."

Take everyone in the conversation to a faraway, safe verbal space that is *light-years away from what was just said*. Yes, it's awkward, and yes, everyone at the table will know exactly what you are doing. Still, this is the best possible course of action in the face of such verbal ruin. Pause, pivot, *go*.

Step 110: If you have said something really offensive, apologize

That is all you can do. Say sincerely, "I'm so sorry—I *really* did not mean that the way it came out." Wait for them to respond, add a quick follow-up sorry if necessary, and then change the subject.

Whatever you do, don't try to justify or explain away what you just said, because then you are holding everyone hostage in the offensive place you've created. Again, you need to move away from there.

Step 111: Use the sandwich method when saying things people may be upset or hurt by

The Sandwich Method of delivering frankness:

Complimentary bread: "It is so sweet of you to ask about me; I appreciate your concern."

Real talk meat: "I'm actually really private about these things, and don't want to talk about it now."

Second slice of kindness: "You're a great friend—thanks for checking up on me."

Step 112: Other people's sex lives are none of your business

...unless you are having sex with them, in which case it isn't other people's sex lives, it's your joint sex life.

Here, via again Miss Manners (seriously, she is the best and everyone should put this book down and go read her now), is an ideal takedown of homophobia and prudery. Someone wrote in asking her what they could possibly be expected to say when introduced to a gay couple. After one of her perfectly curt answers ("How do you do? How do you do?"), she had a great line, which I will paraphrase: "I've come to believe there are only two kinds of people in this world—those who believe other people's sex lives are their business, and those who know they are not."

A non-comprehensive list of stuff that is none of your business:

- Who is fucking whom.
- Who likes what in bed.
- How many people someone's slept with.
- What other people's orientations are, particularly if they've not felt like coming out and telling you. If they have, keep that to yourself unless you are really 100 percent sure that they are completely open and out. Don't assume they are.
- Who might be trying to have kids, or, if they are currently pregnant, the circumstances in which they got that way (planned? unplanned? fertility treatments? et cetera).

Have you ever had someone discuss your sex life? Did you like it? There you go. What other people do with their penises and vaginas doesn't need your analysis or attention. Some things can and should be private except with close friends.

Step 113: Be interesting!

Figure out what your own talking points are—quirky and unique things about yourself that might amuse others and/or help segue into a topic where everyone is comfortable. Also, know these facts about your friends who might be at the party with you—for example, one of my friends is winningly Minnesota-modest, and would never tell people that she was an ice-skating cheerleader in high school. (Which is a thing in Minnesota! Since hockey is the big sport, they need cheerleaders… *on ice skates!*) But you know who *can* tell people that she was an ice-skating cheerleader? Me. And I did, all the time. Because let's face it, ice-skating cheerleaders are the most incredible thing ever, and I'm pretty sure people will want to know when they are in the presence of one.

Step 114: Know how to wrap things up

Every conversation you begin must at some point come to an end, because you do not want to spend the rest of your life talking talking talking in the host's living room, passing the years and growing old together on this one conversation. And, nothing against you, but the person you're conversing with doesn't want that, either. Leave them wanting more, not less, of you. So start to mosey the conversation back to the light, early topics (how fun the party is) and then you can end the conversation on a positive note.

Bonnie broke it down thusly: "It's simple—just say, 'It's been so nice to meet you! Kelly's told me lots about you,' or 'It's been so nice

The Small-Talk Bellcurve

to meet a fellow Oregon State Beaver'—whatever it is—or 'I've really enjoyed our conversation'...ending it that way should put everyone on the same page."

Step 115: Send a thank-you note

Yay! You made it through this party—almost. You are not quite off the hook because you still need to send a thank-you note to the host.

Now, the same thing as with the RSVP applies here—if your host cooked you a delicious dinner, or let you stay at their house, or took you boating, or just generally showed a higher level of care and hospitality and attention than they would for a house party, go ahead and send a note.

The truth is that there is nothing bad and everything good about thank-you notes, so you should send them all the time. In fact, this book's spirit animal is a thank-you note.

Someone takes you out to dinner? Thank-you note. Takes the time to interview you for a job? Thank-you note. Present? You *know* that's a thank-you note, and in the words of an etiquette expert I interviewed

This book's spirit animal is a thank-you note.

Dear So y So,
you are too sweet to think of me! That champagne was delicious and the perfect way to toast the end of my college career thank you so much! Love, you

Let it guide you!

once, the note should be written before you open, eat, play with, look at, listen to, or in any way enjoy the gift.

I saw the apex of thank-you notes several years ago in the Gamma Phi Beta sorority house on SMU's campus. The chapter had a bulletin board full of thank-you notes from other chapters, because of course Texas sorority girls love nothing more than thanking one another on official sorority stationery.

These notes...they were just so *perfect*. I'd been writing thank-you notes for years—good ones, that others always commented on—and I had nothing on these bitches. NOTHING. Comparing their thank-you notes with mine was like watching Michael Jordan play one-on-one against a seven-year-old with a broken elbow. They had, essentially, shut the thank-you-note game down.

I copied their format, and have used it ever since. I will give you an example of me thanking my best friend for inviting me to her wedding, then parse below.

Dear Anne,

You were such an unfairly gorgeous bride. Seriously, you single-handedly stole the show from that delicious salmon, charming decor, wonderful company and excellent/ridiculous dance party there at the end. I had such a great time; it's the best wedding I've been to in years. Thank you so, so much for inviting me.

Love,
Kelly

A breakdown:

• Start with the word *you* if possible, because everyone loves reading about themselves more than anyone else, and this sends a loud and clear signal that you'll be doing just that.
• A couple examples of what you were appreciative of. Be specific!
• How you felt or benefited (so they get the warm fuzzy of knowing they made you feel happy).
• Don't thank them until the very last line, and do it simply. "Thank you so much for this wonderful gift." Et cetera.

Step 116: Determine what you care about, then dedicate some of your time to it

Maybe it's disabled children, or animals, or the environment. Maybe it's the incarcerated, or their kids. Maybe it's the homeless. No matter how black your heart may be, somewhere there is something that you care about the fate of. It is a good, grown-up thing to exert a little bit of energy trying to make things better. It's also a great way to meet new people, bulk up your résumé, and get out of your comfort zone.

"Figure out how much time you've got and then call up a non-profit and say, 'This is who I am, and this is what I'm capable of doing,'" said my friend Jacob, who is an astonishingly talented volunteer.

OPPOSITION

Step 117: Imagine rude people as jellyfish

Someone once told me she imagines crazy mean people as jellyfish, mindlessly floating in your direction, ruining your day with tentacles of unpleasantness, and then floating away. On the upside, when she encounters these awful human beings, she thinks of a jellyfish noise, sort of like *bloop...* *bloop* in her head. I have started doing this as well and find it very satisfying.

Mean Person Jellyfish

Jellyfish do not respond to reason, they usually don't respond to kindness, and they will always show up to ruin a fun party if possible. Therefore, your strategy is threefold: Avoid, neutralize, and, in rare circumstances, poke with a stick.

Step 118: Develop your own Teflon qualities

Oh, this is so much easier said than done. But in the long run, this is the best and most universally effective way to deal with the unpleasantness of others.

From here on out, always, you are a smooth, unblemished surface to which even the most crusty meanness, bitterness, anger, and craziness cannot affix themselves. The gross social output of others slides off you. The bad moods, the dark looks, the curt replies: All of this you process, yes, but only in passing, and not in a way that changes anything in the long run. To move on, you need nothing more than a gentle swipe with a paper towel, not the emotional equivalent of soaking in dish soap overnight.

You're a grown-up, and you get to decide what behaviors affect you for five minutes versus what behaviors change you as a person.

Step 119: Accept that some people are just jerks

Some people have blond hair. Some people are really good at baseball. Some people find nothing more pleasurable than organizing a drawer full of buttons. Some people are assholes. This is the human spectrum.

Step 120: Try to pity them a little, for your serenity

Being a bad, mean person is punishment in and of itself. Think of the most difficult person you know. Do you think they're happy? Do you think it's fun living inside such a taut, prickly shell? Chances are good that they're prickly to themselves, too.

A slightly modified version of the Serenity Prayer:

Lord, grant me the serenity to ignore the assholes I cannot avoid;
The luck to avoid the ones I can;
And the self-awareness not to be one myself

Step 121: It's probably not about you

Let's say you're checking out at the grocery store, and the clerk is dismissive and short with you. Here are the possibilities:

- They hate their low-paying job and the attendant bullshit.
- They had an ugly fight with their significant other this morning and are stewing about that.
- They're developing strep throat.
- They are a sour person generally.
- They dislike you personally and are out to get you, even though they just set eyes on you and you've said nothing to them yet.

Now. Of those possibilities, which is the likeliest? But which one does your mind jump to?

Usually, when people are being dicks, it's not about you; it's about them. Think about the last time you were rude or dismissive to a stranger. It's probably because something else bad was happening and you were in a foul mood. And such is the case with others, too. It's more than likely that either something shitty is going on in their life, or they're just bad, mean people.

Step 122: Just accept that some people won't like you, and never will

...and it's not because they're jealous, either. They can just not like you. Do you like every person you meet? Every song you hear? Every food you taste? Extrapolate that. All around this world, there are people of all stripes—men and women, young and old, of every color and station—who, for whatever their reasons, *do not or would not like you.* Just move on.

As my friend Kate put it, if you don't like someone and they don't like you, that's not a problem, that's mutual agreement.

Next time you find yourself fretting about this, think of someone really, really neat—Albert Einstein, maybe. Then remember that there was at *least* one person who thought Einstein was a colossal dick. I guarantee it.

Step 123: Do not engage with crazy

Here, I am not talking about the mentally ill, but rather people whose perception of the world is so odd and skewed that it is difficult for them to interact with the rest of us. Think people who scream at waitresses. Those types of people.

Engaging with them will never, ever provide the desired effect for you. You cannot make crazy people not-crazy with your reasonable thoughts and words. There is one direction sanity will flow, and it is away from you as the madness spreads, and soon your thoughts and words won't be even slightly reasonable. Drunk counts as crazy here, in both the short term ("Oh, she's drunk") and the long term ("Oh, he's *a* drunk").

The next time you find yourself interacting with someone who is just completely out there, don't tell them they're being unreasonable because that won't do anything.

Remind yourself that you do not engage with crazy (silently, of course; saying this aloud will probably make things much worse). Treat them kindly, and gingerly, and then get away.

WARNING SIGNS

Here is a collection of things that may, in fact, be said or done by crazy people. They can also be said or done by non-crazy people, so just make sure your little ears perk up when you notice these things:

• "Those guys are all out to get me." Possibly, yes. Possibly they are all out to get him because he is a crazy jerk.

• Any sort of slur against a group of people.

• Discussion of conspiracies of any sort in casual conversation.

• Intense, prolonged eye contact.

• Walking any animal that is not a dog.

• Introduction by a name that is clearly not their given one.

• Immediate revelation of an overly personal detail, like the fact that they don't talk to their mother anymore.

• Returning to a topic that you are not returning to, more than twice.

• An unnecessarily cutting comment, particularly if it's disguised as a compliment.

• Discussion of bodily functions, or (true story) telling you that they didn't get any sleep last night because their husband is passing a kidney stone.

• Discussion of something terrible going on in their lives introduced as though it's not a big deal, like a ha-ha thing. But it's clearly not at all a ha-ha thing.

Step 124: Accept, in the deepest part of your heart, that just because you are right or have the upper moral hand does not mean you'll win

You know why movies are so satisfying? Because they reflect back a reality that we all wish were true, that being good is its own reward and that being right means we will win.

This is often the *opposite* of the case in real life. People who have lots of power, people who care less about others, people who are more interested in what they want than what is just—sadly enough, these people tend to do pretty well for themselves, because they are more concerned with what works than what's right.

So if you find yourself the David to whomever's Goliath, fight valiantly. But also...

Step 125: Know when to drop the banana

When my sisters and I were little, we maintained a pretty steady argument for about seven years. I don't know if she got this from a child psychologist or what, but my mother's ingenious strategy was called Drop the Banana.

When we were having a pointless back-and-forth, the first child to say, "Drop the banana" and leave behind the bickering was rewarded. So, if you're stuck in a perpetual pointless-argument orbit, drop the banana and move on with your life.

Step 126: Do not allow yourself to be abused

While preserving your sanity by heading off pointless arguments at the pass is a great skill to acquire, do not do this all the time because you are afraid to fight with someone who picks on you constantly.

Know deep in your heart that you are not someone who tolerates the shitty treatment of others. Or at least don't let it get to you. Again, easier said than done.

But a good way to gauge this accurately is to try to take yourself out of the situation. Imagine that a close, dear friend you love is relaying the circumstances to you. Is it abusive?

STRANGER DANGER, OR AT LEAST INCONVENIENCE

It is so easy to come to the conclusion that every single person in the world whom you don't know personally is out to ruin your day, what with the loud movie-talking and non-turn-signaling and mouth-breathing and every single other repugnant human behavior.

And yes, there is little you can do to permanently alter the behavior of others. But you can be a folk hero who shushes people in the movie theater and doesn't tolerate line-cutters.

Let's start by not being an asshole yourself.

Step 127: Give up your seat to pregnant people, elderly people, and others with obvious physical burdens

Come on. No one needs to tell you that. Just do it.

Step 128: Speak patiently and kindly to people

Even if you feel neither patient nor kind. Just do it. Know that in some way, you will be rewarded for upping the earth's pleasantness level.

Step 129: Remember that you catch more flies with honey than vinegar

Here's one reason to be kind and patient: It gives people more incentive to care about you enough to do what you want. Just because you're kind and good doesn't mean your motives have to be pure.

Step 130: Deal with line-cutters and their ilk as though they are sweet but dim people who need some gentle correction

This can work with people of all stripes who need to straighten up and fly right, although line-cutting is a perfect example. Assume your friendliest, most open expression that lets them know you are all on the same team. Your voice will express *sympathy* that they didn't get this right the first time, but *optimism* that with your guidance, they will manage.

"Actually—" Pause. "—the line starts back that way." Then put a bright happy smile on your face, one with just the slightest hint of steel. Ninety percent of this smile will say, *Glad we've cleared this up!* Ten percent of this smile will say, *Seriously, fucker. Get to the end of the line.*

This also works with drunk bros harassing women, someone who is talking loudly on the cell phone, and teenagers playing loud and terrible music on public transportation.

Step 131: In general, don't cause a ruckus in public

Unless people are paying to see you perform, it's nice to just go with the flow. Be quiet in movies. Don't cut in line, physically or metaphorically. Don't raise your voice to strangers as a means of signaling that they need to pay attention to you, even if they are the worst customer service agent ever. Look at what the people around you are doing, and do that. If you are in a space where people are all walking or moving in one direction, then walk or move in that direction with them. If everyone is being quiet, maybe you should be quiet, too. If you don't care to, then relocate yourself.

Don't be an unnecessary impeder.

Step 132: Wish them well

This is for the long-term sorts of enemies. There is a good bit of truth in that cliché about how acid hurts the vessel that carries it more than any object it might be poured upon. When you carry around ugly negative feelings about someone, guess what? It's your brain that has those awful thoughts living in it, not theirs. Chances are that your hatred does little to nothing to thwart your actual enemy, but rather keeps *you* in a state of icky resentment.

So here is one of those things that is so difficult, but that you can feel proud of. Next time you think something awful about someone, just take a moment and do your best to wish them well. You can wish that their wellness occurs far away from you, but finding a little pebble of positivity to fling in their direction does wonders for one's serenity.

DISCUSSION QUESTIONS AND ACTIVITIES

1. Which is worse to talk about in polite circles: poop or herpes?
2. Name some other things crazy people do, then write a one-act play that includes all of them.
3. What is the most spectacular conversational clusterfuck you've ever witnessed in person?

Seven easy steps to reduce everyday shambles

1. Important information does not live on small scraps of paper for more than the time it takes to hang up the phone and transport that information to its permanent home. Phone numbers go in your phone. Dates go on your calendar. And so on.
2. Keep your phone charged, and on you. Have extra chargers, 'cause why not! One lives in your car, one at work, one at home.
3. Apply a similarly generous strategy to deodorant placement: again, one at home, one at work, one in your car, and one in a strategic fourth location—the gym, perhaps, or a significant other's house.
4. Develop your mantra of Things That Must Not Be Lost. Anytime you leave a place to go elsewhere, run down the list. Mine is phone-keys-wallet. Pho-Kee-Wah, for short.
5. Get online banking, then check your account at least weekly for anything surprising or terrifying.
6. Be on time to things.
7. Call and email people back promptly. These last two steps do more than you can imagine to convey one's grown-up-ness.

5. Get a Job

Getting a job isn't optional unless you are phenomenally wealthy, in which case enjoy hanging out in your own private baby animal menagerie. Mine will have a bouncy castle full of red pandas.

But as seminal Atlanta rapper Young Jeezy put it, if you aspire to stack paper and ball sufficiently outrageous to someday have an adorable private zoo of your very own, you need to get a job. And unlike Young Jeezy, your job will not consist of rapping about Atlanta's cocaine trade.

Jobs are crucial to being an adult. Frankly, jobs are crucial to being a human being. We're social creatures, and we each need to do something that is useful to the other human beings, even if it's in an artificial capacity, like helping other humans get their hot pizzas in a timely fashion.

Side note: I know it is really, really hard to find a grown-up job, and the process can be painfully demoralizing. I promise: I feel your pain. Everyone does, because everyone has to start at this place of not having a job. If you're reading this and don't have a job, know this: You *can* and *will* find a job eventually and someday this will be an icky but receding memory. But for now, there are a few ways to maximize your chances of finding the right thing for you.

Step 133: Keep your head down and cook

This piece of advice, more than any in the chapter, will work no matter where you are or what you do.

An old boyfriend of mine was a cook who was good enough to open up his own restaurant. When he talked about the employees he loved best—the ones who got raises, the ones he would take anywhere—there was one thing they all had in common.

"He keeps his head down and cooks."

If you are the employee who shows up on time without fuss, doesn't cause drama, and quietly but competently does the job you're paid for, then you will always be sought after. Go with the flow when it comes to workplace regulations. Show up in a clean uniform and do the small, stupid things that seem pointless but are part of company culture.

Step 134: Let go of your pride

In the vein of non-Special-Snowflake-ness (see step 1), it is important to come right out and accept that your first job will not be glamorous, lucrative, or fun. It may be one of those things, but it certainly won't be all three.

I have a friend whose work ethic is just unparalleled. It's not even his work ethic so much as his pragmatism: He always understood that having a job is not optional. He worked hard through undergrad, then got into a top-tier law school with a generous scholarship. And then... he decided he hated it and dropped out. Not knowing what to do but knowing that he had to pay rent, he got the first job he was hired for, which happened to be delivering pizzas. And you know what? Because he was the kind of guy who was willing to take on a pizza job just to make things work, when he found what he wanted to do, he rose quickly to the top and now makes lawyer money anyway.

So while you may not be delivering pizzas now, put yourself in a place where you are willing to do that kind of thing. Nothing is beneath you, right now, except doling out handjobs by the watercooler. That *is* beneath you.

This will not always be the case, so (last time Young Jeezy will be quoted) "get on your grind and get it." A metaphorical grind that involves no cocaine, okay?

Finally, this should be obvious, but if you don't have a job and get offered one, take it. As my friend Joce pointed out, there is no reason to think you're too good for a paying job if you are without one.

Step 135: Accept the idea of networking

Networking sounds terrible and suggests the image of carnivorous fish (in people bodies), circling one another hungrily, business cards burning in their pockets.

And sometimes, yes, that's what it is.

But mostly, it's not that at all, in the same way that not all parties are frat parties. Networking is building a community of people you know and care about, and it really is important. You don't have to be an asshole to do it well.

Grown-up jobs, more often than not, come from professional and personal connections you've made.

But also know that networking isn't a transactional thing. It is not step 1: Meet people. Step 2: Said people offer you a job.

"It's not just a bank account you draw from—it takes a lot of ongoing work and maintenance and being willing to offer whatever kind of help and favors you can," Jared, a dude who is one of the few people in the world who is great at networking but also an excellent human being, said. So, in words that he would never, ever use: You are building, twig by twig, a beautiful nest of shared opportunity, cemented by the spit of your helpfulness and enthusiasm. You are not sharking for a job. You're trying to offer your resources to people who can use them, and maybe someday they'll want to do the same for you.

POSSIBILITIES FOR NETWORKING

Lots of business organizations hold mixers. These events specifically designated for young professionals are a great bet in terms of a lower intimidation factor. Conferences are nothing but networking. Job and career fairs, of course, are also great chances to meet people who may want to hire you. You can and should ask your professors, family friends, and colleagues if they would ever be willing to let you tag along on networking opportunities, or if there is anyone they could perhaps introduce you to.

Quick note: All the things that shouldn't be discussed in light social situations from the Fake It Till You Make It chapter are verboten here, too. Heavy political discussions, tales of your health woes, and gossip about who is sleeping with whom should also not be a part of networking.

It's not super complicated: They are there to meet people, and so are you. An introduction can be really simple: "Hi, I'm Kelly," and then, after they've said their name and you've established that it is, in fact, nice to meet each other, and they ask you what you do, you can say something along the lines of, "Oh, I'm graduating from Loyola in a few months and am hoping to work in PR."

Step 136: Ask for a business card when the conversation is winding to a close

"It was so, so nice to meet you. Oh, hey, do you have a card on you? Thanks! Here's mine."

This feels terrifically uncomfortable/intimidating (proposed new emotional state: uncomfimidated), but it's not. People are there with business cards *to hand them out*, and they expect it. Since you've already established yourself as a smart, confident person who would never dream of calling their office every hour on the hour just to hear their voice, they should be happy to oblige.

Step 137: Follow up with people you meet

Send them an email—a brief, non-manifesto-length email—to say what a pleasure it was to meet them and that you hope your paths cross again. You will get the email address off the business card you ask for when the conversation is drawing to a close.

Step 138: Ask those people out for coffee

When you encounter smart people in your industry, realize that it is perfectly acceptable (and encouraged!) to ask them out to coffee, then pepper them with questions. They may say no, but you'd be surprised at how often they say yes. They may not want to give you a job, but people, generally speaking, are happy to answer questions and give advice. The happiness that comes from helping others in a low-stakes way is pretty universal.

Before you go, brush up on their work and what they (not just the industry, but that individual person) have done. Then ask about what they do and what advice they'd give to someone just starting out, and really listen to what they are saying. Buy their coffee and baked good of choice and send a thank-you note afterward (see step 115 in Fake It Till You Make It).

Finally, this step is not just for people new to the working world. There will always be people older/smarter/more talented/farther along than you. Take them out for coffee and listen to what they say.

Step 139: Go on informational interviews near and far

Here is one of the most useful phrases in life: "I'm going to be in town for a few days, and I'd love to stop by and introduce myself."

Here is how you employ that phrase: Whenever you are going to visit somewhere you would not totally hate living, scout out the businesses in your industry that are there, and see if you can't stop by and say hi. Send an email—not to the top boss, but someone who has some power in the division you'd like to be a part of. The "in town for a few days" thing implies that you are a Business-Minded Gal-on-the-Go who zips efficiently through airports and car rental counters en route to global domination. Short skirts, long jackets, and such.

Hopefully, you make a good impression, send a thank-you note (are you sensing a trend with the thank-yous?), and then, when a job opens up, your résumé will float to the top of the pile because unlike the vast majority of applicants, they have a face to put with the name.

This can also work closer to home: Simply say that you know they don't have any openings right now, but you'd just like to stop by and say hi.

Step 140: Make your social media presence as bland as possible

You will be Googled. They will Google you, then move to your Facebook, your LinkedIn, and even your MySpace, which will float around forever. I love that everyone of a certain age has their embarrassing 2007 self trapped in cyber amber. So beat any potential employers to the punch, and if there is anything questionable online, *take it down*.

No one can see my tagged pictures on Facebook. No one can read anything but the slightest hints of my political views. No one needs to know what I look like in a bikini. In fact, new rule: If you wouldn't show or tell your mom, boss, and ex-boyfriend, then don't put it on Facebook.

Step 141: Customize your résumé

Yes, it's a pain. But so is almost every aspect of being a grown-up. How much do you want this job, anyway? Enough to spend thirty minutes tweaking your résumé?

Dana is a recruiter for a schmancy West Coast digital staffing agency, and she recommends that you use the same wording they do in the job description.

Not all jobs have thoughtful people like Dana looking at résumés; instead they employ cold and calculating computer algorithms. And even if someone is looking at the résumé, they're not looking for long unless they see what they're skimming for.

"The average hiring manager takes about seven seconds to skim through a résumé," Dana told me, then added that lots of job postings use computer programs to scan the résumés, and only those that match move on.

"You might have ten different versions of your résumé," Dana said. "Maybe you would think of *managing* being a keyword, whereas the company job description doesn't use one word about managing a team but instead talks about leading a team. You need to change your wording to match theirs."

Step 142: Proofread your résumé

Seriously. Read it out loud, word by word. This is also a good time to mention that writing like you talk works very well. If you're stuck on how to phrase something, find someone you're comfortable with and then try to tell them as directly and simply as possible.

Then get at least two other people to proofread your résumé—the kind of people who will help and not hurt the situation.

Step 143: You can and should send a follow-up email after you send in your application (unless it's specifically forbidden)

Dear Ms. Williams,

I wanted to drop a quick note to make sure you've received my cover letter and application for the general assignment reporter position, and also reiterate my interest in the position. I know you have lots of applicants to sort through, but I hope you'll consider me.

All my best,
Kelly

Step 144: If you are called for an interview on the moon, figure out a way to get there

"Too many times do I see candidates who, when I call them and say, 'Hey, you've got an interview request at this time and this day,' aren't willing to reschedule whatever their something else is and don't get a second chance to interview," Dana said. "The likelihood of them working with your schedule is slim to none."

However, if you really, truly, absolutely cannot get there because you're having open-heart surgery or whatever, come back with several other, similar options. "Oh my gosh. This is heartbreaking, but actually my wedding is scheduled for that Wednesday afternoon and I think my wife-to-be would notice if I were missing. Is there any way we could do the following Wednesday?"

Step 145: Do not bring anyone—not your mom, dad, boyfriend, cat, step-cousin, frienemy, anyone—with you to a job interview

I am sort of shocked this is a thing, but recruiter Dana assures me it is. If you need a ride to the interview, that's fine, but this person must remain invisible to the employer. As far as the employer is concerned, you just emerged, Aphrodite-like, out of the seafoam and into the office park, the winds of your own competence wafting you safely to shore with five minutes to spare.

Step 146: Show up looking and sounding smart

If you've gotten that precious and rare job interview, congratulations! You are so, so close, and needless to say, you are going to blow the interviewer away. They will be left trembling after the presence of such awesome competence, and gnash their teeth when they think of the years that passed when they could've had you, then feel relieved that *at least they have you now.*

So to ensure this is the impression they're left with, think of it this way. This interview is simply asking, "Can you fill this space/gap, this need that we have?" and you replying, "Absolutely." All of your responses during the interview need to convey that "absolutely."

The first way you will demonstrate your absolutely-ness is in appearance. You will look extra sharp in your best suit, unless you are in an extremely casual and creative profession, in which case take cues from those around you (or, even better, ask someone what is customarily worn to an interview during one of those many coffee dates you had earlier).

Step 147: Don't talk about how great this job will be for you, talk about how great you are for the job

Remember, this company or person isn't interested in hiring you because they want you to be as self-actualized and joyful as possible— they're thinking about hiring you because they have a need, and think maybe you can fill it. Your entire job is to convey to them that yes, you can indeed fill that need. Your needs are not important in this step of the process.

It's understandable to forget this—especially if you're fresh out of college. Up until now, your life has been about others teaching and instructing you in the hope that it will help you meet your life goals. But have you noticed that you pay to go to college? Generally speaking in life, the person who gives money is the one whose needs are important, and the person getting money is paid to meet those needs.

Step 148: Don't bad-mouth any past employers. Don't bad-mouth any current employers. Don't bad-mouth anyone

This may seem like a fun, conspiratorial, "Oh, you wouldn't *believe*," sort of thing, but to a potential employer, all bad-mouthing does is establish that you are gossipy and potentially not a team player. It introduces doubt in their mind about you and your abilities—if you're so great, how come this person didn't like you? Remember how the only thing you are doing right now is conveying how capable and essential you are? This does not fit in with that.

No matter how terrible things were with a past job—and they may, indeed, have been really, really bad—it's not valid interview conversation fodder. If you can say good things about the boss or company, then do so. If you just can't bring yourself to say anything even slightly positive, just say, "You know, it wasn't the best fit for me. Anyway, [more statements that convey your professionalism]."

Step 149: Don't forget to ask questions

Frankly, you should have a million questions. This is a place that you will spend forty or more hours per week. This is a place that will assign you hundreds and thousands of tasks to be successfully completed. This is a place filled with people whom you will spend more time around than you do with your own family. Someone who isn't interested in what this means for them is a major red flag. Asking questions doesn't make you a pest; it reveals you as someone who is committed to making sure you are right for the job, and the job is right for you.

Here are some classic examples:

- What does an average day look like for someone in this job?
- What is the most challenging aspect of this job?
- In your opinion, what kind of person would be most successful in this position? (**Note:** Take the answer to this into account, then hopefully tailor your responses to demonstrate that you are that sort of person.)
- What makes your company's culture unique? What, in your opinion, distinguishes you from the others in your industry?

• Is there anything you'd like to share with me about the job that we haven't covered yet?

Obviously, after such a powerful interview performance, they will see there is absolutely no choice but to hire you and offer you exactly what you are worth. At which point you must...

Step 150: Negotiate for your salary

This feels really awkward. We're socially conditioned to not talk about money or how great we are, and all salary negotiations involve talking about how great we are *in the context of money*. If you're not used to it, it can be several layers of uncomfortable. Move past that.

The reason we have jobs is to make money. Yes, hopefully you love and are rewarded by what you're doing, but chances are you wouldn't volunteer there forty (or fifty, sixty, seventy, whatever) hours per week.

There may not be as much wiggle room in your first job as there will be in future ones. If it's clear that there is a particular, non-negotiable salary associated with this job, you will have to accept that.

But if the ad says DOE (depending on experience), then it's negotiation time.

Alan is the director of sales for his company and, in general, a very winning guy. This is probably why he's director of sales. He was willing to weigh in with a few tips on where to start the negotiation process:

• For your starting figure, request the **salary of someone with five years' experience in your particular job.** Ask the Internet what that number is for your job of choice, but for the purposes of this book, let's pretend that figure is $40,000 per year.

• You will also want to have another figure in your head, and that is **how low you will go.** Decide, realistically, what this number is. Alan suggested perhaps 10 percent less than your initial offer, which in this case would be $36,000.

• **Pay attention to the person's reaction when you give your number.** See if they look startled, or blink, or take it in stride.

• **If they say your requested salary is too high, ask for what their budget is, then ask for the top end.** "If you go to work for a big company, there's a salary range," Alan said. "They won't go above it and they generally won't go below it."

• Negotiating only works, of course, if you can **demonstrate your value**, so be sure to figure this out ahead of time. It doesn't have to be a bar graph, but rather an anecdote that demonstrates what a bright young go-getting thing you are. "It could be a story," Alan said. "People love stories."

• Understand that that no one will rescind an offer because you ask for a lot. You may not get it, but you won't be punished for asking.

Step 151: Some industries require an internship; if so, go get one

For a lot of glamour industries, this is the only way in. You don't necessarily need to wait for an internship posting; you can certainly take initiative and ask someone who is not at the very top, but a few rungs down, about the possibility of an internship.

Step 152: Be prepared to do the worst, dullest assignments as an intern/new hire. Do them cheerfully

This is so unpleasant but so true: In almost every profession, you have to pay your dues. Unless your dad owns the company, there is no way around, over, or under it—just through it. And it's not always fun.

But what separates those who will, in time, get to hand off their own boring assignments to future interns is a willingness to do this shit *like it is the most exciting and important task of your life*. You are fucking *thrilled* to type up all the weekly senior center activities in town. God, you would *love* to go get this person some coffee. Et cetera. The key here is not to employ that sorority-style "YAAAAAAY!" enthusiasm, but rather the sort of serious enthusiasm with which you might set off on an epic quest in a big-budget fantasy trilogy. Summon all of your latent acting talent.

Step 153: Pick up on office etiquette and norms

There is a lot of leeway here if you're an intern or a young new hire. Everyone remembers what it was like to be twenty-one and feel really swamped and confused, expected to obey rules and concepts that are invisible to you but so obvious to everyone else.

But! You still need to be on your best behavior, and follow others' lead. That window of wiggle room will close very quickly once you're paid to be there.

Every office has different social mores, customs, and etiquette, and when you walk in for the first time, you will naturally have no idea what they are. It is okay to be quiet and mouse-like for a few weeks. Just watch silently, with your beady but adorable eyes, and observe how and when people talk to one another. Is cursing allowed? Does anyone eat at their desk? Are said desks to be kept spotless, or are they piled in papers? Is lunch an hour long? Twenty minutes? If you leave the office for an errand, do you need to let someone know? These questions have all been answered long before you arrived. Don't go with your gut. Go with what everyone else is doing.

Whatever the standard-issue behavior is, make yours a notch or two more conservative until you are a fully integrated part of the group.

Step 154: The most important of all the above-type questions is "Who is actually in charge?"

This doesn't mean title-wise; it probably won't take that much time to figure out who is organizationally at the top. But there are other leaders, too. There's the one who knows every single thing that happens in the building. There's the person who may not have an intimidating title, but is the boss's favorite and always has their ear. There is the one who is the folk hero of the workers. There is the person you need to talk to when shit hits the fan.

You can't ask most of these things directly, at least not until you find a good friend at work (the kind who would be your friend even if you didn't have work in common). But again, keep your eyes and ears open.

Step 155: Treat casual Fridays as not-casual Fridays

Everyone says it because it's true: Casual Fridays are stupid. Actually, it's just me that says that, but prevailing wisdom does hold that you should dress for the job you want, not the one you have. Unless the job you want is dolphin trainer, and the job you have is funeral home director.

But if you show up looking spiffy (not formal, mind you...just spiffy) on casual Fridays then everyone else looks kind of rumply by comparison. Wear jeans on your own time.

Step 156: Don't be that intern

Internships tend to happen at a point in life when we get to drink lots and lots of alcohol pretty much consequence-free, a golden time that I will dub the Absolut Mandrin Years. And you, intern, have a great and wonderful gift in that unlike almost everyone else at the office, you can get near-blackout drunk at a Saturday-afternoon croquet game and not raise any eyebrows. Life is your schnapps-soaked oyster, so enjoy it.

But the people around you at your internship live in a very different world, one in which the above action would warrant, at minimum, some Serious Concern. You can tell it's serious, because the S and C are both capitalized.

To blend in seamlessly, you must drink as they drink, which is to say sparingly. Actually, no. Drink less than them. Do not be that intern who (true story) got drunk and told all the men in the office that she had no gag reflex. No. Never. No.

Step 157: Do not tell the Internet what you think of your job

Just don't. This is something that can, and likely will, get you fired. No matter how well you think you've veiled it on your anonymous blog, it will come back. It will live forever. The Internet has a big mouth and a long, long memory. Plus, people have an uncanny knack for *immediately* finding the unflattering things you've said about them.

Don't bitch about your boss on Facebook. Don't write emails detailing how much you hate everything on a work computer. Don't think that you can leak things to Gawker without it coming back to bite you in the ass.

If you're over the job, and aren't worried about establishing

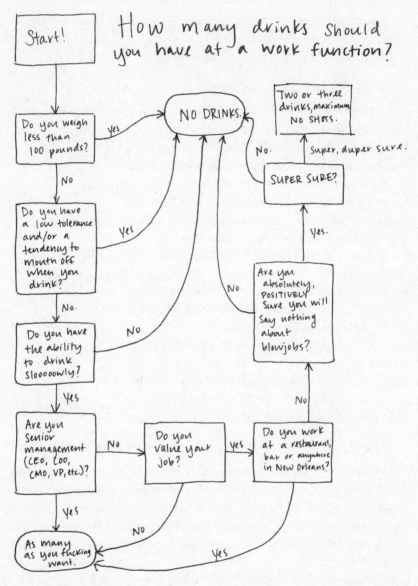

yourself as the kind of person who (publicly) bites the hand that feeds you, then by all means. Otherwise, do what everyone else does and complain bitterly over happy-hour drinks with your coolest co-workers.

Step 158: Don't lose touch after an internship

Now that you've successfully made your way through your internship, congratulations! Even if it seems thankless now (and yes, it most likely is), the Universe sees your diligence and will smile upon you.

Internships can pay unexpected dividends, and give you your first shot at networking. During your internship, there will probably be three or four people who have been especially helpful, or that you feel close to. One of these will likely be your supervisor, but you'd be surprised how many people will reach out and teach you things about what they do. This is an awesome and self-selecting group of helpful, kind people who like you.

Toward the end of your internship, write them a thank-you note that tells them not only that you appreciate them, but also *why* you appreciate them.

And then stay in touch. Not every week or anything, but when something exciting happens in your life or theirs, send a friendly email. And then, when you're a few months out from looking for a job, let them know and ask if they would mind keeping their ears open for you.

Step 159: Ask for a raise

This can happen very naturally at an annual review, or right after you've finished kicking ass and taking names on a big project. For obvious reasons, you should ask at a time when you are doing demonstrably well. You are welcome to ask for as much as you want, though if you work at a big corporation, chances are good they have a set formula. Three percent is usually an acceptable figure to ask for. Again, you won't get in trouble for asking. Send an email asking for a meeting—perhaps during a time in which your boss will be in a jovial mood—and then compress your nervous gases into a steely core, because you deserve this.

Sample dialogue: "Thank you so much for meeting with me. I'm really proud of the work I've been doing here recently, and I was hoping you'd consider the possibility of a raise."

Is this outfit office- appropriate?

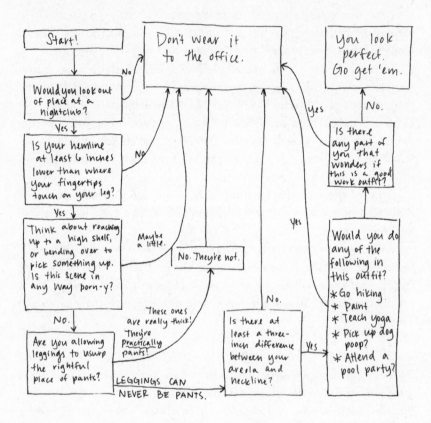

Step 160: Put together a work wardrobe

Chances are very good that

(a) You did not wear office-worthy garb in college; and
(b) You don't have enough cash on hand now to buy a whole new wardrobe.

On the upside, every career lady ever has faced this, and you can certainly come out on top. First, observe what people in your industry of choice wear. Then try to get a few non-cheap base items, and lots of cheaper supplementary options.

You may decide to get nice black slacks, a nice black skirt, nice gray slacks, and a nice gray skirt. Then find a blazer or two that matches all four items, and supplement with cheaper (but also mainly covered-up) blouses.

T.J.Maxx and other discount retailers often have steeply discounted business clothes. Also, chances are good that there is a thrift store in your town run by the Junior League or whatever the local equivalent benevolent rich lady society is. If you are desperately poor, find this store, then revel in seven-dollar Ann Taylor pants with all the tags still on.

Step 161: Get some really nice, expensive black high heels

You know how people say you can really tell a difference with super-expensive high heels? Well, you can. They look beautiful, but, more important, they *feel* beautiful. Save your pennies, five dollars a week for a year, then go to Saks. Get sexy but classic heels. Wear them forever. You will not be sorry.

Step 162: Don't hook up with anyone in your office, no matter how exciting the prospect

Actually, you're probably going to at some point. Almost everyone does. Having a poorly considered liaison with a co-worker is the chicken pox of the working life, so you may as well get it over with. But after that happens, you will look back and wish you hadn't. Have you ever once heard of someone saying, "You know, I'm glad I had that three-week fling with my cubicle-mate a few years back, because it's so great to sit across from him in meetings knowing what his dick looks like"?

After that one mistake, you will realize that it was a bad plan, at which point you will decide to . . .

Step 163: Live your life as though everyone in the office has plastic, featureless doll crotches

This includes you. Your sex life should never be a topic of conversation in the office, and neither should anyone else's. You may reclaim your genitalia once you are on non-company time.

Step 164: You did not come here to make friends

Like every reality show contestant ever, your focus must be solely on winning the heart of a paunchy aged rocker, except you are instead after the corner office. Or at least doing competently the thing you have come to do. You want to be warm and friendly with your co-workers, but this isn't subsidized socializing; you are being paid to do something and you need to do it.

Step 165: Find a mentor

There will be someone you click with, whom you feel close to. If this person doesn't work in the same office as you, all the better; they won't be tainted by any office politics and can always be impartial in their advice. Conferences are a great place to find mentors; after you've met them and sent your follow-up thank-you email (Follow-up email! Follow-up email! Follow-up emails, *forever!*), then it's time.

It may be very difficult to ask outright for mentorship, but this person will almost surely be flattered. After you've had several conversations, say something like, "You know, I really appreciate all the advice you've given me. I know this sounds odd, but would it be okay if I considered you my mentor?"

Their heart will likely melt in the face of this awkward yet touching message.

If this feels too intense or formalized, just keep asking them out for coffee, and on coffee date ten, say, "I'm coming to consider you a mentor" or something along those lines.

Step 166: Develop a good meeting face

I've never yet met someone who likes meetings, but obviously they work in some way, because humanity keeps scheduling them and they are a Very Important Part of the office life. Bring a notepad, and don't let anyone see you doodling.

Meeting face is a curious, interested, yet neutral expression. Practice this in the mirror, especially if your default facial expression is bitch-face. Subtle nods can be good, too, if you actually agree with what is being said. If you're all the way in the back and don't need to pay attention, I recommend trying to list all fifty states as a nice time-burner.

Step 167: Keep your desk tidy

Here, I will officially designate a time for you: At 3:17 PM each Wednesday afternoon, take the next thirteen minutes to tidy, straighten, recycle, and wipe down. Do that last one with the disinfecting wipes you keep in your desk drawer.

Things to keep in your desk at work:

- A deodorant stick
- Hem tape, which works shockingly well, or a sewing kit
- A lint roller
- A bottle of over-the-counter pain reliever
- Non-perishable, non-stinky snacks
- Feminine hygiene products of your choice, if you are a lady or an over-the-top helpful dude
- Disinfecting wipes
- Hand sanitizer
- Quarters
- A travel toothbrush and toothpaste
- Tissues, particularly during the sniffly season
- Mint or gum
- Label maker (Nothing says *baddest bitch in the cubicle game* like matching tape dispenser, scissors, and stapler with color-coordinated labels with your last name. As a bonus, even when you move on and the scissors are handed down to someone else, either the label or its gummy afterglow will remain as a tiny testament.)

Step 168: Distinguish, in your mind, business etiquette from social etiquette

I have a pretty finely developed radar for when people are feeling uncomfortable, and my natural inclination is to make them feel at ease. But as a reporter, sometimes I need to keep pushing. I ask questions that I would not ask if I met this person at a party, because it's my job and *grown-ups do their fucking jobs*. So, while you are not given permission to be a total asshole, you have every right to be curt, business-like, or cold with people when it's called for. Remember: Not here to make friends.

Step 169: Don't verbally undermine yourself

If you were the kind of really cool person who was on the speech and debate team in high school, you know never to start an argument with "I think" or "I feel." Obviously you think it or feel it, or you wouldn't say it.

This can slip away so, so easily, especially if you are new or feel like you don't fully have a handle on what's going on. And you will have this feeling for the first three years of nearly any job worth having.

"Well, I'm not the expert, but..."

"I don't know much, but..."

"I think that maybe..."

Knock that shit off. Seriously. If you're going to share your opinion, *say it as though it were a declarative statement.* Not a question? That you have? Floating around in your head? And you hope others will agree with? But if they don't, that's okay, too? Just say it. And if you really feel that unsure about it, then don't waste that other person's time with verbal waffling.

Step 170: Gchat if you must, but remember your bosses can legally read everything you're saying

Ditto for Facebook, email, Twitter, all of it. If you're doing it on a work computer, you legally have no right to privacy, and you shouldn't expect it. So just imagine these interactions being read aloud to the office.

Hopefully this goes without saying, but *never* look at anything that could even slightly be construed as porn at work. If, for some reason, you unwittingly click to something, go let your supervisor know as soon as possible that it was an accident and won't be repeated.

Step 171: You can only call in fake-sick one day a year

And no, being hung over is not being sick. So choose wisely, friend.

Step 172: If you're coughing, sneezing, or otherwise obviously infectious and cannot take over-the-counter meds to remedy the situation, stay home

Make your co-workers sick and they'll hold it against you forever. When I get someone's nasty ailment, it really makes me want to punch them. This is not an accepted form of workplace communication, no matter how much they may deserve it. So don't set these ugly thought wheels into motion. Stay home and get better.

Step 173: Don't just be likable, be a good co-worker

If you are not a good co-worker—if you don't get things done when they're supposed to be done, if you drop the ball on group projects, if you don't speak up when someone else is being blamed for your mistake, if you don't reply to time-sensitive emails and calls promptly—people will figure that out. Being sweet and charming can cover for a while. But these things will come back to bite you eventually.

Step 174: Accept that there is no such thing as vacation

There's just working extra hard beforehand, spending your vacation feeling that something must be awry, then scrambling for weeks to catch up.

Step 175: Take yours anyway

If you get paid vacation, take it. Even if you're too poor to travel anywhere, you can at least spend your day off lolling around and watching TV and/or being hung over.

Step 176: Do not steal more than three dollars' worth of office supplies per quarter

Pens, I think, are reasonable. But not all the time. And no scissors.

Step 177: Shut down office creepers

First off, you do not need to feel uncomfortable at work. Everyone needs to be there, and no one should make it unpleasant for others to be there. But before you dash to HR, remember this: If someone is making you feel uncomfortable, it is okay to make them feel a little uncomfortable.

I've found that most offices have at least one middle-aged male employee who seems to delight in spending as much time as possible around the new twenty-two-year-olds. Remember, you can be cordial and icy at the same time. Forced, thin smiles that register for half a second then turn into a slightly squinty face, and curt answers without follow-up questions will do wonders.

If this person tends to invade your personal space while you're working at your desk, here is a brilliant strategy, courtesy of Miss Manners. The next time you turn your head and they are way, way too close, let out a little scream. Nothing overly dramatic; just enough that other people do the prairie dog thing of popping their heads up over the cubicle walls to see what is going on.

Then say, "Oh. Gosh. You startled me; I didn't expect you to be that close to me." Period. Don't wave away the awkwardness this sentence will create. Let this painful silence roar, that the dude may remember this natural consequence of breathing in your ear.

If that doesn't work, go to HR.

Step 178: If there is something shady going on, document everything

Not on a work computer, either, because (not to be dire) if you were to get fired, you wouldn't have access to those files anymore. Get time, date, location, specifics, a list of witnesses, and verbatim quotes if possible. These things must be quantifiable.

Step 179: When possible, conflict via email

One, in the workplace it leaves a paper trail, and paper trails are *great* for proving a point, should it come to that.

But beyond that, letters are a great way to deliver a difficult message in a way that gives the recipient a chance to think about and digest what you've said without having to respond immediately. Often, people need a little bit of space when you've given them something difficult, and in the pressure of an immediate response things can come out wrong. If the person you're dealing with is even slightly reasonable, this can be a much calmer way of actually solving problems rather than just feeling angry and self-righteous.

This means that you cannot just write an email and put someone on blast. Email is not your chance to polish every mean thing you've ever wanted to say, lob a digital Molotov cocktail, and walk away without looking at the explosion.

Instead, email should be a place that you can be calm, reasoned, and open to a solution that works for all parties. And yes, if it gets into a back-and-forth eventually you'll need to talk. But this is a good way to say the things you need to say in the way you wish to say them without being interrupted.

Step 180: Let that angry email you composed marinate for a minute

Every single time in my life that I've thought, *Hmmm, I wonder if this email is a little over the top? I should sleep on it*, I could just French-kiss my past-self for her measured control and foresight. Because each and every time, I revise the email.

Yes, it's not satisfying. But it's what grown-ups do.

Step 181: If someone dislikes you off the bat, then do your best to either nip it in the bud or avoid them

This will be a function of power. If the person is beneath you, or clearly on your plane (not just position-wise, but power-wise), then you can adopt an attitude that says, *I'm confused why you're having this problem but it doesn't matter all that much and you need to move through it*. Come from a place of confidence with it.

And you know what? If nothing else, you can let this person's dislike for you fuel your desire to do well, thus eventually putting yourself in a place where you *definitely* have the upper hand.

If they are above you, skip to step 184.

Step 182: Assess whether the work foe is actually an enemy, or just difficult

Yes, some people will genuinely have it out for you, and you may never know why. But when you're encountering someone new and difficult at work, it's best to leave the jury out for a few weeks on the off chance that they are just sort of confused and blunder-ish.

Step 183: Stand up for yourself when someone is constantly dumping stuff on you that is not your responsibility

It's great to go above and beyond at work, but when one person is consistently expecting you to do his or her job, it hinders you from doing yours.

My friend Shantrell once had a co-worker who turned to her for help when he was new ... and then they got into a pattern where she did the work for him. Finally, when he dumped an enormous project on her lap two days before she was supposed to go on Christmas break, she asserted herself.

"I just kind of opted to say ... I don't know what you've been told, and if I'm wrong please clear it up for me, but I'm not required to help out with these projects," she said.

Step 184: If the person giving you a headache is above you, then it's time to kiss a little ass

Yes, yes. It's horrible. Mean bosses are just wretched. Truly, they are the employment equivalent of the stomach flu, in that there is not even one good thing to say about them, and years later you'll still feel nauseous every time you, say, smell linguine Alfredo or hear someone say the name *Bridget*.

But they are what they are. Generally speaking, the boss will always, always be in a more powerful position than you. That's just how it is. And whether it's fair or not, whether they are good or bad, it is in your best interest to be in their good graces. Just do a really excellent job, keep your hatred cards close to your chest, and hopefully eventually you'll be in a position to fire their sorry ass.

Step 185: At a certain point, do your best to disengage

I worked in a toxic workplace in my early twenties, one where everyone new was looked upon with suspicion. The mean girl of the office, I was told, hated all new female employees. "It's just her way!" everyone said, as though this were a funny personality quirk instead of something that made it truly awful to work there.

Sure enough, the first time I was introduced to her, her lip curled and she said in the most acid voice imaginable, "I know who you are," and then left it there.

Things with her got worse. In retrospect, I assume that she felt like I didn't deserve the position I had (which, truthfully, I did not) and resented the fact that the boss really liked me, which provided its own share of difficulties.

It came to a head at the office Christmas party about three months after I was hired. After a few drinks, I was feeling cheerful and felt like perhaps things could finally be put behind us.

"Melanie," I said, "I know things kind of got off on a bad foot between us, and I just wanted to let you know that I think you're a great reporter and I really hope we can work together."

(I'll pause here to allow you to start the horror-movie soundtrack strings in your mind, as she slowly turned a face contorted with rage I did not understand.)

"No one respects you. Everyone knows you're only here because [boss] has a crush on you and we're just waiting for you to quit or get fired." Except instead of saying "has a crush," she said something explicit and gross.

This was just the opening salvo on what turned out to be a surprisingly extensive and well-researched invective. I stood there for maybe five minutes as she continued her awful monologue, paralyzed by shock.

If I could go back in time, I would pause her after she said that very first thing. I would not allow myself to be abused, would not assume that some people can be reasoned with, would not assume that surely I had done something to warrant this.

Instead, I would have found my most crisp and dismissive voice, said "Sorry you feel that way, [c-word][1]," turned on my heel, and walked. I

---

1. Except I would have actually said the c-word, not said "c-word."

was doing nothing useful for myself by staying in that conversation. I was just allowing her, once more, to assert her mean power over me.

Step 186: Discern between dues-paying and abuse in the workplace

Don't expect to be treated with deference or respect in any new office environment. People deserve decency, but you have to earn those other two. You will not instantly be the most respected and beloved person when you walk into a workplace; those things come from months and years of doing your job well, pleasantly, and competently.

So a small amount of prickliness is to be expected while people sniff you out. But if it lasts and lasts even after you begin to prove yourself, then consider whether that's the right place for you.

Step 187: Realize that there is a difference between toxic co-workers and a toxic workplace

There will always be someone you don't like in the workplace, and someone who doesn't like you. This is just the law of averages. Also, a workplace nemesis is sort of fun, especially when you beat them for that promotion.

Step 188: If you work in a toxic environment, find a new job

When you work in a place where the culture is fundamentally flawed—where anger and abuse flow downstream from the boss, where there is a casual sexism or racism, where employees are controlled by fear and intimidation—then you need to go, for your own sanity.

Toxic workplace environments rarely get better. Instead of being hurt, allow that anger to fuel your drive to a new job.

Step 189: Do not move on after less than a year unless there is a really, really compelling reason

Some jobs are not a great fit...but generally, professional-type jobs should last a year, minimum.

If you just can't make it that long, then do your darnedest not to repeat that move within the next five years. You want to look grounded and competent, not flighty.

If after a year, you still dread going in, begin putting out feelers for your next move.

Step 190: Be quiet when you start looking for a new job

Transparency is not your best option here. While you can quietly approach people whom you trust that are not your direct supervisor to see if they'd be willing to serve as a reference, you should not say anything to your bosses until the new job is a fait accompli. As in, offer letter in hand, drug test passed, starting date established.

Step 191: Let people in your network know that you're looking

Remember all that wonderful networking that you did? Now is when it pays off. Hopefully you've been keeping up these ties in a friendly and selfless way, you like them, and they like you. Just send a quick email:

Dear Alan,

Hey! Hope everything's been great. Things here [personal details that are interesting but not lurid].

Anyway, I've really enjoyed my time here at [company] but am starting to think about what the next move will be. I'd so appreciate it if you'd keep an ear out for any openings in [industry].

Take care!
Kelly

Step 192: Write a resignation letter—a nice one

No matter how bad things have been, it's a bad idea to leave on a fuck-you note. So when it is a done deal that you are going elsewhere, you will write a formal, dated letter. No need to pour your heart and soul into it, because presumably you will be talking to your boss in person. But the note should convey a few things:

- You are resigning your position as [X].
- You so appreciate the challenges and growth that you've experienced in the past [X] years.
- Your last day will be [X] *or* you are willing to work until [X] date to help smooth the transition. Two weeks' notice, minimum.

Step 193: Help someone in your professional network out

The first time someone (a friend, or co-worker, or whomever) comes to you saying that they want to switch jobs, and you can say, "Oh, my friend works at such-and-such place, let me put you in touch," you will feel so, so satisfied and helpful. It is really a wonderful feeling. And in this moment, you will understand why all those people were willing to help you out.

You don't need to go crazy, but an email of introduction is always a wonderful start, and spares the person you are helping from having to cold-email someone. In this case, it's a good idea to make sure the person you are putting them in touch with is okay ahead of time. And once they say *yes, pass on my email*, then you can do something like this, adding the second person in the CC: line:

Dear Alan,

    I wanted to electronically introduce Anne, my friend I was telling you about a few days ago. Anne's been working in marketing for a few years, but she's been very interested in public relations and I think is hoping to ask you a few questions. Anne, Alan is the head of communications for Bedwin-Fischer and an all-around excellent guy. Alan, meet Anne; Anne, meet Alan.

Cheers,
Kelly

In this way, it shall come full circle.

DISCUSSION QUESTIONS

1. If you were a carnivorous fish who was good at networking, what kind of carnivorous fish who was good at networking would you be? Follow-up: What is Donald Trump's spirit animal?
2. Did you think I was talking about myself when I mentioned the intern that told everyone she had no gag reflex? Because, for the record, it wasn't me.
3. Do you know of any True Life Workplace Heroes who've called their co-workers on sniffling, kimchi eating, or flatulence? What lessons should we learn from such people?

6. Money

Ugh, money. The worst. Being responsible about finances is terrifically grown-up—it requires impulse control, thinking about the future rather than the present, delaying gratification, and realizing that yes, you probably *can* survive without those vintage sunglasses. And it's really, really hard for some of us.

It's just so much fun to spend money! On delicious food, or ten-dollar drinks, or pretty hats, or airplane tickets, or any of the sixteen billion things in this world that are a blast to purchase, own, and experience. And it's so soul-crushingly dull not to spend it, knowing that it's right there, calling to you. "Hey [your name]," it begins. It uses a whispery, conspiratorial voice like it's your senior prom date or something. "Hey. Wouldn't it be great to take me to that new boutique? And maybe stop for macaroons? Didn't you need some stuff at Target? Oh my God, you know what? I am so hungry and I think the only thing that will make me *not* hungry is sushi. Like, a *lot* of it."

And then you spend it and it's gone because most of us aren't lucky enough to have lucrative jobs or independent wealth at twenty-three. The one advantage you have is that poverty in your twenties has a certain kind of glamour that cannot be said of, say, tuna fish casseroles in your seventies.

Do not underestimate the great pleasure that comes from outsmarting poverty, from looking nice even though you can't buy a forty-dollar pair of pants, from hosting a party on the cheap, from being able to actually handle a financial emergency without depending upon your parents.

The best reason to be good about money is that not being good about money is so, so painful. There is no moment that forces you to think about your poor choices more than when your debit card is declined when you are trying to purchase fried chicken at Popeyes. This is not something that I'm saying *has* happened to me, but I'm not saying it *hasn't* happened, either. At least the drive-through lady forgot she'd already handed over the Diet Coke so, hey! Free Diet Coke in exchange for any dignity I may ever have felt!

> If you have never eaten at Popeyes Famous Chicken and Biscuits, you are missing out. Did you know that famous New Orleans chef Paul Prudhomme developed their menu? And that their biscuits taste like they are deep-fried? Run, don't walk.

Step 194: Set reasonable expectations for yourself, money-wise

Before we delve into the sexy, fast-paced world of financial responsibility, take a moment and decide to be gentle on yourself if you are not yet a financial Viking. Money is an arena where it's all about expectation setting.

Some people reading this are people with diverse investment portfolios—in which case, yay for you, go enjoy your yacht or whatever. And some people reading this live with their parents. And some people are one type now but have been another. We will all experience circumstances that are not entirely within our control, especially when it comes to money, so don't judge yourself too harshly.

Just decide, realistically, where you are and what you can do. But mainly decide that you *can* do something, that there are small pieces of this very important thing that you have control over. And do not get stuck in a shame spiral. *No matter what you've done, you can take steps to fix it.*

I don't know what the constellation of qualities that make someone good with money is, but I certainly don't have it.

I am never going to be, by nature, a frugal person, or someone who can honestly say she's never strategically bounced a check. If, God forbid, I were ever to be rich, I know I'd be a cautionary tale. The local TV news would play a clip of me crying when they repossessed the pair of hot-air balloons I commissioned in the shape of my and Rick Ro$$'s heads.

But I can be someone who doesn't ring up seven thirty-five dollar overdraft fees for transactions of less than five dollars apiece. I'm probably never going to be great with money. But I can be okay with money, and you can be, too.

Step 195: Ignoring money issues won't make them go away. In fact, the opposite will happen

It's so easy to allow money to flow away from you if you aren't paying attention. And the prospect of keeping a vigilant eye on each cent in your possession can feel like an unpleasant combination of shrewishness and drudgery. Shrewdgery. But it must be done. The only way you can have control over your financial destiny is to face it head-on. And the first, best, most important tool is...

YOUR BUDGET

Budgets are right up there with meetings and annual gynecological exams in both unpleasantness and unavoidability. But like any good Pap smear, you'll feel capable and in charge once all is said and done, even if the during was no fun.

Step 196: Know exactly how much money you have coming in

The first step to determining how much money you can spend is to figure out how much money you have coming in on a monthly basis. For most of us, our salary will make up the bulk of this figure, but certainly add in any side income, from freelance writing gigs or your business selling earrings made of tiny plants on Etsy.

Now. See that number? You may not spend more money than that. Period. No ifs, ands, or buts.

Step 197: Know what you are spending money on

Make a list of your non-negotiable monthly expenses—rent, bills, however much you spend on groceries, gas, any recurring expenses—and then add a 5 percent cushion for all the unexpected expenses, plus your ten dollars per paycheck to add to your rainy-day savings account (see step 209). This will be your monthly living expense. This number doesn't include long-term savings and discretionary income.

Step 198: Take a long, hard look at the things you don't need to be spending money on

Conrad, who is a mortgage broker and, generally speaking, a super-responsible dude, said that it's a good plan to get six months' worth of bank and credit card statements on the table.

"Tracking where you currently spend your money is absolutely the first step," he said. "You can go back and make a list: *Here are the places I spend money. I'm spending X on food, I'm spending X on gas, I'm spending X on entertainment, I'm spending X on shopping.*"

Man, is this humbling, but highlight every unnecessary expense on your monthly bank statement. Look at the sea of jabby neon decisions. Is *jabby* a word? The adjective form of the verb *to jab*? Because that's how $57.89 on coffee in a month feels. Very jabby indeed. Stop bleeding money.

Step 199: Stick to your budget not because it's the right thing to do, but because it gives you an out

This may seem counterintuitive, but one lovely thing about having a budget with built-in savings is that once you've been adequately responsible, you don't have to feel guilty about spending the extra, discretionary income on earrings made of tiny plants. They grow on *air*!

A wise blog reader put it thusly: "Like crash dieting or quitting something cold turkey, it's often harder to stick to something that feels like a punishment, when what a budget can actually give you is freedom...If I look at all my expected income, then subtract my necessary expenses and plan in some savings...then everything that's left over is mine to do with as I will! If I budget in a hundred dollars of 'me money' a month, then I can spend that dough guilt free."

Step 200: Give yourself a per diem

Decide how much screwing-around/discretionary money you get per day—maybe five dollars, maybe fifteen—and then stick to that. Money can roll over, but you can't borrow against future per diems.

Step 201: Start writing down every time you spend money

If you want to lose weight, write down everything you eat. If you want to gain money, write down every time a penny leaves you. This is like that highlighting you did in step 198, but ongoing.

This small act of self-accountability means that you probably won't take a spoon to the frosting, metaphorically. You will have a much harder time unnecessarily parting with cash if you have to take a moment to think about what you're doing.

Step 202: Think of shopping like drinking

You know what's just real, real fun? Shopping because you can. Shopping because it feels good. Shopping because if you do it long, hard, and smart enough, then it is possible that you will someday own every single pretty thing in the world, and wouldn't that be *terrific*?

But shopping can be like drinking. You can do it in a normal way, you can do it maybe a little more than you should but not veer into self-destruction, or you can *fucking ruin yourself.*

Are you shopping and buying things to make yourself happier, to quiet your sadness? Are you doing it despite consequences? Do you go through that icky mental progression where you think, *Oh, I shouldn't [shop/drink]*, and then you think, *Okay, just a little bit*, and next thing you know you're down two hundred dollars and have a crushing fiscal hangover?

Step 203: Develop your anti-shopping mantra

You need to get your non-shopping game face on.

I have honed this skill until it glistens, particularly in IKEA. IKEA is a high-pressure crucible of young adulthood, and only the strong can hope to survive.

For four hours, my inner monologue sounds like this: *You don't need that. You don't need that. You don't need that, either.* And so on.

Step 204: If you don't have money to shop, do not window-shop as though that's a real thing

That's like advising people on a diet to watch other people eating steaks for a little pick-me-up.

I *love* thrift shopping, and seeing how cheaply I can find things is part of the thrill. But when I was twenty-two, making twenty-four thousand dollars a year, I *didn't* have that extra ten bucks. I learned, the hard way, that I will always, always fall in love with something at a thrift store, and there was no point in torturing myself by finding it and then having to leave it behind.

You are not going to want to shop less when you're in a store! Don't tempt yourself! Go somewhere that won't make you feel sad and poor, like a park, or your equally poor friend's house.

Step 205: Do not charge shopping sprees and other such foolishness on your credit cards

Just don't. I'm serious. Not for the work wardrobe that you are sure will get you the job you need. Not for the most perfect item in the world.

Debt is the Voldemort to financial responsibility's Harry Potter, which is to say, no good, very bad, all-powerful, doing awful things. You should do everything you can to vanquish it.

As my dad once said, being in a credit card situation where you can just barely make the minimum payment every month is as close as you can come in our modern world to being in debt peonage. And, historically, being a peon is rough. Do not allow yourself to become one.

It's fine to buy a small something on your card every month or so—in fact, you should do that, then pay it off in full to build credit. But do not pay 30 percent interest forever on anything.

Let's say you're the kind of person who isn't great about paying off your credit card in full every month. It's okay if you're not, but accept that you're not that kind of person and that you are actually paying maybe three times the sticker price each time you put something on the card.

If you're *really good* at paying off your credit card every month, then by all means, use them—you get cash back, airline miles, rewards, and so on. *This only applies if you are an A+++ student when it comes to paying it off.* Airline miles are not a good reason to rack up insane debt.

Step 206: Freeze your credit cards

Thank you to blog reader Leah for this one: Literally encase them in ice. Put them in the bottom of a bowl full of water, then stick that in the freezer. If you want to use them, thaw it out. Once again, it seems unlikely that you will ball outrageous through Sephora if you have to spend hours and hours first considering your decision.

And even if you've got the money, and it's not a problem, you should still . . .

Step 207: Pause before you buy something

Lots of people say you should wait a week before you buy something, to determine if it's really necessary and gauge how badly you want it. This always seemed a little harsh to me, and I'm certainly not a saint about it.

But at least take a moment. Leave the store, maybe, and go somewhere else. By removing yourself from the immediacy of the situation and the item you want, it sort of sobers you up, takes you back to a time when you didn't desire or even know about this tiny tchotchke that has stolen your heart. Then and only then can you thoughtfully decide whether you actually need that item, or just want it.

Step 208: Get what you came for

If you are in the kind of place where you go needing one thing and leave with fourteen (I'm looking at you, IKEA, Target, Whole Foods, and H&M), then make a list and *do not allow the siren song of thirty-dollar coffee tables to lure you onto the rocky shores of eating ramen until your next paycheck.*

Step 209: Put away ten dollars per pay period in savings

I don't care how poor you are, you can handle ten dollars every two weeks. Of this I am certain. It really, really, really should be twenty dollars, but ten is the absolute minimum. So make it non-optional. From now on, your monthly expenses include twenty dollars for savings. Because you're not saving for retirement, though that is important too. No, no. You are setting yourself up to have that teeny cushion.

Step 210: Be prepared for the three-hundred-dollar emergencies

Here is the beauty of putting away ten dollars per paycheck: At the end of the year, you'll have $260, which incidentally is how much minor emergencies always seem to cost.

These emergencies are and always will be part of your financial landscape, at least once per year until you are dead. Your car will need new tires, or you'll owe the government some money, or your roommate will flake out at the worst moment. Just this little tiny bit of money will be of assistance at some point. And the first time you handle one of these without busting out the credit card or, worse, calling your parents (see "A Short List of Things Your Parents Are Not," in the Family chapter), you will give yourself a well-deserved high-five. Which looks to the outsider like clapping, but you'll know the difference.

Step 211: Ideally, someday, you will have three months' worth of living expenses squirreled away. Or, if you're a superstar, six months' worth

I have never been one of these people, but that is what you're supposed to do. There are many names for this pool of money, ranging from the polite ("safety net") to the not-so-polite ("fuck-you money"). But no matter what it is, remember that money represents freedom to leave a terrible situation—an abusive job (see step 188) or your horrible boyfriend whom you live with or whatever it is.

Financial planner Ron Kelemen calls this the "opportunity-slash-emergency fund."

"Maybe a job opportunity presents itself in the next town, or maybe your car breaks down and this would help you avoid getting into more debt," he said. "Or maybe it's a shove-it fund, so you're not stuck in a job where you have to stay forever and can't leave."

Step 212: One month's expenses is better than none

Don't let great be the enemy of good when it comes to saving. Something is infinitely better than nothing.

MAINTAINING DECENT CREDIT

Yes, yes, everyone says this, because it's true. To do things that adults want to do (get loans, buy a house, get jobs) you need to have decent credit. There are several things that go into your credit score, but the basics are simple.

Step 213: Cut up credit cards, but don't close the account

The ratio of debt to credit you have makes a big impact on your credit score. You want to aim to have a very small debt balance and large limit. So aim for a $30 balance on a $1,000 credit limit, rather than a $450 balance on a $500 limit.

Step 214: Do not ignore a bill

Here are the ways that a bill will leave your life:

1. You pay it.
2. ...

Here is a way that a bill will *not* leave your life:

1. Leave it unopened on your hall table, then look at it anxiously every now and again.

Duh, bills are awful. No one likes receiving a bill, no one in this whole world. In this way, bills and tapeworms are not so very different. But they must be paid or, like an untreated tapeworm, they will get larger and more powerful. And with that, you can calmly enjoy what will, from here on out, be a tapeworm-free book.

Now. There is a certain group of people in the world, of whom I am one, that has the money to pay their bills, but just doesn't, because bills are dreary. If you are this sort of person...

Step 215: Pay your bills on time. Pay your bills on time. Pay your bills on time

That means putting it in the mail *several days before it's due*. If you pay it online, pay it the day before, latest.

I don't care what you have to do—set a monthly alert to go off on your cell phone, have the money automatically withdrawn, pay a friend to nag you, whatever—but make it a ritual. On the seventeenth (or whenever), you pay each and every bill.

Pick a day and a time to pay *all* your bills. That way, you won't have to do that thing where you get a call from an 800 number and don't answer it just in case it's AT&T wondering where their $45.27 is.

Step 216: Know which bills you can be late on

In a perfect world, none of us would ever pay a bill late. Collection agencies would disappear, because every grown-up would pay their bills, in full, three business days early.

But. Suppose—just suppose!—that sometimes you are getting to the end of the month and cash is tight. This is pure, pure hypothetical territory we're moving into here, the quantum mechanics of grown-upness.

Maslow's* Hierarchy of Bills

* Not actually

Reminder: start at the base, then work your way up to financial responsibility fulfillment!

Shopping! Sushi! Fun!

Cell phone. Cable.

Student loans. Insurance.

Credit cards. Power and water.

Rent. Groceries. Necessary medications.

But if that were to happen, make sure you have your own internal order of who gets paid, first to last.

Rent and credit card companies should be right up there at the top, rent because it's the biggest and most important expense and credit cards because they will slap you with a thirty-dollar late fine or a nastily high interest rate so fast your head will spin. Toward the bottom should be cable/Internet/cell phone because if things became truly dire, your world could continue to turn without them.

In the middle will be utilities, insurance, and student loans. Again, utilities and insurance are really important, and student loan companies are nearly as quick to tattle to the credit agencies as credit card companies.

Step 217: If you find yourself in a serious bind, call and ask the people you owe money to for help

If something really bad has happened in your financial life, be proactive and *call companies ahead of time*. The truth of the matter is that even though they seem cold and impersonal—and many are—they are run by human beings, and these human beings understand that sometimes bad things happen.

A while ago, I had an enormous hospital bill—we're talking an amount that could buy a decent used car—out of nowhere. Rather than waiting until I got the horrible bills and freaking out, I called the hospital in advance and let them know that it was going to be really hard for me.

And in return, they helped work out payment plans and even forgave some of the debt, based on my income level.

But the key is that you need to be *proactive* here. Do not wait until your bill is ninety days past due to call your creditor or service provider. Call as *soon* as you know there's going to be a problem, and say that you want to figure out a solution, you want to be a good customer, and you want to get them their money.

"It's good for you, the borrower, but it's also good for the lender," said financial planner Ron. "What they ultimately want is their money back, and it's going to cost them money to try to get blood out of a turnip. It's in their best interest to find something accommodating."

Step 218: Get comfortable with the idea of refinancing

Refinancing is another one of those frightening-sounding words, but it can be something surprisingly simple. Refinancing is moving your debt from one place to another, resulting in lower interest. A while ago, I had about two thousand dollars of credit card debt with high, high interest rates. An extremely practical friend of mine suggested that I look into taking out a small consumer loan from my credit union, and sure enough, I took a 20 percent interest rate down to 4.75.

Side note: Credit unions are awesome. They're not-for-profit, member-owned financial institutions, and they tend to have much friendlier, less predatory terms—think lower fees, higher savings rates, and so on. They can be less convenient, with fewer offices and ATMs, and some of them have closed membership, but it's at least worth looking into whether you qualify for one. You might qualify through your job, or your college, or even just your state of residency.

HOW TO BE POOR

Okay, so now you're not allowed to spend much money anymore.

"But wait!" I hear your tiny, shrill voice. "Wait! That sounds like no fun at all!" Rest that piercing voice, and realize that the poor can have plenty of fun, they just have to be smart about it. On with the fun, or at least bearable, poverty!

Step 219: Get good at shopping for clothes on the cheap

Given enough money, anyone can look stylish and amazing. Have you ever noticed that there aren't many ugly rich people?

But you can also be cute and poor, I promise. Think about this in terms of spending time rather than money, because it's much easier to find the something that is just the perfect fit for $110 at Nordstrom than for $3.50 at Goodwill, but you can do it.

• Shop with a specific item in mind, then search single-mindedly for that one perfect thing. You shouldn't clothes-shop aimlessly, ever—that's a good way to buy a lot of stuff you don't need. So figure out what you do need, then go get that. You can rifle really quickly through racks if you know you're looking for a white lace blouse or a high-waisted gray wool skirt.

• When possible, buy vintage clothing. I can't afford new interesting clothing, but I can pay for old interesting clothing. When I'm in a thrift store, I rifle through looking for *old* stuff. Get familiar with what old material looks and feels like—what the stitching looks like, the buttons, the zippers, and then look for that.

Or find quality, designer duds for less. Again, look for good stitching, quality fabric, and so on. If you need to, creep around Saks Fifth Avenue surreptitiously checking out what nicely made clothes look like. Then leave, because no one besides Beyoncé should be shopping at Saks.

Step 220: Hold a clothing swap

These are so satisfying, you have no idea. All you need is an apartment, some similarly sized friends, and hopefully a bunch of wine. Everyone brings clothes, jewelry, and shoes they don't want and dumps them on tables or the floor; then you root around like pigs searching for truffles. Clothing swaps are the best. I can't tell you how satisfying it is to see that beloved dress or skirt that just isn't right for you anymore go to a happy home. And, obviously, it's a bunch of new (to you!) clothes, for free.

Step 221: Get familiar with happy hours and, failing that, the Sides menu

Yes, I understand that wait staff doesn't like this, but it's a valid money-saving strategy. If you get an invite for a night out and you absolutely, positively cannot afford it, then turn it down. If you can afford about 50 percent of it, eat ahead of time! Eat an almost-but-not-quite meal at your house, then go and order something small.

You can get a salad, or a side, you know! Or an appetizer. Make sure that when the bill arrives you aren't a total jerk about it.

Note: You still must tip properly. Tipping properly is not contingent on how much money you have, it's contingent on whether or not you accepted service. If you don't have enough to tip—and in Amer-

ica, that's 15 percent at casual restaurants, 18 to 20 percent at fine din-
ing, and a dollar per drink at a bar—then you do not have enough
money to go out. Period.

However, no matter what, you need to...

Step 222: Pay your fair share cheerfully at restaurants

If you want to split up the bill seven ways, ask the wait staff if
that's okay before you sit down. Or, better yet, bring cash. At the end
of the meal, figure out how much you *think* you owe (don't forget tax,
tip, and beverages!), then add two or three dollars and say you will pay
that amount. For God's sake, don't spend half an hour quibbling to
make sure you don't overpay by thirty-seven cents. If you're out with a
friend who got an entrée that was a dollar more or whatever, *just split
it in half.* Friendship is long, and you'll recoup your losses eventually.

Also, if you must pay your check with several different cards, here
is a convenient thing to do for your server: On the bill, write the initials
and amount each will be paying. So it would look something like this:

KB: $23.50
RL: $16
SB: $21.25
Plus
$15 cash (no change, please)

Ultimate adulting move: Just pick up the check for the table, knowing the favor will eventually be returned...and that doing so won't
bankrupt you.

Step 223: If you are dying to go to a schmancy restaurant that you could never afford, go for lunch

I have no idea why more people don't do this. It can be so luxe and
fun, and just as delicious as dinner for maybe 60 percent of the cost.

Step 224: Get good at having cheap fun

Get a French press and learn to make coffee for your friends. Buy
cheap wine and three-dollar frozen appetizers from Trader Joe's. Host

potlucks at your house in the winter, picnics in public parks in the summer.

Going out for drinks is going to cost you at least fifteen dollars, every single time. But you know what? You and your friends can totally split a decent bottle of wine for ten bucks and play a board game and have a delightful time for a third of the cost.

And if you have rich friends who are always suggesting that you go out bar-hopping or out to expensive restaurants, it's okay to—without laying a thick guilt trip—say something demure about trying to stick to a budget.

Step 225: Don't borrow money from your friends

Just don't. It will never, ever turn out well. Don't lend your friends money, either. If you want to help them out, just plan on making it a gift. Or do something non-monetary, like spotting a friend dinner. It'll come back someday.

Step 226: Discern things that are worth spending money on

My brilliant friend Sarah once explained to me that paying to get her dog's toenails clipped is an absolute necessity. It's worth it in terms of not dealing with a terrified and potentially bloody dog. Paying for someone to change your oil, spending extra on a good-quality winter coat that actually keeps you warm, and not buying a janky old bicycle off Craigslist if it's your only mode of transportation all fall into this category.

Here are some things to consider:

- How reliant am I on this good or service?
- Is this something that I could *theoretically* do myself but in reality am more likely to mess up and cause possibly costly damage?
- Is this something that will last me four times as long if I spend twice as much?

Step 227: Think in terms of how much things cost over their lifetime

Going out to dinner is great, but that money is gone in one night. All forty dollars will be dedicated to that extremely short period of time. Even if you are an excruciatingly slow eater, it's over in two and a half hours, max.

Goods and services have varying degrees of durability, and it's reasonable to think about how much worth something provides over its lifetime. To pick the most frivolous example possible, when I can afford it, I buy nice foundation. Yes, it's thirty-five dollars at the department store rather than eleven for the drugstore brand, but that thirty-five-dollar bottle lasts me for at least seven months. Is it worth five dollars per month for me to have decent foundation? It's a pretty low cost for something I use every single day. The key here is that I can't apply this to everything, only things I'm willing to sacrifice other spending opportunities on.

Step 228: Remember the other side of the lifetime-cost rule

But here's the thing: You can use the lifetime-cost trick above to justify nearly any purchase (except maybe lingerie), but remember that if you don't have thirty-five dollars to spend, then it wouldn't matter if that incredibly luminous, acne-fighting, skin-perfecting shade lasted you for the rest of your life. Remember your budget? *If it's not in your budget, then it doesn't matter what a great buy it is.*

Okay, so there you have it. That is how to be poor. And it isn't so bad! But you know what's better than being poor? *Not* being poor. And you can do it. If you are straight out of school, know that, barring having a kid or drastic job loss, in five years things will not be nearly so painful.

ADVANCED ADULTING

So now you're sort of in control of your finances, and are getting a handle on how to be poor. Now it's time to imagine a day when you're not poor. It will come. Now is a great, great time to talk to a financial planner. You don't have money, but you do have something that all the money in the world can't buy: time. It makes a big difference to start this process when you are twenty-two, versus thirty-two. A financial planner can also help you figure out how to get out of debt, which is not only the Voldemort to financial security's Harry Potter, but also the Ursula to financial stability's Little Mermaid and possibly even the Gaston to financial relaxation's Beast.

What is a 401(k)? The 401(k) is, essentially, a big pile of untaxed money; really, it's an investment account that often encompasses a broad range of mutual funds (a mixture of stocks, bonds, and so on). Lots of employers will match your contributions up to a certain amount; if they do, what we're talking about is essentially free money, and it will compound faster than you'd think. This is also one of those things that benefits hugely from starting early, say starting a 401(k) at age twenty-three versus thirty. We're talking a massive difference in terms of savings, in the tens of thousands of dollars over the years.

Seriously. Contribute. Do not allow yourself to be frightened by that little (k) in parenthesis. Pretend it stands for "kumquat," or "koala," or another friendly k-word. It is your 401(koala), just idly munching upon eucalyptus of employer-matched income, and you *love* it, and want it to be happy and fat.

In general, financial things stress me out and bore me. So my coping mechanism is to tie the concepts to things that relax and delight me, which is to say, animals. We've already met the 401(koala), but let's dip into the rest of the Financial Zoo.

Compound-Interest Cheetah moves way, way faster than Simple Interest Snail when it comes to changing piles of money. If you are lucky enough that this benefits you—say, your savings interest is compounded—it's great. But if it's a debt situation with compound interest, then Compound-Interest Cheetah's swiftness can be as devastating to you as a regular cheetah's is to a gazelle.

IRAguana is a retirement plan that, like real iguanas, is not required to pay taxes. So whatever money you give to him isn't counted as income for the year. Usually, IRAguanas are somewhat picky and you have to qualify to have one that counts as a tax deduction.

Savings Sloth: He grows very, very slowly, but Savings Sloth should have a place in each and every one of our lives. Do not let predators like Cute Art Print Cobra or Going Out To Bars Bobcat eat your Savings Sloth.

Pension Panda: Just like regular pandas, Pension Pandas are now sadly rare. A pension is an amount that a company pays a retiree regularly; they were much more common in our grandparents' generation. Social Security is a sort of pension.

TAXES

Step 229: Calm the F down, they're not that bad

Taxes are way, way less scary than they seem. Truthfully, if you just have one job, it should be pretty simple and you can probably do it on your own using an online filing program like TurboTax or H&R Block. Especially when you are young and poor, April 15 will probably result in the government giving money back to you. I *love* filing my taxes. I recommend listening to some sort of money-themed hip-hop while you do this. It's not required, obviously, but should get you feeling nice and rich and in control.

Some good ones:

- "Money Ain't a Thang" by Jermaine Dupri featuring Jay-Z
- "Got Money" by Lil Wayne and T-Pain
- "Money to Blow" by Birdman, Lil Wayne, and Drake
- "Gin and Juice" by Snoop Dogg
- "C.R.E.A.M." by Wu-Tang Clan
- "Duffle Bag Boy" by Playaz Circle featuring Lil Wayne

Step 230: Pick an online tax-filing site of choice

Those programs are pretty straightforward; they simply ask you to fill out the numbers in the various tax documents you've been sent, then ask questions that should be easy to answer, like, "Did you buy a home in the last year?" Sometimes, it's free to file your federal tax return, but then you have to pay eighty dollars or so to file your state tax return, or vice versa. Either way, this is probably a simpler solution than having someone do your taxes for you.

Common tax documents include your W-2 form, which your employer should mail out toward the beginning of the year, plus the 1098-E form—a statement if you've paid a certain amount in student loan interest, or if you've donated money or goods to a non-profit.

If you have a more complicated tax situation—think lots of income from investments, self-employment, filing jointly if you just got married—then think about going in person to a tax preparation place. It really is affordable and worth skipping the headache.

Question: Do I need to save my receipts?

Saving receipts seems like the height of adulthood. Really, there are two good times to save your receipts:

1. Before the charges clear on your credit or debit card, so you have proof of the amount paid in case there is a dispute.
2. When you would like to write something off as a tax deduction.

There are about a billion and one things that can be written off—in addition to donations, there's moving expenses, business expenses including gas mileage, medical expenses, state income taxes, and so on. But it's a nice idea, if you're planning on writing something off, to keep the receipt around. Just get a shoe box, cut a hole in the top, write TAX RECEIPTS on it in big, friendly letters (or, better yet, glued-on rhinestones to add much-needed glamour to the tax preparation process), and pat yourself on the back.

Step 231: Wealth isn't that complicated

At the end of the day, it's a radically simple thing: There's just one way to save money, which is to spend less than you earn.

DISCUSSION QUESTIONS

1. What is the most expensive item of clothing you've ever purchased? What was the pleasure-to-guilt ratio?
2. Have you ever had your credit card declined? Did you just slink off sheepishly, or offer a super-implausible explanation? Did you say, "Oh my God! I have to contact my bank! Something terrible has happened!" then rush off, as though the only possible explanation was that your bank account had been drained by an elite international ring of thieves? That's what I did.
3. Why can't we all just be rich already?

7. Maintenance

Everything is falling apart. Some things (like mountains) fall apart slowly, while others (like cars that never get their oil changed) fall apart quickly. At least compared with mountains.

It's frustrating that you can't do something once and have that be enough. It feels like once a problem has been solved, it should *stay solved*. But this is not how things work. Our universe constantly trends toward chaos, and adulthood often feels like nothing but solving the same recurring problems, over and over, again and again, forever.

On the upside, maintenance is not as big of a pain in the ass as you might initially think. Most items in your life need no more than two minutes of love per day, or perhaps an hour of affectionate attention every few months, to stay happy. These boring bits of time have immense payoffs.

So tattoo this on the inside of your eyelids: Spending a little time and money now protects you from experiencing great expense, inconvenience, and heartache later. Take the extra few minutes to hang up delicate clothes to air-dry so your shirt doesn't hang limply on you like a dead jellyfish. Change your car's oil on time not because you are a super-responsible person, but because you do not want it to break down on some backcountry road en route to a wedding.

If the mere thought of checking on something (your finances, your health, a friendship) stresses you out, take it as proof positive that you need to check up on it sooner rather than later.

This chapter is more about physical items than finances, relationships, and other intangibles, which are covered elsewhere. Just remember: You can have nice things...if you treat them like the nice things they are.

CARS

If your life requires a car, then that is likely your most important possession. No, it's not your beautiful vintage coat, your guitar, or your grandmother's wedding ring. The loss of the other things would hurt infinitely more in the long run. But the loss—even temporary—of your car will make almost all aspects of your day-to-day life super inconvenient, in a way those other losses do not.

While you can't prevent car troubles, you can take steps to lessen the possibility of it bursting into flames ten minutes before you're supposed to be in an important meeting across town.

Step 232: Name your car

With gas, insurance, maintenance, and whatever it cost you in the first place, you throw something like 15 percent of your income at the thing. So discover, in your heart, a deep love for this mass of metal, plastic, and gears. Name it, perhaps after yourself. Cherish it. Adopt a protective, benevolent attitude toward it. You and this car are on the same team.

Don't stomp down on the gas pedal two seconds after you turned it on, or pull out so fast that you squeal the tires. Drive it like you love it, because you do. It takes you from place to place, keeps you safe and warm, holds your Diet Coke, plays you the songs you want to hear, and all it asks in return is to be driven decently gently and given some new oil every now and again. Is that too much to ask?

Step 233: Find a mechanic you love or, more realistically, who will not rob you

Before you get that as-yet-nameless car, ask around for recommendations. Mechanics are like lawyers in that people will happily gush about a good one and spit venom about the bad ones. I lucked out massively in the form of Shane, who has all the crucial mechanic qualities: He's honest, never tries to upsell unnecessary repairs to my automotively ignorant self, and charges less than almost everyone else in town. He was also willing to sit down and explain how to take care of the damn things.

Step 234: Avoid used-car lots in favor of private sellers

Unless you own a Jet Ski or take trips to Vietnam for fun, you're probably in the market for a used car. So look for a good previous owner.

"Car lots tend to have the worst cars on them, because...no one will buy it, so [sellers] have to trade it," Shane said, adding that Craigslist, Nickel Ads, and newspaper classifieds are always a better plan.

You can certainly ask for maintenance records—not only to know the car's been serviced regularly (more on that later) but also to find that delightfully anal quality you should seek out in people from whom you wish to purchase an expensive, used, and hopefully well-cared-for thing.

Per Shane, do all the following when assessing a used car:

1. Start it, and make sure the engine turns over and starts right away.

2. Look for a big puff of smoke out the tailpipe. If there's smoke, that's an indication of burning oil, which is a major problem.

3. Drive it, being sure to get up to at least forty-five miles per hour. If it's a standard transmission, make sure it shifts into all the gears smoothly. If it's an automatic, listen and make sure the car shifts itself at the correct time. Listen for any grinding, clunking, or banging, as these are all Bad Signs. "Go over some bumps, see if it feels solid; see if the steering wheel shakes," Shane said.

4. Park, then look under the car to see if anything's dripping. You should also look at wherever it was originally parked and make sure there are no suspicious stains.

My friend Sam has an interesting strategy for buying used cars: She always looks for leather seats in good condition. She doesn't particularly care about this, but the seats' higher price says that the car itself was likely to have been nicer when it was first purchased, and their preserved state shows her that the car's previous owner took pride in their possession.

Step 235: Do not buy a used European car

European cars are sexy and rare and a terrible plan unless you have piles of money for maintenance. Or are the type of person who likes to date people that unexpectedly and violently melt down.

Step 236: Do buy a used Japanese car, or American if you feel so moved

"Any Japanese car is a better-quality car than a European car— they're priced more reasonably, they're easier to work on, and easier to get parts for," Shane said, adding that domestic cars are second place to Japanese cars.

Step 237: Take it to a mechanic to look over

It doesn't cost that much—Shane said his shop charges $42.50 for half an hour of labor. This is a very, very small bill compared with the investment you're making. Whatever the mechanic says, listen to him or her. Do not allow your desire for this car to blind you to the dangers he or she may warn of. If it's something that can be solved fairly easily and he or she gives you a repair estimate, then go back to the seller and ask them to either fix it first or discount the amount from the purchase price.

Step 238: Do not skip oil changes

This is the very best thing you can do to ensure your car has a long, happy car life. Check your owner's manual, because lots of cars only require oil changes every five thousand miles. This counts as something that is Worth Spending Money On.

Do not remove that little sticker that says when you'll need another oil change, either. Leave that sticker be. If you look at it and feel guilty, go get the oil changed.

If you truly cannot afford an oil change, at least go get some oil and top it off. It costs maybe five bucks for a quart; you can do it.

Step 239: Know how to check your car's oil

Every car has a dipstick under the hood. Check your oil when it's cold, which is to say, after the car hasn't been running for a little while. Pull it out, wipe it off with a paper towel, then put it back in and pull it out. There's the full line, and then the add line. If the oil is below the latter, your car needs more oil.

Step 240: Get scheduled maintenance every thirty thousand miles, or as indicated in the owner's manual

Spending $350 on car maintenance is the second most boring use of $350 in the whole wide world. (First place: Dental work. Third place: A visit to the vet to get the dog to stop vomiting, which at least has elements of danger and urgency.) But it has to happen.

"Every thirty thousand miles, there are usually some significant things that should be done. It depends on your budget, but you should change the coolant, you should change the transmission fluid, and you should have the car looked at"—especially brakes, belts, hoses, and tires, Shane said.

Step 241: Watch warning lights, especially the red ones

If a light comes on, pay attention to your car—is it driving differently than it did before the light was on?

Car warning lights are amber if they require attention, and red if you are in imminent danger of permanently fucking your car. The worst light to come on is the red oil light, which indicates that your car has lost oil pressure and is not lubricating itself. This is very, very bad. Imagine extremely vigorous, unlubricated sex, except everyone's genitals are made of steel and powered by exploding gasoline.

Your car tells you things via those little lights, but in ways you cannot fully understand unless you have a magic scanner. Which you don't. Mechanics and auto parts stores have them.

Many national auto parts stores don't charge to run the scan, whereas most mechanics do. Call ahead to make sure it's actually free.

Car warning signs

Here's a rundown of some ways that your car can be acting weird, and what it may be trying to tell you in its car way:

- If you're going slow and the wheel is shaking, or it feels like you're driving over speed bumps, that's probably a tire problem. It's usually pretty obvious when you have a flat—if it's in the front, Shane said, you'll have a really difficult time steering. If it's in the back, the whole thing will drive mushy. Pull over and change your damn tire. (Or better yet, call AAA [step 399]!)

- If it's driving normally except there's a thumping or jerking when you step on the brake, or a squealing sound, you may well need a new brake job. This is not as expensive as it sounds unless you let it go on too long and start to wear down your brake disks, in which case it can get very expensive indeed.

- If you hear a *clunk, clunk, clunk* when turning but nothing when going straight, that probably means a front axle is going bad.

> • "If you're accelerating and you hear a backfire or popping sound, a little *pop, pop, pop, pop,* that's usually a spark plug that's gone bad," Shane said. If there's no sound but there is jerking, that could also be a spark plug, but also potentially an injector or coil problem.
>
> • If you let go of the steering wheel and the car immediately decides on a new course for itself, that's likely an alignment problem. You can also have problems with alignment that don't manifest during driving—check out your tires every now and again, and make sure that they are wearing evenly. The treads should be pretty even, but if the outer treads or inner treads are notably shorter, HEY. Go get it aligned.

Step 242: Get new tires when necessary

Remember when I said that car maintenance is the second most boring expenditure in the world, after dental work? Well, I lied. Tires are the clear winner of Things That Are Really Expensive But Not Even Slightly Fun To Purchase sweepstakes.

Once, when I was especially angry about how expensive and boring tires are, I called a spokesman for a major tire manufacturer named T.J. Now, T.J. is a true believer in tires—at one point, I asked if he ever got tired of talking about tires all day, and he said—this is a verbatim quote—"No! I can't believe you would even ask me that. No, tires are so cool. I cannot express to you the coolness of tires."

Anyway, one really smart thing that T.J. pointed out is that tires are the only part of your vehicle that is actually connected to the ground.

The major sign you need new tires is that the tread has been worn down to less than one-sixteenth of an inch. You can check this with a penny—stick Lincoln, head-side down, into the tread. If you can still see his whole face, then the treads are too low.

You *can* buy used tires if you're crunched for cash and it's an emergency, but you should just pony up for new ones. Lots of tire stores offer free rotations and warranties, so ask ahead. Ask specifically what the warranty and lifetime care covers—if you get a hole, will they patch it? How long does the warranty last? On more than one occasion, I've gone to Les Schwab, where I get my tires, with a flat and walked out without paying a dime. Figuring these things out now is a good way to ensure that you won't have to spend any more of your precious, exciting money on boring tires than is absolutely necessary.

CLOTHES

Think of someone you know who always appears capable. Think of someone you know who often has stains on their clothing. Chances are close to 100 percent you are not picturing the same person.

You don't have to spend a lot of money on clothing, as we established in the Money chapter, to look swell. You do need to take proper care of the clothes you have—wash them in the temperature and manner they want to be washed, with similar colors. If they were human, this would be racist, but since they're inanimate items, let it slide.

Some things to have on hand for proper care of clothing:

- A liquid laundry detergent that doesn't fade colors
- A stain remover (I find the OxiClean ones tend to work very well)
- A mesh garment bag that you put your undies and tights in when washing
- Non-wire hangers

Step 243: Don't be wrinkled

243(a) Get a good steamer.

Not the handheld, travel kind, the sort that have a reservoir base and a wand that you use to steam.

Steaming clothing is incredible. All the wrinkles fall out, it makes your clothing smell fresh and clean, and it just . . . it just *revitalizes* it. A steamer makes old clothing look new.

To steam, you want to just run the steamer slowly on the inside of the clothing, angling so that the steam rises up. You absolutely want to watch your fingers, because steam burns suck. One strategy is to hold an oven mitt in your non-steamer hand, although know that the steam can and will go right through that. SAFETY FIRST WHILE STEAMING.

243(b) Get a basic, but not cheap, iron.

Irons are great for when you want the crisp details: a beautifully starched collar on a white shirt, for example. Get one that has steam and spray functions, which most of them do.

When ironing, be sure to set it at the appropriate heat level for that garment. Do *not* go higher, or you can easily burn the clothing. Don't forget to move the iron slowly but constantly, and—not that you would—never leave it sitting, hot-side down, on the piece of clothing. Lots of people like to start with the smallest panel of clothing (the collar, say, or the cuffs) and work to the largest. But if you're going to iron, be sure to iron all of it, because any wrinkles will stand out clearly against the vast smoothness.

Step 244: Let your deodorant dry before you put on clothing

Put on your deodorant, and let a few minutes pass. Also, when you're done wearing it, spray the pits with hair spray (see step 249) or your stain fighter of choice.

Step 245: Wash most things in cold water

Unless something is really and truly dirty, there's no reason to use hot water—it fades colors, can shrink some things, and isn't energy-efficient.

Step 246: Sort by colors to wash

This doesn't mean that you have to have a load of light-violet-only garments, but you should sort whites, darks, and colors, paying special attention to clothes that are likely to bleed. Newer items should always be looked at with more suspicion than those that have proven themselves colorfast. Highly saturated cotton clothes tend to give off color, as does tie-dye.

Step 247: Master hand-washing

Anything delicate can and should get hand-washed. It's not that difficult, and is in fact easier than hauling a load of clothes to the Laundromat.

You do it with those often-mentioned, rarely understood delicates: Think lace, silk, fine sweaters, bras, and almost all nice lingerie.

Here's how it's done: Fill your sink or tub with cold water, then add some washing detergent. If there's food or grease stains on the item, add some dish soap (more on that below).

Put your items in the soapy water and give them a good swish. Let them soak for at least thirty minutes, swishing every now and again, then let them drain. Fill up the basin again with cold water to rinse, then hang them up to dry.

Step 248: Don't throw everything in the dryer

Dryers do a great, great job of prematurely aging clothing. Dryers are like the American presidency. Clothing goes in looking youthful and vigorous, and emerges slumped and gray-haired.

Some things are just fine in the dryer: Jeans, socks, T-shirts, and other similarly rugged clothing items will have no problem with it. Things that rely on elastic or stretchiness—think swimsuits, and garments with lots of synthetics in them—and anything delicate should also be kept out of the dryer.

Invest in one of those folding, old-fashioned drying racks, or string up a clothesline.

Note: Do not hang something very heavy when it's wet, because the weight of the garment can pull on the shoulders and stretch it out. Things like sweaters and heavy dresses should be set on a towel, then sort of tugged gently into shape to dry.

Step 249: Use hair spray to get stains out

Sam Hart has run LiL' Gypsy Vintage Boutique for twenty years, and because of this she is a pro champion at removing stains and smells from clothing.

Sam swears by cheap aerosol hair spray—"Whatever I can get at the dollar store"—to get stains out. She said she's found stain removers to be hit-or-miss, whereas just spraying some hair spray on does the trick much of the time.

If it's a food or grease stain, use some clear dish soap. That Dawn you bought back during the Domesticity chapter should do you proud.

"There's nothing that cuts food better," Sam said, adding that if it can get grease off your pans, it can get grease off your pants.

As soon as you get the food stain, get it wet and rub some dish soap in, then put it in the laundry. When you wash it, wash it on cold and do not put it in the dryer. Washing on hot makes the stain a permanent part of your clothes, but with cold there is still a chance to salvage the item.

Step 250: Use vinegar to get smells out

Throwing a cup of white vinegar into a full load of laundry neutralizes odors. Sam said a paste of vinegar and baking soda can also do a great job on stains, especially armpit stains.

Step 251: Get over your fear of bleach

I spent years living in bleach terror. How did it work? What did it do? If I had some in my house, would my clothes develop splotchy bleach stains by a process of osmosis? I imagined bleach fumes floating menacingly through my house at night, searching with slit bleach-fume eyes for potential sartorial victims, not unlike Hexxus, the evil spirit of pollution cloud voiced by Tim Curry in the seminal 1992 animated classic *FernGully: The Last Rainforest*.

Needless to say, this is not how bleach works. Bleach is simple. Bleach is your friend. Use it on whites, and whites only. Let the washer fill completely, without putting your clothing in it, then add three-quarters of a cup of bleach and make sure it's mixed well. Add your white clothes in.

Afterward, Sam said, it is absolutely wonderful if you can hang the whites outside in the sunshine to dry. This does an excellent job of getting them extra, extra white.

Step 252: If you are going to wear white, you must[2] commit to it

This also goes for baby blue, baby pink, spring green—basically, any color that would be at home for an Easter service.

Before you put on that white garment in the morning, ask yourself if you can refrain from the following until that item is safely back in your closet:

• Eating any sort of tomato-based broth? Especially the kind with that deadly orange grease floating on the top?
• Painting?
• Using Sharpies in any but the most subdued and careful manner?
• Consuming any food that isn't Nilla Wafers while driving?
• Any sort of interaction with your car other than delicately pumping gas? (Think tire and oil changing, or nearly anything that requires you to pop the hood.)
• Acknowledging the existence of mustard? Seriously, don't even look at it.
• Ground-sitting?
• Chili-cheese anything?
• Carnivals? Carnivals combine everything above, plus face painting, into one dangerous brew.

Also, if you manage to vigilantly protect your white garment from harm, *take it off when you get home.* Your house is safe for you, yes, but 37 percent[3] of indelible stains happen in the home.

---

2. You don't *have* to commit, as every single white garment I've ever owned will attest, but you *should.*

3. I made that up but it seems right.

Step 253: If something is delicate or squish-able, find a way to safely store it

Hats go in hatboxes. Purses can be lined up neatly on a top shelf in a closet, but shouldn't always hang by their straps. Give purse straps a much-needed break, because purse straps are the middle-aged waitresses of the clothing world. They are working hard.

Bras should be gently nestled within one another. Do not allow stockings to invade your lingerie drawer, or they will get all twisted around your nice lingerie.

Step 254: Hang up or fold things, as they prefer

Things that get hung up:
- Nice pants and slacks
- Skirts, except the very most casual, un-wrinkleable kind made of synthetics
- Button-up shirts
- Jackets
- Anything else that is constructed through the shoulder—think shoulder pads, or 3-D construction
- Dresses
- Coats
- Ties (do not leave them tied, either; untie them)

Things that get folded:
- Sweaters: This is important
- T-shirts
- Underwear
- Gym clothes
- Jeans

Step 255: Store jewelry like the expensive thing it is

Nice jewelry should be separated from its Forever 21 kin and delicately coiled individually in a jewelry box, ideally lined with velvet or some other similarly luxuriant fabric if it's something easily scratched or delicate. Remember that pearls are finicky and should never, ever have anything (like perfume, or lotion) near them—they lose their luster and sulk.

Step 256: Don't put tacos in your purse

A short list of things that should not be stored in your purse, backpack, or murse, even if you don't have anywhere else to put them and you can't imagine the worst that could happen:

- Tacos.
- Cans of soda, or bottles of any liquid, really, unless you are extra certain that they are hermetically sealed.
- Leaky pens. In fact, once a pen has leaked (even once!) treat it as you would a boyfriend that slept with your sister (even once!) and throw that busted shit out. You don't need that in your life.

• Bright red lipstick when the temperature outside is over ninety degrees.

• Stainy liquid makeup in general (foundation, bright lip glosses, liquid eyeliner), unless it is zipped safely into a case that has proven itself reliable.

• Calzones.

• Any meat, really. Beef jerky is okay.

If you've ever arrived somewhere to find everything you own covered in shampoo, you understand the importance of packing such things in ziplock bags.

Step 257: Find a good tailor

Okay, don't do this for a little while, because it's easy to get addicted to tailoring. But if you have something nice—think a suit, or a really beautiful dress—that you've spent a lot on, there's no reason not to spend fifteen dollars more and make sure it fits you perfectly. If you work in an office, ask around. A good tailor, like a good mechanic, is someone that people are deeply dedicated to, but you are unlikely to find them on your own, and certainly not via the Internet. Ask around the office, or your parents' most stylish friend, if they know anyone good.

Step 258: Before you write it off as ruined, take it to the dry cleaners

Dry cleaners are magical. They are sorcerers. They are a man on the moon. Something can seem completely unsalvageable, and not only do they fix what's wrong with it, but they make it look new again even though it was floppy and faded and sad when you dropped it off.

Case in point: One time, I got bright lip liner all over a camel-hair coat. Every single panel of the coat had cruel coral streaks. I was crying in the gym locker room and complaining to anyone who'd listen that I'd ruined my one nice coat, which is *not* an effective problem-solving strategy, until a kindly naked lady took pity on me and suggested I take it to the dry cleaners.

I still have that coat. Because dry cleaners operate outside normal laws of physics, at least when it comes to stain removal.

HOUSEPLANTS

There is something quietly admirable about people who capably take care of plants. Plants are the ultimate passive thing: They never tell you what they want, they just sort of wilt and die if they don't get it, like tiny green Katie Holmeses. Pre-badass, vanquishing Tom Cruise like it's not even a thing Katie Holmeses, obviously. So perhaps houseplants have similar cores of steel they just never demonstrate, but in the meantime, you need to water them.

Despite this pathetic tendency of theirs, they are a lovely thing to have around. They make oxygen, they serve as a nice counterpoint to your animated self, and there is something deeply satisfying about watching something that only needs two minutes of your time per day flourish.

Step 259: If it's going to be indoors, get a houseplant, not the outdoor kind

There are many, many plants that love nothing more than to be inside, maybe on a northern-facing window with indirect sunlight. Before you go to the nursery, scope out your living space and see where they can get at least a little natural light. Is it sunny there for six hours a day? Two? Is it shaded, or is it direct light? This will go very far in helping the friendly nursery people figure out what will work for you.

Easy indoor plants:

- Succulents, including aloe
- Most small cacti
- Sago palm
- African violets
- Ficus trees
- Philodendron
- Spider plants

Step 260: Find out how often your plant wishes to be watered, and do not overwater it

It's really, really easy to drown a plant, whereas if they're underwatered, they just sort of look droopy and sad and Katie-esque. But among the many endearing qualities of plants is that even if they're thirsty, they quickly cheer up once watered, usually within twenty-four hours.

Stick your finger in the pot. If you can still feel moisture, they probably don't need any more water yet.

If the soil is very dry and the water just runs out of the bottom of the pot, place a bowl or plate under it and add water. This allows the dry soil to rehydrate, and your plant will soak up the water from the bottom.

Step 261: Do not repot them right away

Just like people, plants find moving to be very, very stressful and don't want to do it unless things have become unbearable in the old place. It's possible that it'll be ready to move on immediately (see below), but if not, you're probably just stressing it out by repotting it.

After you take a plant home from the nursery, leave it in the pot it came in, at least for the moment. Chances are good this is a hideously ugly plastic pot, so by all means buy an attractive planter that's one size larger. They usually get larger in two-inch increments; if it's planted in an eight-inch pot, buy a ten-inch pot. Then put its current pot inside its future home, and maybe scatter a little moss around the top to disguise this arrangement.

Step 262: Repot when they become root-bound

Eventually, your happy plant will swell and fill its home with roots (if it hasn't yet when you bring it home). To see if it's ready to move on up, take it outside, tilt it partially upside down, and gently shake it out of the pot. If the roots swirl around the edges of the soil, it's ready.

Add a little of its soil of choice to the bottom of the new pot. Set the whole thing in gently, and pat soil into the sides. Give it a good, loving, and thorough watering.

PETS

So you've not killed a plant and are ready for a step up in the responsibility department! Yay! Pets are wonderful, and you should go for it . . . if you are ready and have the right motivations.

I got my beloved cat Marigny Treme Brown-Gervais just as soon as I moved out of the dorm room and into my first apartment. I'm ashamed to say that my thought process was not *Do I have the money to take her for yearly checkups? Who will watch her if I go intern somewhere for the summer? What will my life be like for the next fifteen years, which is how long she may live?* but more along the lines of *My life would be happier if there were a cat wandering around in this apartment.*

Eight years later, we still enjoy each other's company. But there are apartments I can't get because I have a pet, and pet-sitting to arrange when I go away, and vet bills when she gets a kitty ailment. I still wouldn't be able to spend thousands of dollars if she needed surgery, which makes me feel like a bad owner, but having four thousand dollars squirreled away seems an unreasonably high bar to pet ownership. She's 800 percent worth it to me, but these are things I wish I'd given more thought to.

And dogs are way more care- and cost-intensive than cats. Cats, I am pretty sure, are closer to houseplants than to dogs on the care-requirement continuum.

A couple of quick reminders:

• A pet is not a living safety blanket. It is a small being with hopes, dreams, and a frequent, ongoing need to poop.

• Moving is not an excuse to take a pet to the shelter. Chances are good that your pet will not be adopted, particularly if they're older, a mixed breed, or have any behavioral issues. If your options are to leave your pet by the side of the road or take them to a shelter, then obviously you should take them to a shelter. But their chances, once there, are not great.

Step 263: Free animals are not free

Especially when they're little. Brittni Lipscomb, who helps run Orchard View Veterinary Center, pointed out that kittens and puppies need vaccines every three weeks, and de-worming every two weeks until they're sixteen weeks old. One benefit to adopting from a shelter is that your pet will already have lots of the necessary procedures under its belt.

But it's more than just the first few weeks: Pets are expensive.

First things first: Before your pet comes home, go to the bank and get a hundred-dollar bill. Put this in an envelope, then write [YOUR PET'S NAME] EMERGENCY FUND. Keep this around. This can't pay for everything, but it'll help.

Know that to do the bare minimum, health-wise, for your pet will be around three hundred dollars per year. Can you set aside twenty-five dollars per month? What if you didn't have cable? Or a gym membership?

Step 264: Find the right vet for you

Brittni said she thinks interviewing potential vets is a great idea. "Remember that you are hiring them to do a job for you. Visit the practice, tour the facility, ask if you can watch a procedure, check prices, ask what their philosophies are," she said. "Make sure you are going to a veterinarian you trust."

Step 265: Don't be afraid to talk to your vet about the most cost-effective options

First, vets are not out to screw you. They are not getting wealthy off their glamorous, dog-vomit-rich lives. And they understand that not everyone can afford everything. Saying, "I love my pet and I want the best for her, but I can only afford X" is a fair statement. Ask if there are less optimal, more affordable ways to solve whatever the issue is.

Step 266: Buy decent food for your pet

It doesn't have to be the super-high-end stuff they sell at the vet's, but some brands are more nutritionally sound than others. My vet recommends Royal Canin, Science Diet, or Eukanuba.

Step 267: Treat your pet for fleas, especially during the summer months

Vets recommend that you treat year-round, but if money's tight and you live in a cold climate, you may be able to get away with spring/summer treatments. The key here is that there are a few things that are very effective, and a whole host that are not. Buying a four-dollar flea collar at Petco will do nothing for you.

You can certainly get prescription-strength stuff, but Vectra, Advantage, and Frontline are all over-the-counter and work well.

Read *all the instructions* before you apply the stuff. You are about to put some pretty serious poison on your beloved pet, so take the ten minutes and make sure you're doing it correctly. If your house is infected with fleas, get a bug bomb. Do not try to do any all-natural stuff. Just get a bug bomb.

Step 268: Pay attention for signs your pet may be sick

"Anytime your pet is acting differently than normal it can be a concern," Brittni said, adding that changes in eating or drinking, sluggishness, and having accidents in the house can all be signs that they're sick. One reason it's important to feed your pet the same amount of food at the same time is that you can immediately tell when they're eating less than usual. She also pointed out that many illnesses aren't obvious to the owner, so regular checkups are important.

Take your pet to the vet (or even the hospital) ASAP if any of the following is happening:

- Acute abdominal pain
- Uncontrolled bleeding or bleeding from the neck
- Coughing up blood

- Breathing problems
- Broken bones
- Burns or electrical shock
- Car accidents
- Collapse or fainting; loss of consciousness; seizures; paralysis or lack of coordination
- Diarrhea that goes on for more than a day (especially in young animals)
- Distended abdomen
- Eye swelling or injury
- Frequent vomiting, or unproductive retching
- Frostbite
- Neck injury
- Pale gums
- Poisoning
- Straining to urinate

If any of these things are happening, call your vet right away.

Step 269: Consider pet insurance

This is way cheaper than you'd think—there are lots of plans for between twenty and thirty dollars a month that cover the basics, and for maybe twenty more you can have catastrophic insurance, in case they got hit by a car.

It is a legitimate thing to own a pet even if you couldn't pay for a forty-five-hundred-dollar surgery, if it came to that. It doesn't mean you don't love your pet. But it is not a legitimate thing to own a pet if you can't afford the very, very basics—vaccines, spaying and neutering, and flea treatment.

AROUND THE HOUSE

Most day-to-day house maintenance is basic cleaning (see all of chapter 2). But there are a few things you can and should do that go above and beyond to keep things in good working order.

Step 270: Clean out underneath the burners if a lot of oil or food has spilled down there

Unless you like grease fires, in which case, you know, do what you do.

Otherwise: If you have a gas stove, this is pretty easy; if it's electric, you'll need to pull the burners out first. Grab them at the point where they plug into the stove, then wiggle and slowly pull them out. Use dish soap and hot water to break down the grease underneath, then a dish towel to dry it off.

If the saucers under the electrical burner get really funky, as they will every couple of years or so, every big-box store with a home-improvement section sells replacement saucers.

Step 271: Pay some attention to your fridge

Beyond just not letting the stuff in there rot into a nasty, dripping mess, there are a few things you should do every four months or so. They're easy and don't take long.

First, make sure the coils on your fridge aren't covered in dust. They're located either behind or under the fridge; if they're underneath, you'll have to remove the front panel. Dust them off with a broom if need be.

Then wipe off the plastic edges that create a seal with disinfectant. Make sure they aren't cracked or warped, otherwise the fridge will overwork itself to make up for the lost cold air. If a dollar bill falls down when you close the door on it, the seals aren't working well.

Finally, clean the inside and wipe it with white vinegar, which prevents mold. Put a new open box of baking soda in there to keep it fresh smelling.

Step 272: Don't put hair down your drains

Or oatmeal, or anything else likely to glob up into a gunky mess. But if you do notice that your sink or tub is draining slowly, do not wait until it's totally stopped up. Go get some Drano, and *read the damn directions.*

BODY

It's impossible to phrase this section in a way that doesn't sound like nagging, and people nagging you about your health is the most guilty squirm-inducing conversation there is. It's so easy to reach the "Fuck it!" saturation point. Because of course they're right: There is no more important physical thing in the world than the body you happen to inhabit. You only have one, and some things you do to it are not fixable.

But it's so fun (in the moment) to abuse them. It's more fun to eat Doritos than bananas. Diet Coke tastes better than water. Staying out late and drinking always seems like a great plan, at least until the next morning. Believe me, I get it: I used to be a chain smoker, and I *loved* it. I loved every single one of the hundreds of thousands of cigarettes I've smoked to date. But while I loved cigarettes, I hated myself a little every time I chose to smoke.

You have to take care of your body. You have to. You have to. You have to. Yes, right now if you're in your twenties then it seems like nothing will ever be wrong with it, other than hangovers and non-reality-based concerns about your upper arms looking fat. But even if you can't feel or see the consequences now, they're there.

Plus, think back: There is probably at least one time in your life when you were being healthy—eating right, exercising, and getting enough sleep. You really do feel and behave better when you do these things. You don't have to be an all-organic yoga instructor to be good to your body. Just make one small, good choice every day, and you will slowly but surely become healthier.

My friend Elisabeth, who, when she is not being my friend, is a surgeon (seriously: She professionally cuts people up. That is her *job*.), was willing to chat about how she treats her body, which is pretty different from how I treat mine.

Step 273: Being healthy is actually pretty simple, if not easy

"Think about it this way: You have a couple of holes where things go in, a few where things come out, and you're surrounded by breathing, dynamic skin," she said, then added that the whole key to health is watching what you put in, monitoring what comes out, and protecting that skin.

Step 274: Never start smoking and if you have, quit

"I tell my patients that I'd almost rather they use heroin with clean needles than smoke," Elisabeth said.

She pointed out that cutting down is better than not cutting down, and suggests to her patients that however many cigarettes they smoke daily, the next month they smoke one less per day.

You can't quit unless it's your time. No one else, and certainly not a book, can pressure you into it, because that isn't a decision for other people to make. It's yours. But you can choose, in smaller ways, to turn your back. You can choose, next time you want a cigarette, to say, "You know what? I'm not going to have this one. I can have one later, if I want, but this one I do not need."

Step 275: Purchase real food

The reason we're all fat is that so, so much money and research has gone into making food that tastes delicious and makes us want more.

"Anything that tastes really good—think twice about," Elisabeth said. "Try to eat seven bananas, and your body's going to shut down and say, 'You know what? I'm done.' You can eat the same caloric amount of McDonald's and your body will want more."

Elisabeth mentioned the old trick of shopping around the edge of the grocery store, which is where the things that humans have eaten for thousands of years tend to be located: fruits, vegetables, meats, and a few carbohydrates.

The less a giant food company is adding to your food, the healthier you will be, the more energy you will feel, and the more you are likely to maintain a healthy weight.

Step 276: Keep an eye on weight gain

We are all differently shaped and sized, and a big part of being a grown-up is accepting your body for what it is, and not spending mental energy anguishing over something that's just a feature of you. If you have seriously unhealthy feelings about your body, obsess about food and weight (not health: weight), and base your self-image on how thin you look, that is called an eating disorder and generally requires mental health counseling to recover from.

That being said, obesity is a serious health issue. And it can sneak up on us: For hundreds of thousands of years, the human beings who survived were the ones whose bodies could effectively retain energy (read: fat) through the lean times. Then, in the past hundred years, that has gone right out the window. Don't blame your body for this tendency. It makes perfect biological sense, and it's not a reflection on anything except millennia of evolutionary selection.

But it does mean you need to find a way to maintain your body where it is, what your particular balance of exercise to calories should be.

"Let's say you were 140 pounds last year, and you're 145 this year," Elisabeth said. "If you don't change your habits, in four years, you're twenty pounds heavier, plus you've established four years of habits that lead to five pounds of weight gain per year...It happens so subtly. If you divide five pounds by 365 days, it's not something you'll see on any given day. But in ten years, you'll be fifty pounds heavier."

Step 277: Find a couple of healthy things you can cope with snacking on in lieu of the delicious stuff

Somewhere in this big wide world, there are at least two healthy snacks you can tolerate. Find them. Maybe they are frozen raspberries, or tangerines, or low-fat string cheese, or shelled edamame. These are the things that are allowed to live around your home in vast quantities, laying in wait for you to mindlessly eat a big bowl of (or, in the case of the string cheese, two packets, peeled very slowly).

It's easy to say, "Don't eat unless you're hungry! Don't eat if you're stressed! Don't eat if you're watching TV!" but for a lot of us, those habits are very deeply ingrained. Eating something that's low-calorie and good for you can be a nice compromise.

Step 278: Pay attention to portions

After putting on about twenty pounds, I decided to lose it. I didn't have to stop eating the things I liked (anything that includes animal fat and is favored by old Southern men), but I did have to start eating the amount humans are supposed to eat of the things I liked.

A twelve-ounce steak is not a steak. It's three steaks. Half a big bag of chips is not a serving of chips, it's a quarter of the daily calories you're supposed to eat.

The trick to smaller portions is (a) to eat them slowly, and (b) to wait a little while before going for more. A lot of times, you can be nearly as happy slowly eating your 14 chips as you would eating 140 in the same amount of time.

Step 279: Find an exercise you like

Bodies need to move. That is their whole point, besides eating, pooping, and sexing; that is what we all have this extensive and beautiful musculature for. So just make sure your body is in motion, at least sometimes. Ten minutes a day is better than nothing.

You don't have to go to the gym to do it, either. There are yoga videos on Hulu, walking is free, you can go dancing, you can bike ride, you can jog around your apartment—even though that sounds like a direct path to madness to me. Do a bunch of things. You will feel stupid and out of shape when you do them. But eventually, you will do something that does not feel like working out. You will do something you enjoy, something that makes you feel more at home in your body than you did the day before. Keep doing that.

Remember, you don't have to go balls-to-the-wall to get the health benefits and lose weight. Tina, who is the group fitness coordinator at my gym, pointed out that if you're at that very, very high point in the workout—the anaerobic part, where you can't talk except in gasping breaths—you're actually not burning that much fat, because your body isn't getting oxygen effectively.

Also, remember that you don't need to spend money to find expert advice and help—there are tons of great online resources, like Couch to 5K, and apps for everything from counting calories to quitting smoking.

Step 280: Consider taking vitamins and probiotics daily

Yes: If you eat nothing but lean proteins, fruit, and leafy vegetables in all colors of the rainbow, you are probably getting all the vitamins you need. Is that how you eat?

Elisabeth pointed out that vitamins and nutritional supplements are not monitored or researched by the FDA, so it's worth your while to find ones where the manufacturers have done the studies and research themselves. She herself takes omega-3 capsules, a daily probiotic, and prenatal vitamins.

- **Omega-3:** "Take omega-3, not omega-6," she said. "This is actually proven by the FDA and drug companies to restore a good balance of triglycerides in your bloodstream...I take it to justify the fact that I'm also taking in pizza and beer. It's the least I can do for my body to make up for all the shit I put into it."
- **Probiotics:** These are the healthy strains of bacteria that make up your body's flora and keep tabs on all those malevolent bacteria. "Between 60 and 70 percent of your immune system resides in your gut," she said. "So every time I take one of those, I have thirty billion more little bugs fighting in my favor."
- **Prenatal vitamins:** "A prenatal vitamin is critically necessary if you are a woman of childbearing age—even if you are on birth control, even if you have an IUD," Elisabeth said,

Even if you have no intention of having a baby, they contain all sorts of healthy, useful vitamins and minerals and make your hair and nails healthier. You may as well.

Step 281: When you get a prescription, read all the enclosed information

Make sure that it doesn't interact with other prescriptions (or habits) you may have. Some antibiotics make birth control ineffective. Others will make you violently ill if you drink more than a glass of wine. Ask your pharmacist about it.

Finally, even though prescriptions seem safe despite the thousands of possible side effects, know that there are side effects and that this is a risk you take. A small pill that effects a systemwide change is not something to mess around with, particularly if you're taking other ones, too. Take it as prescribed, and if you have any concerns about it, call your doctor before you take it. Also, if you're taking antibiotics, take all of them, as prescribed, even if you feel better. Otherwise, your urinary tract infection or whatever it is may well retreat and come back stronger and crueler than ever.

Note: Carry around a little card in your wallet that lists any medications you take, as well as the dosage. This could save your life if you're in a car accident. You need to be able to tell doctors what is already in your body so they can make the correct decisions as to what will be safe and what won't.

Step 282: Don't time-travel on the weekends, especially if you do an eight-to-five schedule on weekdays

"If you don't go out until 11 PM, you get in at 4 AM, and sleep until 2 PM...and you go back to your eight-to-five schedule, that's like traveling to another time zone every time you do that," Elisabeth said. "If you think that jet lag is bad and messes you up, think about the fact that you're doing that every weekend."

This is not to say you can never go out. But think about if it's possible to do that in ways that aren't radically different from your weekday schedule.

Step 283: Wash your hands. Really. And don't touch your face

"All day long, I touch sick people. And truthfully, the one way to avoid getting sick yourself is to wash your hands frequently, and get out of the habit of touching your face," Elisabeth said. "You have a beautiful face. Look at it all you want, but don't touch it. Just say no."

A reminder that good hand-washing involves at least thirty seconds and vigorous scrubbing—that's what breaks down the cell walls of the bacteria. Also, if you can avoid touching things that a million other people have touched—if you can open the door with your hip, for example—you'll be better off.

If you don't get sick that often, then yay! Continue to not worry about it. If you do, and if missing a few days of work isn't possible, then get good at hand-washing.

Step 284: Keep hydrated, especially on airplanes

I used to get sick every time I stepped on an airplane, because airplanes are essentially germ canteens hurtling through the sky. But my uncle Tom suggested that I get a saline nasal spray, and it's worked wonders.

"You naturally secrete antibodies in all your mucous membranes," Elisabeth said. "And of course you can blow your nose and flush that stuff out. But when [the membrane] is dry and cracked, the germs stay there and flourish."

Side note: If you're blowing your nose and the output is anything but clear, that's a sign that you may have a sinus infection.

Step 285: Wear sunscreen (or stay in the shade)

Decide now which is more important to you: a tan or skin that still looks nice when you're fifty. Some of us don't have a choice, because we're genetically deficient redheads that can't be in direct sunlight for more than ten minutes. But even if you didn't lose the melanin lottery, it's still a good plan to put on sunscreen daily.

Yes, even the expensive stuff tends to feel sticky and gross and pore-clogging. But like healthy snack foods and exercise, somewhere in this world there exists a combination moisturizer–daily SPF protectant that won't bother the hell out of you. Get used to putting it on every day, even (especially) when it's cloudy.

Step 286: If there is an optional choice you're making that's hurting your body, knock it off

Here, I think about cheap high heels, but this applies to all sorts of things. Pain is your body's way of registering that something bad is happening to it. If that pair of heels makes your feet cramp up every time you wear them, then stop wearing them. It doesn't matter how cute they are. The whole point of maintenance is making sure that you're not permanently fucking something up through carelessness, and that includes active carelessness as well as the passive kind.

DISCUSSION QUESTIONS

1. Why are healthy things so boring? Why are comfy shoes so ugly? What is the meaning of all this?
2. What's the most responsible, dull expenditure you've experienced in the past month?
3. What is the most high-maintenance item that exists in the entire world? Do you think it's the Large Hadron Collider? I do.

8. Friends and Neighbors

You probably already learned this through any number of cheerful preschool songs, but friends are some valuable-ass people.

They don't need to hang out with you, they're not obligated to give you their affection, they don't have to have you in their life. *They choose to.* Most of them don't even want to have sex with you! So treasure them. Work hard to deserve their affection, and give them yours freely. Initially, you don't owe them anything, and they don't owe you anything. Once you've chosen each other, decide to care about them enough that you'll get up in the middle of the night to drive them home after they get freaked out by a regrettable hookup's bird-eating spider. Don't Google that.

When you're little, friends are like weather. Some are better, some are worse, but they're more or less always there. But it's harder than we expect to make and keep them once you're working and living on your own. As my friend Nancy pointed out, she could go to a bar any night of the week and find a man to sleep with her (Note: She does not actually do this. But she *could*). Meeting friends, not so simple. Finding and solidifying a friendship isn't difficult, but it is daunting and ill defined, unlike the obvious course that bar hookups travel. But the rewards are great, and less likely to send you to the ob-gyn to figure out what, exactly, is happening in your crotch.

Also, know that when you get out of school, it's likely—not certain, but likely—that if you move to a new place, you will spend a while feeling very alone. One of the many shocks that come from graduating is that for the first time ever, we're not surrounded by a giant cohort of clear potential friends. Sure, there are work friends, but from here on out it is going to be a little trickier than it was in your hometown or at your college. You have to push through this—you can and will make friends. It just won't happen at summer-camp speeds where you meet someone at noon and by 5 PM they're your best friend ever.

Step 287: Assess honestly your own friendship needs and wants

Some people have the time, energy, and boundless affection to have thirty-seven really close friends. Some people want two close friends, and fifteen people they can call to go out dancing with on a random Friday. Some people want one really tight-knit group. All of these are 100 percent reasonable social needs.

Our model for someone who does well in friendship is someone with a zillion friends, who is never alone, who can conjure twenty people at a bar with nothing more than a mass text. For some, this is indeed what they want. But it's okay if that's not what you want—if you're a quieter, shyer person who would rather have a small handful of people you're genuinely close with.

Step 288: Decide that you are going to have an amazing group of friends

Sarah Von Bargen of yesandyes.org is one of the best friends I know—not in that we're best friends (although I would be delighted if that were the case) but in that she is great at being a friend, and as such had some choice insights.

The first step to making friends as a grown-up, Sarah said, is to decide you want it.

After grad school, she said, she found herself in a new city. "I literally was like, 'I want this sort of social life where I go to backyard parties and barbecues, and I want a group of friends that's smart and interesting and engaging, that does fun stuff, and I'm going to find a way to make this happen,'" she said. So how did she do that?

Step 289: Go to places that have the kinds of people you want to be friends with, then ask them on a friend-date if they're even vaguely promising

Friendship-making is not all that different from dating.

"You put yourself in situations where like-minded people are going to be, and then you talk to them," Sarah said, adding that she would do things like go to the all-women climbing night at the local rock climbing gym.

"I'd take an existing friend with me, and then we'd chat with other girls while we were waiting to belay, and then I'd say, 'Do you guys want to go get a beer with us?' "

Not everyone is as outgoing as Sarah, and this is stressful in the same way that asking someone on a date is stressful. Anytime you say to someone, even in a very veiled way, *I care about you. Do you care about me?* it's scary.

But almost everyone will be pleased that you took the initiative. And if they're not delighted by your straightforward friendliness, there you go! That is a bad friend candidate, and it's good you won't be wasting any more time.

Step 290: If you like them, announce your intention to become friends

Sarah suggested this, and it instantly made me burn with desire for someone to say this to me.

"If I really connect with someone, I just full-on say, 'We're going to be friends.' And 100 percent of the time, they're like, 'Yeah!' . . . I navigate life by saying the super-direct, awkward thing we're all thinking. I'll say, 'You're awesome, I want to be friends. Let's hang out.'"

So if Sarah had met this person, say, at a house party, she'll announce intentions to find them on Facebook, then send a message saying, "Hey, it was great to meet you. I know you're also into amazingly awful movies, and my friends and I are going to go see a screening of *Showgirls*. Wanna come?"

Step 291: Find friends through your other friends

If someone is smart and fun, chances are good their friends are similarly great. If there is a friend-of-a-friend you see a lot in group social outings, go ahead and grab coffee or a beer with them one-on-one and solidify that friendship.

"Take the initiative to hang out with them individually, to be friends outside the circle," Sarah said. " 'It's great to see you at these parties; I want to be friends for real.' "

Step 292: If you and your friends all want to expand your social circle, think of creative ways to do that

Sarah said that once every few months, one of her friends has a dinner party where she invites maybe five people, and asks everyone to bring someone new, often someone who has just moved to town or maybe recently broke up and is in the market for new friends. Which brings us to...

Step 293: Be nice to new people

Being new to a place or job is like being really sick. When people show you a small amount of kindness, it feels like a great deal of kindness, because you're so nervous/stressed/anxious/lonely/unable to swallow solid foods.

You don't need to go over the top, but stopping by to introduce yourself and issue an invitation goes a long way. If they're new at work, invite them to grab a cup of coffee that afternoon. If they're new in the building, let them know that you'd love to answer any questions about the neighborhood—where the best pizza is, which scary neighbors to avoid, and so on. You can even pull the old-fashioned, still-classy move of bringing the new neighbor a pie.

If you've ever been new in a non-friendly place, you know how awful it is. All of us, sooner or later, will be new somewhere, hoping there are decent people around. Be those decent people.

Step 294: Find a thirty-something (or older) friend

One of the distinct pleasures of being a grown-up is that all of a sudden, the age range of your friends widens drastically. You can actually be friends with someone old enough to be your mom, and not in the "You're my friend's mom and you like me as a secondary child" kind of way. Also, truism: People who are older than us are smart, and interesting, and know so, so much more about life than we gave them credit for when we were asshole teenagers.

A big part of my inspiration for this book came from a trio of friends I had at my first reporting job in Mississippi, when I was twenty-one. Nancy, Henrietta, and Rachel were all between five and nine years older than me, and they were *so fucking smart*. They would do things like (gently) tell me not to wear cocktail dresses to work, or why a certain relationship would or wouldn't work, or, in one Very Special Episode of Preparing Kelly To Fend For Herself, how to cook a chicken breast.

These things, in retrospect, seem obvious, but they weren't to me. Not because I was stupid, or ill prepared for life, even though I sort of was. There are just lots of things that someone who is twenty-seven knows, thanks to the five extra years of experience being on their own. There are even more things that someone who is thirty-two, and has ten years under their belt, knows. If you apply this principle to the work-place, it seems obvious that someone with years of experience will under-stand things a new guy won't. But we don't give others the same amount of credit when it comes to understanding general life preparation.

So if you can find one that will tolerate you, and take you under their wing, this is the way to go. And someday you, too, will patiently explain how a French press works to a bright-eyed but confused young thing. It's the circle of basic competence.

Step 295: If you haven't seen someone in a while and you miss them, spend the thirty seconds to reach out rather than angsting about the lost friendship

Getting in touch doesn't have to be a huge deal. Text them and say, "Hey, I miss you, we're overdue for a drink; let's catch up."

"You can think, *Why don't my friends do that to me? Why do I always have to be the one who does that?*" Sarah said, but then pointed out that a lot of people just aren't like that—they're busy or just aren't conscientious about that sort of thing. But they'll almost always respond if you start. If they don't respond two or three times in a row, then know that the burden of communication will probably always be on you. Some people are flaky but totally worth it. Some people aren't. Make that call.

Step 296: Do well in your long-distance friendships

Distance is what shows you whether or not something has long-term value. It's easy to fall away from someone who is out of your fish-bowl, who no longer works with you, who every time you talk requires fifteen minutes of updates to be on the same page. But if this person is still a vital part of your life, they're worth holding on to.

A long-distance friend is like a cactus. They don't require a lot, but they do require some. Call on their birthday, or better yet, send a card. Be pen pals, because a forty-cent stamp plus ten minutes of effort is a great way to make someone's day. Make sure you don't go more than three months without talking on the phone. Gchat. Keep someone in your life's orbit, and stay in theirs. Best of all, go visit.

Step 297: Be a fun-thing initiator

If you want to do more fun things, take some initiative. Usually, there's at least one social chair in any given group of friends—the person who seeks out fun things to do, then figures out who wants to come. Even if this isn't normally your role, step up to the plate at least once in a while.

Also, do not be discouraged if not everyone you invite shows up—people are busy. It doesn't mean they don't love you or don't want to see you.

Step 298: If there is something you want your friends to do, and it's important, spell that out ahead of time rather than being angry when people fail to read your mind

We are conditioned to minimize how important something is to us. But if it really is important, go ahead and say that—"You know, I know everyone's busy but it would mean a lot to me if you could make it."

If your feelings will be hurt if people don't show up to something, tell them that. It's an okay thing to say, so long as you're not doing it all the time. And, of course, so long as you are the kind of person who shows up for the things that are important to them, even if maybe they don't tell you that directly. A strong way to do that is...

Step 299: Pay attention to how your friends show affection

If you have a friend who fusses over you on your birthday, then fuss over them on their birthday. If you have a friend who is always, always ready to drop everything and talk to you when you're upset, do the same for them.

"If someone is really important to you, one of your closest friends, pay attention to how they show affection to you, because that's probably how they want affection shown to them," Sarah said.

For example, Sarah noted that she couldn't care less if someone came to watch her run a 5K, but for some of her friends, it's really important. And that's legitimate. Just because something isn't particularly important to you doesn't mean that it shouldn't be important to someone else.

Step 300: Tell the people you love why you love them

"My friend Darcie is the singularly most capable person I know," Sarah said. "And I tell her, to her face—'You are the singularly most capable person I know, you're great at everything.' I love her and I want her to know that."

I try, once a year, to write a letter to each of my closest friends and let them know why they mean so much to me, and why I am so damn lucky to have them in my life. Everyone wants to be acknowledged. Everyone wants to feel loved. There is no reason to withhold this from the people who are worthy of it.

Step 301: For fuck's sake, keep your friends' secrets

This is not negotiable. If someone swears you to secrecy and you break their confidence, you are being a bad friend. I don't care how big your mouth is, figure out a way to keep it shut.

Remember that a lot of times, people sort of assume there to be a free and open exchange of information between significant others. So when someone tells you something, you can say, "Is it okay for me to tell Dave about this?" And if they say no, respect that. To protect yourself, if you are confiding in someone, be sure to ask them specifically not to tell their boyfriend or girlfriend if you don't want that person to know.

Step 302: Don't gossip about a friend with someone who doesn't love him as much as you do

I have a core group of five really close friends, and we've all known each other since we were twelve. If I tell one of them something, unless I swear them to secrecy, I'm sort of telling all of them because we're incorrigible gossips and spread secrets via osmosis. But the key here is that we all really love one another, and so when we talk about one another's actions, it's more a familial tightness than a need for idle gossip.

But I would never talk about one of those friends with someone who didn't love her like I did, because that would be disloyal. If her name came up in conversation with someone who wasn't as close to her as I am, I'd probably say something along the lines of, "You know, Amy is one of my very best friends and I don't feel right talking about her." Loyalty is one of the very loveliest of qualities, so do your best to show it.

Step 303: Don't freak out when friendships wane and wax, especially the long-term kind

If there's someone you've been dear, dear friends with since you were twelve, that's fucking tremendous. There is a very finite number of people in the world with whom you can honestly say that you've been friends forever, so that small handful of people is tremendously valuable.

That being said, sometimes you'll go through periods where you have less in common, and see less of each other. It happens. Especially if you're in really different situations. If they just got married, say, or you have a kid, or one of you is in grad school while the other is working hard as an aspiring actor, you will probably have less to talk about. Don't throw it away or write the friendship off.

The value of the relationship is not in the uninterrupted continuity of same-level friendship, but in the fact that you can be friends at twelve, twenty, twenty-five. So don't freak out if you're not close friends for six months when you're twenty-three. You won't ever make any new old friends. Don't get mad at them, or yourself, if it's not exactly the same as it used to be. A lot of times you'll find that after a few years, you'll feel closer again.

Side note: Everyone knows that moons wane, but not everyone knows that they wax (get bigger). I move we reclaim the verb *waxing* from the painful hair removal sense, and instead use it to refer to the process of getting almost imperceptibly but steadily larger. This makes everything sound disgusting but also hilarious. "Y'all, my armpit fat is waxing something *tremendous* this summer."

Step 304: Monitor your friendships like you do romantic relationships

Friendships are more intuitive than romantic relationships, so we give them less scrutiny. But a lot of the same questions you ask yourself in a romantic relationship are valid in a friendship.

"When you're in a romantic relationship, people are proactive about communicating their needs and evaluating, 'Am I getting what I need from this relationship?'" Sarah said. "I don't think people do that with friendships, and they should."

To that end, she said, she pays attention: Has this friendship run its course? Is this person a toxic presence in my life? Are both of us getting what we need from this?

"If every time I hang out with them, I come away feeling down or like I'm just their unpaid life coach, what's the point?" she said.

Step 305: Do not treat your friends like your unpaid life coaches

It's just not fair. This should be a give-and-take, and if you are always taking, your phone will be quieter and quieter.

Your time together should be a heady brew of inside jokes, discussion of shared interests, interesting bits of gossip that are too juicy to share with the general public, and, yes, talking about things that are important to you. Discussing something that's forefront in your mind when necessary is one thing. Making every interaction into a soliloquy about Your Troubles is another. That shit gets exhausting. You know that.

Friends can and should be there for each other, and sometimes one party needs a lot more support and love than the other. But your friend can't be your psychiatrist, and it's not fair to ask them to be. If you have large, ongoing issues that take far more to work through than can be sorted out by venting over cocktails, it's a good idea to seek professional help (see step 407).

And if a friend always, always turns to you with problems that are beyond your friend-healing abilities, then it's fair to say— gently!—"You know, I know this stuff with your family is really, really hard for you, and I want to be there in any way I can. But I feel like a lot of this is deeper than what I can help you with. Have you maybe considered talking to someone?"

Step 306: Be supportive of depressed or heartbroken friends

Straight up: It is rarely as fun to be friends with someone when they are clinically depressed as when they are their normal selves.

But everyone, everyone, everyone goes through a hard time every now and again. Do not bolt when this happens. Do not interpret their silence or their sadness as a rejection of you. It doesn't matter that it's a pain in your ass; it's just what you have to do.

Step 307: Remember that your new love interest is only moderately interesting to your friends

There are few times in life when you have So! Much! To! SAY! as when you've just started dating someone you're excited about. And since your friends love you, chances are that they are happy for you, too, and want to know all about this new person.

But remain aware that although this is a ten on your interest scale, it's probably a four on your friends', especially if you try to shoehorn your love into every topic they introduce ("Oh, you got a promotion? I think one time *Matt* got a promotion!"). Tell them about him or her and feel free to gush, but pay attention to their receptiveness/ enthusiasm level. When it starts to flag even a little, it's time to change the subject. Life is long, and if it works out, you'll have plenty of other chances.

Here are some people whom you should not share your buoyant enthusiasm with:

- People who've recently filled their friend obligation of listening to you prattle on for one reason or another
- People who have suffered heartbreak and are unhappily single
- People who wish that *they* were the person you were now seeing

Step 308: Don't date your friend's ex

Should you date your friend's* ex?**

START!!

Is your friend actively sad that they are not in this relationship? — No → Did they date seriously and/or for more than a year? — No → Is your friend in a relationship now that they are psyched about?

yes / yes

No

Have they had at least one relationship since the breakup? — Yes → Are your friend and the potential date on cordial terms?

No

no — NO. There are lots of attractive people in this world that aren't friendship-ruining.

no

yes

Ask your friend if they are cool about it. Do not just listen for what they **say**, listen for what they **mean**. Are they cool with it?

* Note: this chart applies to friends that are verbal-invitation-to-birthday-party level or higher. The acquaintance's ex flowchart is different.

GO FOR IT. But know that things will still be at least a little awkward.

Yes

** Yes, long-term/ongoing hookups count.

Or do, but know Things Will Be Weird, almost no matter what.

Step 309: Tell your friends the truth about important things

When it comes to things of consequence, you need to be honest or you're not being a good friend. It's an issue of respect. They can handle it, and they deserve it. Be on their team. If your friend is dating someone who treats her badly, and asks your opinion of him, you should give it to her. If he wonders aloud about whether he has a drinking problem, and you think he does, say it. Once someone has ambled down an avenue of conversation, even if you think they will be upset by the answer, you should still give it. If they opened the Pandora's box, chances are they want a look inside.

These things are not comfortable or fun to say, particularly if you've been socialized to avoid bluntness. When you speak a painful truth aloud to a friend, it doesn't just hurt her, it hurts you, too. Because of this, it requires bravery, and it requires a vast ocean of love. Find them within yourself, for that person's sake.

Sometimes tell the truth about unimportant things. Sometimes, dodge

When someone asks you a question where the answer isn't, ultimately, important—Does this dress make me look fat? Do you like this new person I'm dating that you've met once?—sometimes they want a real answer, and sometimes they just want someone to tell them they're okay.

If it's the former, be diplomatic—"You know, that's not my favorite dress on you." If it's the latter, unless you feel like they are really and truly not okay, then say, "He seems great." If you're going to lie, lie convincingly and briefly, because the more you qualify, the more obvious the lie becomes.

Step 310: If a friend is fucking up their life, open your mouth and tell them

This may never happen, but if it does, you'll know because you will worry about them constantly and feel guilty about remaining silent. This happens rarely, because it's not particularly your job. This is a layer of responsibility above just answering honestly if they ask you about something. Unsolicited advice is rarely welcome, and should rarely be given. If people want to know what you think about a given topic, they'll ask you.

However. However. If your friend is on the precipice of making (or continuing to make) a really, really bad, permanent decision, it's your job to tell them that. If they are throwing their life away to move across the country for someone who doesn't care about them, if they are about to marry a raging asshole, if they are missing work because they're too hung over from doing coke on a Wednesday, open your mouth, pass air through your vocal cords, and speak your piece.

This could mean an end to the friendship, at least for a while. This, too, will be painful, especially if your friend doesn't see the truth in what you've told them and doesn't make any changes. Know that sometimes, that stuff has to settle in, and that doesn't happen overnight. That can take months, or years, and they have to want to know the truth of what you've said. But eventually, hopefully, they will come around and realize that you did it out of love. Or maybe you were wrong, and you'll come around. Only time will tell, but if you don't say something and it will eat you up, then say something. If it's a really good friendship, it will survive.

Step 311: End a friendship, if need be

You are not obligated to be friends with someone, nor they with you, and sometimes friendships run their course. If you don't take pleasure in their company, if they always blow you off, or if they act too much like any of the frienemies (see below), then you can end it without guilt. If you find that you're regularly not happy in their company, that's a deal-breaker.

If it's a casual friend and they call repeatedly, you can either do a boundary-setting get-together ("You know, I'd love to get a drink but I really only have time for one because I have to be somewhere at seven thirty") or just avoid them.

But sometimes, people will poke at the wound, keep calling, wish to be absolutely and completely positive that you don't want them. If this is the case, an explanation may be in order. If you were close friends, an explanation will nearly always be in order.

If it boils down to "I just don't have that much fun with you," then that should probably go unsaid, since that will only hurt the person and not particularly do anything for them long-term. If there's something more specific, and sharing it will (a) not cause undue hurt and (b) have the potential to help them with future friendships, then phrase it diplomatically.

"Lisa, I feel like we spend a lot of time fighting and not that much time just being friends, and that our friendship seems to have this conflict always at the center of it."

"You know, you're always really down on yourself, and it makes me feel sad and down, too. It's hard."

Step 312: When faced with a frienemy, determine which type it is

Is this the undermining frienemy? The one who hangs out with you to feel better about her own life? The dear childhood friend who has become slowly but surely toxic in your life? A lot of times, we feel upset at someone but can't tell why exactly. Do your best to crystallize this to yourself, and your plan of action should become clearer.

The Seven Dwarfs of frienemies:

- **Flaky:** Do you two have plans? How about now?
- **Flirty** (to your significant other): This girl needs you to accept the fact that she playfully jostles your boyfriend every few minutes because that's just who she *is*! She's just *friendly*! Oh my God, it doesn't even *mean* anything! You're not *mad*, are you?
- **Boasty:** This frienemy says something boastful but phrases it as a complaint about themselves so you're forced to comfort her, even though both of you know damn well that she isn't upset about looking too thin.
- **Crabby:** This frienemy can never, ever enjoy a single thing, but instead keeps up a monologue of misery and disdain. Never bring this person to a fun dance party, or a goofy movie, or to meet your new significant other. Spoiler alert: She won't like them. Because she doesn't like anything.

Flirty

Flaky.

Boasty

Backstabby

Crabby

Underminey

Doc

- **Backstabby:** This friend loves you soooooooo much! Except when you are between her and something she wants, in which case, fuck you!
- **Underminey:** No, that dress you bought looks…great! So you! It's awesome that you feel so comfortable with your body!
- **Doc:** This frienemy knows *exactly* what you're going through, and has all kinds of advice. It doesn't matter whether or not you're actually going through this, because Doc has diagnosed so, so many things wrong with you. She's only trying to help. She's just doing this because she cares.

Step 313: Decide whether there are deal-breakers at play

There's better and worse things about all of us. And every single person you will ever engage with will have some less-than-ideal qualities. These are, as the brilliant Dan Savage put it, the price of admission.

So the question of whether or not this price is too high is a valid one. On one side, you've got whatever foolishness this person is pulling, and on the other you've got all their great qualities, difficult though they may be to see at this moment. And, of course, the difficulty and potential awkwardness of ending a friendship.

Step 314: Don't bicker on Facebook

Seriously, that is the worst. You know how, when someone is being unpleasant and nasty at a party, everyone else in the room is sort of cringing? Well, just remember that Facebook gives you the ability to make people all around the world cringe in unison.

Step 315: Learn to apologize

You know who loves apologizing? Nobody. Well, that's not true. There is a certain segment of the world that enjoys nothing better than a cringing mea culpa, and they will apologize all the damn time for anything. But the rest of us hate it.

But everyone must accept the fact that, at least on certain issues or certain actions, you will most assuredly be in the wrong. Many times! You're going to do something wrong today, I guarantee it. Which is okay, but if your wrongness hurt someone else, you need to acknowledge it, apologize, and try to do better next time.

How to make a good apology:

• Realize precisely what you have done wrong. You can't apologize in a meaningful way unless you actually regret what has happened. So tumble that in your mind. What did you do, what should you have done, what would you have done if you could do it again? These things all matter, and you can pick out themes to fold into the apology.

• You just need to be as humble as possible while at the same time not making excuses. You can explain yourself, but don't try to excuse yourself. That is their job.

• Be sincere in your regret.

So here is how a sample apology looks:

"Amy—listen, I just feel terrible about [action] because [reason why what you did is shitty]. I don't know what I was thinking, except [if there is a *very* pertinent bit of exculpatory evidence it may go here so long as you make it clear that this is not an excuse]. Honestly, if I could do it again [something that would have been better for everyone]. I'm very sorry, and I hope you'll forgive me."

Step 316: Graciously accept the apologies of others

It is so, so hard to cough them up. So when someone has gone through this difficult gestation, labor, and delivery, you need to be gracious about it.

Even if you are still really angry, you can say, "I forgive you." Say it with the amount of sincerity that you will feel about the apology in two months.

Step 317: Do not graciously accept apologies for the same transgression again and again

Remember in the step about apologizing, how you need to do better next time? Well, that holds for other people as well. Some things are human nature. Some things are people's nature and will not be changed. But if you keep getting the same actions, followed by the same apology, you need to accept that this is a thing this person does.

Step 318: If you really can't accept an apology, then let them know in a calm way

Some things, put simply, are indeed unforgivable. They are friendship-enders. There is no need to go through a list of them, although I think it's fair to imagine that at least 60 percent of them involve a significant other and/or the opposite sex.

Now. If you feel like you can forgive them eventually but are just really enjoying the groveling, then by all means, let it continue and enjoy. But if you know that no amount will make a difference and you are done with this person, then you need to say something like this:

"Listen. I know you're sorry, and I appreciate you letting me know that. I really don't feel like we can be close anymore, and I need you to respect that. If things change, I'll let you know."

Step 319: Find a strong, deep sea of insincerity to be sort of sweet to people you dislike

For the regular, run-of-the-mill enemies, you should conceal at least some of your distaste. You don't need to treat them like an actual friend. The key word here is *cordial*. Never be openly hostile. Exchange unenthusiastic pleasantries, then, sort of scoot away and you have fulfilled your decent-human-being obligations.

FRIENDS AND ENEMIES IN (OR NEAR) THE HOME

Being friends with your roommates and neighbors is the absolute best, because not only can you get drunk together and then totter home down the hall, but you also always have a perfect pet-sitter. And vice versa (see step 30, on giving them a key).

But the incredibly close and, in many cases, unchosen proximity is a petri dish for the bacteria of chilly resentment. No one wants this—after all, one of the best things about being at home is that there is no one there to hate.

Step 320: The first time you see a new neighbor, introduce yourself

You don't need to be Welcome Wagon about it (although you should; see step 293). Just say, "Hi, I'm so-and-so. Did you just move? Oh, neat. Yeah, I've been here a couple of years; it's a great building. Well, if there's ever anything you need, just let me know!" Then, give them your phone number unless they seem crazy. This way, they can call you rather than the landlord when you're listening to music too loud.

Step 321: Follow standard escalation procedure with neighbors who are doing wrong by you

1. Don't make your first step the landlord. That's chickenshit. Give the offender the benefit of the doubt. Knock on their door and state your issue in a calm voice that says, *Hey, you probably didn't know this was bothering me, but it is. Would you mind helping to solve the problem?*

Sample dialogue for a neighborly problem:

"Hi, sorry to bother you. I'm Kelly and I live upstairs in 4D. I just wanted to let you know that your music is pretty loud [**Note:** If it's sex noises, just say that there's a lot of noise] and I was hoping you could turn it down; I work early."

Then, when they apologize, smile graciously and say, "Oh, it's not a huge problem. I figured you didn't know," which lets them feel thoughtful and kind when they comply with your request.

2. If it happens again, write a note. Yes, notes are the most passive-aggressive form of communication possible. But at least they don't have to respond.

> Dear so-and-so,
>   I have to tell you that the loud music is still bothering me. The walls are thin, and I work early. Could you please turn it down around [specific nightly time]?
>
> > *Best,*
> > *Your name*

3. If it happens a third time, get the landlord involved.

Hint that you are terrifically unhappy and will have to reconsider your living situation if the problem doesn't improve, and you know that you're not the only tenant bothered by this. You hate to get them involved, but could they please say something?

Step 322: Be a good, quiet neighbor generally

The music and sex noises of others are never as great as the ones you produce. It is nearly guaranteed that your neighbors feel the same way. So keep that in mind, and be reasonable about quiet hours.

Step 323: If there is an issue with a roommate, discuss it calmly and do not allow pressure to build until it explodes

If you're living with someone, chances approach 100 percent that there will be at least one thing you disagree on, and that is okay, and you can discuss it and find a solution like adults. But not if you first spend 11.5 months fuming and compressing your anger into a brilliant diamond of rage.

The third time you notice the thing that upset you, calmly put it out there in a non-judgmental way, say that it bothers you and you want to figure out a solution.

Example: "Hey, I feel like the dishes aren't always being done in a timely manner."

Step 324: Don't leave passive-aggressive notes for your roommates

That is for stranger neighbors only. If it's your roommate, you can say it to their face.

Step 325: Leave before things become unbearable

Moving is a total pain in the ass (see steps 48–58). But sometimes it's the only way. If you find yourself dreading your at-home hours, then consider whether the living situation is right for you. Don't ride it until the wheels fall off and the friendship is ruined.

Step 326: Be the kind of friend that you want to have

This is what it all boils down to. Listen when they bitch. Tell them they'll be okay. Go over and check in on their cat when they're on vacation. Call them on their birthday, or better yet bake a cake in the shape of their initial. Keep their secrets. Treat them like what they are—the rare person in this world who gives a fuck about you not because they have to, but because they want to. Give a fuck about them.

DISCUSSION QUESTIONS

1. If you are going on a friend-date, is it appropriate to try to hold hands during scary parts of the movie? (No. [Unless they're a super-cool friend, in which case they'll be down with it and HOLD ON TO THEM TIGHT, FOREVER.])
2. Which is a more important friend quality, honesty or someone who wears the same size shoe as you and is willing to lend and forget?
3. Agree or disagree: The most amazing friend move of all time is to make someone a homemade Pegasus-Unicorn piñata on their birthday and hang it above their desk? I love you, Ruth.

9. Love

Oh, love. It's great, except when it's awful. Let's talk about how to maximize greatness while minimizing the terrible.

OVERARCHING DOWNER LOVE THEMES

Love is so complicated, so chaotic. But there are a few ways to responsibly approach what is, in the end, the point of humanity (or at least the future; if everyone stopped having sex tomorrow, eventually there would be no more people).

Step 327: Accept that heartbreak is inevitable, and realize that the only way to be a full human being is to experience it at least once

Let's get the bad news out of the way right up front so we can move on to the delightful aspects of romance. There is nothing you can find, read, or do to guarantee you find true love or prevent you from experiencing pain in the course of its pursuit.

But if you are paralyzingly terrified of heartbreak (and her sister, loneliness), then you will never really experience the good stuff, because you'll be too consumed by the specter of the bad.

No one likes pain (emotional pain, anyway), and everyone feels it. The quicker you accept that your heart *will* get broken at one point or another, that you will *not* die from it, and that it will in fact make you a fuller, more compassionate human, the better off you'll be. You don't need to dwell on it, just like you don't need to constantly think about your own mortality. But you need to be at least somewhat cool with it.

Terrible Awareness-Society Idea: The Mortality Awareness Association (MAA), dedicated to reminding people they'll eventually die. This will be the least popular cause ever, and everyone will dread when it's pledge-drive time. ("Hello, this is Kelly calling from MAA. Can I speak to you for a moment about the ever-present threat of death? Did you know some-day, no one will ever remember you existed?") Granted, so far this chap-ter has been a little MAA-ish, but it'll get more positive soon, I promise.

Step 328: Don't unnecessarily cause others' heartbreak; don't perpetuate or cause your own

Don't casually hurt people who love you, even if you don't love them. This is not good for your soul. And yes, lots of times the best way not to hurt someone (or to minimize the damage, anyway) is to break up with them.

On the flip side, you need to have enough dignity and self-worth to walk away from something (or, more likely, someone) that is bad for you. If you stick around and accept less than what you deserve, that's on you. You cannot rely on others to do what is best for your heart. It's yours, not theirs.

Step 329: Fuck it. Love is worth it

You know this. I don't have to tell you what love means. The pain-to-payoff ratio could be four times worse, and we'd still do it.

On to the steps! We'll start with singleness, then move on to dating, relationships, and (sigh) breakups.

Step 330: Be cool about being single

A few people really love being single. You don't hear it much from them, because people who are *actually* happy with singleness don't spend a bunch of time telling everyone how great it is. They are too busy going out dancing and having exciting sex with attractive strang-ers. Or they're the kind of self-fulfilled, joyful people who have an all-consuming yet productive hobby, like yoga or parasailing. They feel no need to defend themselves, because we're all jealous anyway.

And then there's the fairly large mass of people who are single who aren't super-duper excited about it, and that's just fine. Don't let all the jokes about sad single people get to you. Not having a significant other and wanting one doesn't make you a sorry cliché or traitor to feminism.

It's reasonable to feel lonely if you're single and don't want to be. *Sometimes.* But you should also take pleasure in the freedom to flirt, and have the adventures/misadventures that will happen before you find your favorite. Ahead of you lie not only first kisses but also first-make-out-against-a-wall-for-twenty-wonderful-sloppy-enthusiastic-minutes sessions. Those are *great* and rarely happen after month three of a relationship.

Step 331: Learn to enjoy your own company

The valid solution to sad singleness is not an end to the singleness, it's an end to the sadness. Buck up and learn to enjoy the pleasure of your own company. Remember, you could find the world's most perfect dude or lady, be insanely happy with each other, and then he or she could get run over by a bus tomorrow. Be a full, intact person on your own.

The best part is, when you're okay being alone, you *choose* to be with someone rather than *needing* to be with someone. And choosing is key. When you fall in love, you choose them and they choose you. No one is stuck somewhere they don't want to be. Strive for that, not partnering up out of desperation so you don't have to be alone with your thoughts.

Bonus step: Have dance parties for one when the fancy strikes. Ideally, your soundtrack will be a bunch of songs about how great you are, like Daft Punk's "Harder Better Faster Stronger" or pretty much anything by Beyoncé.

LOOKING AROUND FOR SOMEONE

Step 332: Ask someone out

This goes for both ladies and men. The process itself is pretty simple if terrifying, sort of like giving birth. But it gets easier with time.

If you're interested in someone, and you think they're interested in you, the only way to find out is to ask them out. Then you'll have your answer. Don't spend a bunch of time pining for someone who's either unavailable or too dense to pick up on your fine, fine qualities. The key here is to not be ambiguous, even though that makes it even more nerve-racking, because the intention in asking someone out is to clear up any remaining ambiguity. And, mainly, to get you a date.

Here's how it should work:

"Hey. I think you're great. Do you want to go get [coffee/drinks/dinner] sometime?"

Don't qualify it with *if you're not busy* or *you know, just a casual thing*. No need to undersell yourself or anticipate rejection. Just put a period at the end of that statement. A metaphorical period, obviously, since it's a question.

A short list of people with whom it is 99.5 percent guaranteed to end badly:

- Someone you find physically but not emotionally attractive (or vice versa)
- Someone who is married
- The significant other of a close friend or family member
- Someone you have already broken up with at least twice
- Someone more than seven years behind or ahead of you in Emotional Maturity Years
- A person you find insanely attractive but is so-so about you
- Someone who is mainly attracted to a gender that you are not, but is making a rare exception
- Scorpios

Step 333: Don't be friends with someone you're romantically interested in, hoping they'll change their mind

I've been on both sides of this equation, and can safely report that it will result in nothing but frustration and/or hurt feelings.

When you are the object of affection, it introduces unsettling questions about whether someone genuinely enjoys your company or is just hoping that if they persist for long enough, they'll see you naked. Guys, y'all do this a lot and it is *not* a great strategy. It forces straight women to give every intergender friendship the side-eye.

When you're on the other side, those tiny bright bursts of happiness you get from seeing this person will never equal the slow trickle of anguish that comes from pretending they'll come around.

If you like someone, say it. And if things don't go your way, then at least you aren't throwing good feelings after bad.

Step 334: Just because someone rejects you does not automatically make them a bad person

Is the person who rejected you a decent human being, or a sack of poop?

In our minds:

Does the person I want to date also want to date me?

→ NO → WHAT A FUCKING DICK/BITCH

↓ yes

This person is deeply good. Like, donates-anonymously-to-charity good.

In real life:

Does the person I want to date also want to date me?

→ yes → Maybe he/she is a cool, decent person,

→ NO → or maybe they're not. Only time will tell.

It's counterintuitive, but just because someone doesn't want to date you (or continue to date you) does not mean they are an awful person with no taste who will likely die alone.

So while rejection always hurts, pay attention to the *way* you were rejected or broken up with. Was the culprit decent about it? Were they straightforward? Did they behave in a way that implies that they understand you are a person, with feelings and pride?

If the answers there are yes, yes, and yes, then that person is a fine individual who, for whatever misguided reasons, doesn't want to be with you. Forgive them for it (in time) and accept that they aren't some kind of heartless monster. It will help you get closure (see step 379) insofar as that even exists.

Step 335: Don't be unkind to someone because they're interested in you

If they like you and you don't like them, they don't deserve scorn, they deserve kindness. (Please note that kindness does not equal giving false hope. In fact, that is the opposite of kindness.) Don't laugh in their face, don't automatically hate a club that would have you as a member. Be flattered, be kind. But don't lead them on.

HOOKUP ETIQUETTE

Let's acknowledge that not all sex is in the interest of finding a soul mate. Sometimes, we don't have time for a relationship, or we're still hurting from a past one, and we just want to get laid. *There is nothing wrong with this*, so long as you're doing it in a way that isn't destructive to you or the other person.

Step 336: Friends-with-benefits situations can work, but only if the following conditions are met:

1. You genuinely like and respect them as a person but;
2. You have no desire to date them and;

3. They have no desire to date you but;

4. This doesn't hurt anyone's feelings.

This doesn't happen all the time, but when it does, it can be fantastic. Chances are good that within a few weeks or months, someone's heart will change and this will be washed away, a sand castle into the sea. So enjoy it while it lasts.

Be honest with yourself if emotions get involved, and talk to your partner if you see heartbreak on the horizon. If you don't feel comfortable talking honestly to them about what it is, ask yourself why. Are you secretly in love with this person and hoping your magical vagina will eventually bring them around? If so, that's not fair to them. Open your mouth and say what's actually up.

Step 337: It doesn't have to be a walk of shame. It can just be a walk

The morning after can be rough. Even if the person's being great, even if you had a good time, even if you're not even slightly hung over. If you're feeling bad, take a minute and remind yourself that you probably won't feel this way in a couple days. It is what it is, which is Not the End of the World. You did what you wanted to, you had fun, and that's that. If you feel this way over and over, skip to step 341.

Step 338: If you hooked up with someone the night before and they're being anything besides gracious and awesome the next day, fuck 'em

Should you find yourself greeting the morning in an apartment both unfamiliar and unwelcoming, there is no reason to slink out. I mean, you don't need to high-step, but whatever, you've done nothing wrong—they're the one who is being a jerk.

Gather your things—double-check that you are not leaving any beloved items behind, because the last thing you need is for this unworthy person to think you're fishing for a reason to contact them. Then square your shoulders back, thank them frostily for the nice time, and march on out.

Step 339: If you've been sexual with someone, treat them with respect and kindness

No need to have flowers delivered or anything, but you should be cordial and kind. This means acknowledging when you see them around, not shit-talking their performance or allowing your own complicated feelings to translate as unkindness.

Step 340: Don't kiss and tell (except with your closest friends)

It's just not terribly dignified. Adults don't brag about their sexual conquests. If someone asks, smile coyly and say something vague like, "Oh, yes, Seth is a wonderful guy. I'm very fond of him." Period.

Step 341: If hooking up makes you feel bad about yourself, don't hook up

There shall be zero slut-shaming in this book, because allowing others to experience their sexuality however they see fit is important. There are some people who hook up with minimal emotional attachment and they *love* it, and if you're one of those people, enjoy the hell out of it with like-minded people, and skip these next few paragraphs.

But there are other people for whom hooking up—that is to say, messing around with someone without commitment or the sort of affection that comes with a relationship—is just no good. And generally speaking, you won't really know which kind of person you are until the morning after you hook up.

People in the latter category think to themselves, *This time.* This *time, it will be different, and fun, and I won't feel guilty, like all those other times*, but then, sure enough, they feel guilty. If you're one of those people, then acknowledge that about yourself and don't be self-destructive. Wait for the right thing. It'll happen.

Step 342: Don't use your sexuality as a weapon

Sexuality, obviously, can be super constructive. It leads to love and pleasure and intimacy and all sorts of other things. But sex can also be a wrecking ball. You can use it to damage others, to swing back at someone who hurt you, or to punish yourself.

If the way you are behaving sexually causes you or others anguish, then examine that and do your best to knock it off.

Step 343: Don't be a piece on the side

Think back on friends who have been the other woman or other man. Think about how many of them have said that the experience was *awesome*, it worked out *exactly as they were hoping*, and, once they finally had the cheater in their grasp, they found his or her character *totally changed*.

If you like someone who's in a relationship, it's okay to tell them, loud and clear, that you're into them. ONCE. Don't touch them while you do this. Then you must *drop it and move on* in the hope that they'll extricate *themselves* from a relationship that they were maybe not totally into.

Someone cheats on a significant other they're really into if they are a cheating kind of person. Hence the no-touching policy. But no one's going to break up with a significant other they're really into for the chance to date you.

Do not purposefully break up someone else's relationship. Not only is it a bad idea in the abstract karmic sense, it will also be bad for you in the immediate term.

If you get involved with someone who is attached and accept a secondary "piece on the side" role, you establish yourself as someone who doesn't respect yourself enough to demand all of someone's affection. Also, make no mistake that you are getting involved with a cheater. People who cheat with you aren't doing it because they find you so irresistibly hot. Maybe you are, but they are the kind of person who finds *many* people irresistibly hot because they have poor boundaries and self-control.

If you don't want anything serious, don't care about how the third party feels, *and* the idea of bombing someone else's relationship really doesn't bother you, then fine. But it's silly to consider a future with that type of person.

Step 344: Don't date someone you're not crazy about, or who isn't crazy about you

This bit of advice came from my friend Max, and I honestly couldn't have put it better.

People project their feelings onto others since the feelings in their own head are the only emotional condition they are ever *fully* exposed to. So when we are just so, so burningly into someone, it feels like they must be so burningly into us, too.

But that isn't how feelings work. There is not an even exchange rate going there, so the best you can do is to look for someone who at least has a similar exchange rate to you. If your feelings are euros and theirs are vouchers for buy-one-get-one McFlurries, get out.

When you stay with someone you adore, and they don't adore you, you run your heart through a can opener. Constant tiny punctures until it's eventually a pulpy mess.

If the exchange rate is reversed and they are so super excited about you but you aren't excited about them, do the right thing and let them go. Do it for yourself, too, because it is painful to know you are slowly dashing someone's hopes and making them sad.

Note: This does not apply to the first couple months of a relationship. You do not need to be batshit crazy in love the first time you hang out (though that is nice).

Step 345: Don't get into something you already want out of

During an episode of VH1's seminal *I Love the '90s: Part Deux*, celebrity dreamboat Michael Ian Black was discussing *Titanic* and unintentionally gave a perfect metaphor for these kinds of relationships.

"I was on the edge of my seat through that whole movie, saying, 'What's going to happen? *What's going to happen to this boat?*'"

What's going to happen to this boat, indeed.

Step 346: Don't try to feel something that isn't there

This one is big. Most of us have met someone who would be *perfect*...if only we were into them. It can be so frustrating to meet someone who seems ideal on paper, but who sparks in you little enthu-siasm, like tofu. The temptation can be to date them in the hope that something will develop.

And you can do this...for a while. But if nothing grows, eventu-ally you need to break it off. You will likely hurt this person who has been nothing but wonderful to you, and you will feel like a big piece of poop.

Your guilt is natural and indicative of the fact that you're not a sociopath. But the heart is complicated and doesn't ever fully explain itself. If you could have those feelings, you would. Don't beat yourself up if you don't.

DATING

Yaaaay! You like them and they like you and now it's time to *date*.

Step 347: Try to go on at least a couple of actual dates

Here are things that are not dates:

- Meeting up at a party
- Going to someone's house to watch movies
- Getting stoned and watching *Arrested Development*

All those things are fun, but they are also not, technically speak-ing, dates. Now that you are a grown-up, your goal is to get to know each other, and hopefully you don't need too many substances to enable that interaction (though a drink or two is permissible).

Things that are dates:

- Meeting for coffee one-on-one and then chatting happily for a few hours
- Strolling around a park, making entertaining observations about other people you see
- Going out to dinner, then sitting at a table for two and trying to impress each other by ordering the jellyfish

Step 348: Don't get drunk on the first date

Limit yourself to a few drinks. A drink, even. If you're too drunk to take a Breathalyzer, you're too drunk for a first date. No matter how much you love the booze, just take it easy for a couple of dates. This also makes you less likely to have sex on the first date, which is, generally speaking, another bad plan.

Step 349: Hold your cards close to your chest, at least at first

The older you get, the more backstory there will be with the people you date. They will have been in love before, had their heart broken, gotten an STD, or experienced a serious loss that they still hurt from. And so will you. The trade-off, of course, is that as you get older you also get better at love.

But the first few dates are a time to circle each other, sniff cautiously, make sure no one is planning on making a suit out of anyone else's skin, and *then* commence the process of really getting to know the other. No need to reveal your deepest, darkest bits on the first few dates. Try to establish that you're both reasonable, levelheaded people first.

Note: You really should disclose any relevant health (read: STD) issues before you have sex. That is the decent, grown-up thing to do. To do this with accuracy, you need to get tested at least every six months.

In return, when and if someone reveals them to you, don't flip out. Lots of people have them, and if you're safe and cautious, they can be a total non-issue.

Don't drop this card on the table right before you have sex, either. People aren't good at processing important things when they're naked.

Step 350: Do be yourself on dates

Yes, you should be a good-behavior version of yourself, but don't make up a new persona. It's a fine line but you must, must be yourself. You can't fake being someone else forever; it just won't work. You don't want someone who is into a contorted projection of who you are; you want someone who is into you. So make sure they have a chance to see that. Remember, if you fake it, they will not think, *Oh my God, an incredibly hot astrophysicist who shares my love of the Seahawks! WHAT ARE THE CHANCES!*; they will think, *There is something off about this person and I don't know what it is.*

Step 351: Do give the necessary disclosures before or concurrently with any discussion of exclusivity

Here are some things that someone you are dating—really actively dating, and into, and maybe headed toward a relationship with—deserves to know:

- Any past marriages
- Any children
- Any chronic health conditions that may affect them, including mental health stuff

Things that you are never, ever obligated to reveal:

- How many people you've slept with
- Things you liked better about exes
- Unchangeable things about their personal appearance that bother you

Step 352: Don't discuss past loves overmuch

It seems so relevant. You're romantically involved with this person! You *were* romantically involved with *that* person! Maybe this would be a great time to introduce them into the conversation.

But it's usually not a great time, especially not on the first few dates. Bringing up an ex broadcasts that that person still looms large in your mind. More often than not, the other person will interpret your comments to mean that you are still not over your ex, and grown-ups don't date when they're still hurting over someone else (see step 384).

Step 353: Don't assume you're dating exclusively unless there's been a discussion

If it's been a month or so and things are going really well and you decide you *want* to be exclusive, then just say, "Hey, are we exclusive? I want to be." Chances are good that this will be a relief to both of you and the other party will appreciate your initiative.

And if they're not wishing to be exclusive, well, there you have it.

Step 354: Beware the dangers of New Boyfriend Narnia, and limit your own disappearance

It's so easy to disappear down a rabbit hole the first few months of a new relationship. If you're newly in love, it just doesn't make *sense* to do anything besides lie in bed together for days, gently stroking each other's faces and behaving in ways that are so uncool and so fun. It's the best, and lucky, lucky you. But remember that, although you may be so, so deeply and significantly in love in ways that no one else could ever understand, outside obligations do not disappear.

Your friends still want to see you, your mom still wants you to call, your work still wants you to show up, your cat still wants to be fed. Do all of those things you usually do, so that you may sail away on your dreamboat without guilt once those duties are met.

Step 355: Your significant other is not your best girlfriend

This assumes that you're a girl dating a boy, although this could also go for boys dating girls and girls dating girls and boys dating boys.

There are lots of things that are *fascinating* to you but maybe not so much to your significant other, and vice versa. Acknowledge that just as you might not want a blow-by-blow of the Giants game, he may not want every single detail of the latest interaction with your work nemesis, who is an unrepentant trout-mouthed bitch.

One person can never be everything to someone else. So talk about the things that interest both of you, feign semi-interest when the other one goes off on something unbearably boring, and eventually, gently re-route the conversation. And pay attention when they are re-routing you. If they are not giving responses when responses should logically be given, that means they are hoping you'll move on.

Step 356: Be cool doing things on your own. Actually cool, not just saying you're cool

Let's say you're a part of a couple like my friends Sarah and David. Both are social, outgoing people-people, but Sarah has a pretty firm window on how long she wants to be at a party.

Toward the beginning of their relationship, she let him know this.

"I said, sometimes we're going to go to a party, and after a few hours I'm going to want to go home. I'm telling you right now, it's not a trick; I'm not saying, 'No, it's fine!' when it's not fine. I'm going to go home and fall asleep in your bed, and when you come home I'll ask you about the party. I'm not going to be angry. You're enjoying yourself; why should you not stay and enjoy yourself?"

Do not take not wanting to spend every second pressed to each other's sides as evidence you're not a good couple. The best couples are cool when they're together and cool when they're apart. Wanting to do the same thing at every moment is a sign of nothing except a lack of imagination.

Step 357: Do not date someone because of what dating them says about you

When you think of significant others as status symbols, you likely think of trophy wives and Botox. But there's more to it than that. Sometimes you'll date someone because of how hot your friends think he or she is, or their status in the community, or how rich they are, or whatever outside rubric applies. This is not the right thing to do.

Date someone because of who they are and how they make you feel, not because of the external stuff. And trust: If you base your self-image and -worth on the fact that you are dating Mr. X, things will almost invariably go poorly for you. Remember that thing about the possibility of Mr. X getting smushed by a bus at any moment?

Step 358: Treat good-personhood as a basic dating qualifier

…which means, of course, that bad-personhood should be a deal-breaker. If someone treats other people poorly, eventually that behavior will extend to you, too.

This means different things to different people, so I can only speak in generalities that mean something to me. But is this person a good person? Are they kind to people regardless of whether that person can do something for them? Do they value honesty? Do you feel they are guided by an internal compass that is at least mostly in line with yours?

These qualities aren't necessarily the sexiest, and they don't reveal themselves immediately. You can look at someone and tell right away if they're hot. You can't look at a person and know what their internal architecture is like. Those are things that will reveal themselves, in ways big and small, and you *need to pay attention*. Because no one is hot when they're eighty. But some people will still be internally beautiful, and others will still be assholes. Which do you want?

Step 359: Ask yourself if you could happily chat with this person when you are eighty

This tip came from my friend Emily. As noted above, eighty-year-olds don't care as much as we do about fucking. But when scorching chemistry is gone, you know what will remain, and even improve? Your companionship. How happy you feel lying in bed next to this person, each reading a book the other has zero interest in. Your ability to work together to overcome obstacles. Your ability to understand and forgive each other, to accept the other's quirks, to chat happily over dinner. So assess those qualities. They are the important ones.

If all your friends hate your significant other, BREAK UP.

They see something — something important — that you do not.

…but you will.

Step 360: Before you get in too deep, make sure you want similar things

Falling in love with someone who isn't right for you is as easy as falling down the stairs, and they both end pretty much the same way.

While the Big Questions of what you want—Marriage, or no? Kids, or no? Monogamy, or no? Living in Manhattan or a small town?—don't need to come up immediately, they definitely should at some point. And if it turns out you two are fundamentally incompatible, then you need to move on, painful though it may be.

Step 361: Don't date someone who is mean to you

Another one of those clichés that is true is that it's a cruel, cruel world we live in. But it's tolerable, because we find and surround ourselves with people whom we love and who love us, and together we function as a cushion against that cruelty.

But if the person you date is contributing to, rather than subtracting from, the sum total of unpleasantness and cruelty in your life, it's time to move on. Then maybe take a little while and figure out why that behavior is acceptable to you.

Lots of times, we act out dysfunctions we picked up when we were young in relationships. We all have buttons, good and bad, that people push. So if you're into someone, and you realize that you're into them *because* they push your fucked-up buttons, then take a minute and work on yourself.

Step 362: Know that it's not always easy or fun

Here is a list of things that are always easy:

- Lying in bed
- Watching reality television
- Eating a bunch of delicious pastry

Here are things that are always fun:

- Jet Skiing
- Looking at puppies frolic happily
- Eating a bunch of delicious pastry

You'll note that "long-term relationships" doesn't appear on either of those lists. Because yes, sometimes they're easy and sometimes they're fun and they should be both of those things much, if not most, of the time.

But if you bail the second it's not one or the other, you'll wind up lonely. Being in a real, grown-up relationship means deciding every day to love another person, even though sometimes they will annoy the everlasting shit out of you.

Everything needs maintenance. Loving someone is not a onetime thing, something earned once then secured forever. It's more like a human six-year-old, something delightful but also in need of vigilance and attention lest it fall out of a tree and break its wrist.

Step 363: Don't try to change people

If you need an improvement project to take on, then start a garden or take up woodworking or volunteer. Do not make someone your project, unless you are really into endless amounts of bitterness and frustration on your part and theirs.

Accept the person you are dating for who they are and who they are not. If that's not acceptable to you, then break up with them.

People can and do change. When *they* want to. You cannot do it for them. You can give them some Real Talk. If you love someone and care about them, romantically or otherwise, this is a responsibility you have to them. But you can't, in the end, make them into what you want them to be. It prevents actual growth on their part.

Step 364: Don't undervalue the importance of sex in a relationship

Good sex isn't a valid reason to stay in a relationship, but bad sex is a valid reason to leave one.

There are certainly people for whom sex doesn't matter that much, but for most people it's pretty central, perhaps since it's kind of the point of human existence. It doesn't make you a shallow or carnal person to view sex as an important part of a relationship. The main thing that concretely distinguishes this relationship from every other relationship in your life is that either you sleep with this person or are planning to. If you are promising to just have sex with one person, maybe for the rest of your life, *it should be good sex*.

If you have a high sex drive and they have a low one, that is an issue that warrants discussion, just like it would be if you are someone who loooooves to spend money and they're a saver. It's a facet of incompatibility, and while you can certainly overcome it, you can't overcome it by being too squeamish to even bring it up.

Step 365: Say what you want in bed, without shame or fear

If this person is a decent guy or girl who cares about you, they will want to know how to make you happy in bed. If they don't give a fuck about what kind of time you're having, that's a good sign this is not someone you should be having sex with.

But the only way they'll know what you want is if you tell them, either non-verbally or, if it's something a little more complicated, verbally. This can feel reeeeeeeeally awkward and terrifying, because our sexuality is this very private, quiet part of ourselves, and the idea of someone rejecting it is so painful.

But again: A decent partner will want you to be happy in bed. And unless what you're asking for is really, really out there, they'll probably be excited to try something new.

Step 366: Have frank discussions about possible consequences of sex with the people you're sleeping with

You should be able to talk about the fun stuff in that previous step, but also the not-so-fun stuff. You must be able to have a rational, non-squirmy (or at least minimally squirmy) discussion of contraceptives, STDs, what would happen if someone got pregnant, and so on.

Don't talk about these things in bed, either. Talk about them when no one's mental energy is consumed thinking about the fun sexytimes that are about to be had.

Sleeping with someone *is* a big deal. It's easy and fun and you should do it when you want to, but it's a big deal. This will be the most mom-ish sentence in this whole book, but sex is one of those arenas where there can be consequences, and those consequences can be life-altering. Make sure you're on the same page.

Step 367: Fight like a grown-up

Those people who say they never fight with their significant others are semi-full of it. It is in fact possible not to fight, although it's impossible to never disagree on anything unless one person is so doormat-ish that they refuse to have opinions.

Here are some ineffective fighting tactics:

• Yelling, name-calling, or anything else that brings to mind over-protective parents arguing with a Little League coach
• Bringing up past, unrelated resentments
• Not admitting what is really wrong, and what you feel the solution is
• Refusing to accept a sincere apology

Here are some effective techniques:

• If it's the heat of the moment and you are too furious to talk without yelling, take a break. Say, "I love you, I'm going for a walk, let's talk in half an hour." Then call one of your friends, or a parent, and vent to them. Get feedback, too.
• Stating, clearly and concisely and with minimal judgment, what you are upset about, and why.
• Listening and being open to what the other person has to say, and not going into the argument with a winning-no-matter-what mentality.
• Not raising your voice. This is a person you love, not a dog that you're scolding.
• If you're going around in circles, drop the banana (see step 125).

Step 368: Hold off on the big stuff (in ascending order: living together, pets, mortgages, children) until you are really and truly positive

Sometimes, if things are rocky, it feels like maybe making a Grand Life Gesture is a way to prove to the world (and yourself) that things are okay. This is the worst possible thing you could do.

In the grand scheme of things, most problems aren't really problems, and most mistakes aren't really mistakes. But having children or buying a house with someone you are iffy about is a Problem and a Mistake (so much so that they become proper nouns, capital letters and all), and you shouldn't do it.

Living with someone prematurely isn't quite as big a mistake, but you know what is? Making your lifestyle dependent on a relationship that isn't written in stone.

COHABITATION

Living together! The idea is pretty exhilarating—just the two of you, nestin' it up, livin' and lovin' in sin. Moving in can be great, a successful trial run demonstrating that you can dwell together without descending into madness. Or it can be calamitous. If it's calamitous then, hey, at least you figured that out now. But there are some things you can do to smooth the way.

Before you do it...

• You should probably date, *very successfully*, for several months after the honeymoon phase ends before moving in together. *Successfully* in this case can be defined by the things that aren't happening: No big ugly fights, no almost breaking up or *actually* breaking up and then getting back together, no nagging feelings that this relationship is doomed. Moving in together will not solve any of those problems.

• Make sure you're on the same page when it comes to the home itself. Is it always going to be sparkling clean, or are socks draped over a lamp shade par for the course? Can you compromise on decor (or, ideally, have one person who couldn't give a fuck less about color scheme)? Is your house loud and full of guests, or quiet with an early bedtime? You probably know a lot of these things about your boyfriend or girlfriend already, but an ounce of discussion ahead of time is worth a pound of yelling at each other to pick up those goddamn shoes.

• Are you doing this for financial reasons? Sure, you can save a lot of money, but if you're setting yourself up for ruin in the event of a breakup, that's a bad call. A much more adult decision would be to get your finances in order so you don't need to depend on a relationship (see chapter 6).

During...

• Make sure you have a good system worked out for paying bills. One great idea I've heard is to have a joint checking account for rent, bills, and groceries that each of you can deposit money into or pay from. If one person makes a lot more money than the other, does she or he contribute more toward expenses?

• Figure out an equitable, or at least fair, way to divide up chores. Nothing breeds resentment like someone shouldering more than their fair share. That shit is the petri dish of anger, and before you know it, colonies of slow-burning rage will crop up everywhere.

• Do you prepare and eat meals together? Who cooks? Who cleans? Who grocery shops?

• Will your pets be cool together? I'm just saying. Pets have feelings, too.

After...

• Should things go south in the relationship, try to have an exit strategy in place. Is there someone you could move in with temporarily? Could one of you continue in the lease if the other one leaves? If not, give that yearlong lease extra scrutiny.

Step 369: If you do get engaged, do not announce it to the important players over Facebook

Before the social media press release, you need to tell families and close friends yourselves. Social media, in general, is not a reliable means of broadcasting important news, and you will be guaranteed to hurt feelings in the process. But once they know, feel free to tell the whole world. Hooray for you!

ENEMIES IN LOVE

That title doesn't refer to actual enemies in love, though that sex would be pretty, pretty hot. Instead, any time you have a significant other, they will probably tote along at least one person you don't care for.

Step 370: You don't get veto power over his friends, sadly

Ideally, this is a dumb friend from high school or something whom he doesn't see that often and you can just sort of not hang out with. Guys need lots of time alone with their friends anyway, and most men aren't super-duper sad if their buddy's girlfriend can't come along for the night.

Don't talk shit about this person to your boyfriend. He will probably be able to pick up on your dislike, anyway. Knowing one person you love dislikes another person you love feels like two stones grinding against each other in your stomach, especially if there's nothing you can do to improve the situation.

Step 371: Make peace with his closest friends and family members

If this person is a major feature in his life—a best friend or close family member—then just accept and make peace with the fact that you may really dislike each other, but you both like him. Mustering up all your inner strength and serenity is the price of admission for this guy.

Step 372: All of the aforementioned must go both ways

This must go both ways. This must go both ways. This must go both ways. This must go both ways. He must accept and be gracious about your dear people whom he is less than fond of. This must go both ways.

WHEN IT IS OVER

This is not meant to imply every relationship ends in failure. Many lead to marriage or long-term partnership; many dissolve in a way that is natural and leaves both parties feeling relatively happy, with fond memories of the other.

But let's face it: Lots, at least in the early twenties, end in sucky sucky breakups.

There are two distinct (though sometimes overlapping) roles in a breakup: the breakupper, and the breakuppee. Sometimes, you've gotten to the point in a relationship where neither person gives a shit that it's over (or never cared much in the first place) in which case your only job is to not shit-talk (see step 385). But for the most part, after a breakup, one person hurts and one person hurts a lot more. Let's start with the slightly hurt party before we move on to the really hurt.

Step 373: Don't stay with someone because it's emotionally convenient

When you realize something is over, you need to end it. It will never get easier. There will never be a time that severing a relationship that has lasted years will be no big deal.

Think of it this way: When you're in a relationship with someone, you sort of grow into each other, like two closely placed trees. The farther you go, the more entangled you get, and the more impossible it becomes to extricate yourself without cutting away big swaths of yourself.

Signs that it's over:

- You're less interested in sex.
- You have a deep, unshakable feeling that there is something just not right.
- It is hard to remember why you liked them.
- Even endearing things they do annoy you.
- You want to or are having sex with someone else (in which case, come on, stop being like that; be a grown-up and end it).

Step 374: Start an emotional distancing process a little bit ahead of time

When you start to feel like it might be over, then you have permission to start withdrawing a little bit—for a while. No more than a few weeks, though, because really what you're doing there is buying time to get over it while this person suffers through uncertainty and dark premonitions.

That said, it's the mark of a sociopath to go from being 100 percent into it to over it within a few days. Take the time, start putting a little space between you and your partner, start getting your things out of their apartment, and then pull the plug.

Note: If you are in an abusive relationship of any kind, this does not apply. Ditto for breakups involving obvious fault (substance abuse, cheating, and the like). You can and should bounce immediately. If you live with this person and think they may harm you, then get out right now. When they leave for work, call upon all your friends and move your stuff out now. Seriously. Do that now, read the rest of this book later.

Step 375: Break up with someone in a kind yet direct way

Here are the sorts of things you should not say when breaking up. They may seem kind but are actually awfully cruel as they leave the heartbroken in a terrible holding pattern, thinking that something will change and they will get clearance to come back to the relationship.

- "I just don't want to be in a relationship right now." (So someday you might want to? I shall languish in heartbreak purgatory until you decide.)

- "I just want to be friends." (Yesss, very good. We will stay friends, until I can trick you into falling in love with me again.)
- "I need some space." (But if you need space *now* then I'll bet you won't need space *later*, so I'll just be right here.)

If you want to break up with someone, break up with them. You don't want to cause unnecessary hurt, but saying things that make you feel temporarily better and them much worse is not the way to go.

Here's how a grown-up breakup should go:

- "Listen. I know this is really, really hard. But I want to break up."

Don't listen to begging, don't equivocate, don't give this person false hope.

Step 376: Do give an ultimatum, if that's what matters

If you really and truly *would* be willing to stay with this person if that one thing changed, then by all means, tell them that and set concrete guidelines for success.

"I can't keep dating you while you're drinking. If you want to stay together, you need to quit and I need to see that happening *now*."

This can happen once every five years. An ultimatum is supposed to be a game-changer, not a dysfunctional pattern to be repeated endlessly.

Step 377: But if it's truly over, don't give reasons

Your reasons for breaking up with someone, unless there is obvious cause, probably boil down to "this just isn't right," and "we both deserve a better fit." Which you do. Your not being into them automatically qualifies you as a bad mate for them, and that is something that cannot be changed.

Yes, maybe there are specifics, but unless sharing them will really and truly help this person grow and be successful in their next relationship, don't share them. Knowing that you can't stand the way they chew their food or that their spit doesn't taste right won't help them; it'll just be the cherry atop the emotional agony sundae.

Step 378: If someone is breaking up with you, do your best to walk away with your dignity intact

Quick: Take a moment and go over your personal-worst-moments highlight reel. Chances are decent that at least one of them involved a breakup. And yes, during the actual breakup you have permission to dissolve into a trembly, snot-drenched mess.

But. When you leave that terrible room and conversation, take a moment and decide how you want to comport yourself. You are broken up. So now, even though everything is shitty, you can stay on that steady level of shittiness *or* you can lose your dignity to boot and add a new, shitty dimension.

You don't have your boyfriend or girlfriend anymore, but you do have your dignity...right now. If you spend the next weeks and months calling, texting, begging, pleading, driving by their house like a crazy person, et cetera, then you won't have that, either.

Step 379: Don't expect "closure," ever, on anything

We all want "closure." But that doesn't make closure any more of a real thing than, say, a kind and gentle Pegasus who is eager to read your unpublished novel.

Because what you mean when you say *closure* is "magical verbal bullet that will make me not feel like shit, even though I've just been dumped." And that, sadly, is not something that exists. In real life, closure comes from months or years of perspective, reflection, and insight. Or it doesn't—some things close, some things don't. But there is no closure to be found via excruciating conversation with a very recent ex.

Here is how you imagine a conversation that will provide "closure" would go:

> **You:** Why did you break up with me?
> **Person Who Broke Your Heart:** Because you were too incredible, and way funnier than I am, and I felt like you could fly ever higher once you weren't weighed down by me. I loved you so much that it felt selfish to spend one more second with you, because you have already brought me five lifetimes' worth of joy.
> **You:** Oh. Well, when you put it that way.

But if someone were going to be honest about the reasons they broke up with you, here's how an actual "closure" conversation would go:

You: Why did you break up with me?

PWBYH: Because I knew I couldn't stand a lifetime of that humming noise you make when you chew, and I'm tired of having sex with you and want to have sex with other people—people who *aren't* you, and who *don't* make that humming noise. Also, my mom doesn't like you.

You: Oh. Well, when you put it that way.

Really, your ex's reasons probably can't be verbalized, and if they could they wouldn't be nice. Think about the last time you broke up with someone without obvious cause (cheating, substance abuse, or the like). If that person demanded an explanation, could you give one? And would you want to? No and no. This answer, if it even does exist, will not bring you peace. It will just allow you to spend a lifetime hating something about yourself that a future love interest may find endearing (or at least not mind).

So wait for closure if you wish, but you will save yourself a good deal of time and angst by accepting that it doesn't matter *why* it didn't work, only that it didn't.

Step 380: Do not talk to someone who has broken up with you

This advice was in *It's Called a Breakup Because It's Broken* by Greg Behrendt and Amiira Ruotola-Behrendt. I *cannot recommend this book highly enough* to those who have recently had their heart smushed. It is so, so helpful, although also embarrassing when someone spots it on your bookshelf. The authors argued that you should absolutely not talk to someone who's just broken up with you for two months, minimum. No calling, texting, passive-aggressive Facebook status updates—nothing.

This will start the painful but necessary process of accepting your life without them. When you're in a relationship with someone, you mold your life around them. Then they're gone, and there is this rag-gedy, raw edge where they used to be. What you need to do right now is smooth out that edge and make yourself a complete person without them. *Because they are gone.* It's just you. So be alone, try to heal, and stop prolonging the pain with contact. Remember being satisfied with the pleasure of your own company? Draw on those reserves of self-sufficiency.

Step 381: If need be, have your friends spread news of the breakup

There are people who should know about it, but if you can't bring yourself to have the same anguish-inducing conversation fifteen times in a row, ask a friend to do some PR on the breakup, saying that it hap-pened but you don't really feel like talking about it.

Step 382: Forgive yourself if you go a little crazy

Heartbreak can induce insanity in the very sanest of us. It's okay to be so, so deeply sad. You can feel sad for years, if need be. What will not help is berating yourself for having that sadness. If you could wave a wand and make yourself not feel it, you would. Constantly remind-ing yourself how pathetic you are doesn't need to be a part of it.

That sadness is evidence that you had something good, even if it ultimately wasn't right for you. You won't feel it forever, but it's okay to feel it for now. It's okay to feel it next week, next month, next year. Just know that no matter how endless and constant it seems, eventu-ally it won't be there. Someday you'll open that emotional drawer, and it will be empty.

Step 383: Remember that your ex will never, ever again be a source of that feeling you felt

In my early twenties, I was batshit crazy in love with a dude. Just ridiculously head-over-heels, wouldn't shut up, couldn't believe my luck, et cetera. One time, I remember, we'd been talking on the phone and after we hung up, I sat down on my couch and just screamed and screamed, like a twelve-year-old at a Beatles concert.

And yet, I was not happy in this relationship because he didn't really love me. Or maybe he did, but he didn't love me enough, or in the way it counted. He was unsure about me, and *it eroded me in the most painful way possible.*

And guess what? Yeah. We broke up.

Afterward, every time I ran into him at the grocery store, every time I saw him across a crowded room, I felt a tiny flash of what I'd once felt followed by crushing pain. I was like the rats in a study on opiate addiction. Sometimes, when a rat pushed a lever with its little rat foot, it would be rewarded with cocaine, and sometimes it wouldn't.

And what the scientists found was that the rats would push, push, push push push push push that lever indefinitely, thousands and thousands of times, for the rest of their lives, even if the cocaine never came again.

And thus, the experience of being recently but no longer in love.

I finally realized that when I pushed that emotional lever with my metaphorical rat foot, I got nothing. Eventually, I accepted that I would never, ever feel that feeling again, at least not from him. The sound of his voice through my cell phone would never make me scream on a couch again. *There was nowhere in the world I could go that would make me feel that way, least of all parties where I knew I would "accidentally" bump into him.* And I needed to stop pushing the lever.

Step 384: Don't rush to replace someone if you're still really hurting

People are not bits of watch machinery. They are not interchangeable; you cannot simply go out and find another one exactly like the last one and expect things to work the same. If you are really, really missing someone, then miss them. Don't hurt a bunch of other people by imagining they can seamlessly plug the chunk that was scooped out of your heart. It won't help you and it's not fair to them.

Step 385: Don't shit-talk your ex in public

This doesn't apply to close friends, with whom you have complete permission to shit-talk, but rather strangers, acquaintances, nosy co-workers, and so on.

It can be *so tempting.* But don't. Whether you broke up with them or they broke up with you and you're indifferent/crushed/delighted, here are the talking points:

- Actually, so-and-so and I aren't together anymore.
- But they remain a dear friend (optional, and you have permission to use the term loosely).
- Period. Use vocal tone to imply the finality of what you've just said, then move on to another topic.

No matter why you broke up, reasons valid or not, here is the Official Reason:

"S/he is a really wonderful person, but we just weren't right for each other."

This is unassailable. "Not being right for each other" could be anything! Cheating! General boredom! Horrific screaming fights! Hating their family! Really enjoying the relationship but having the unshakable feeling that something is not quite right!

No matter which it is, this is someone you once loved, and airing whatever happened to satisfy a random person's desire to rubberneck is poor form.

Step 386: Be cool with your ex continuing to exist

Guess what? Your ex, despite your wishes, will continue to exist. You are entitled to feel the natural, logical desire that they move to a chilly Afghani mountainside and adopt a new life as a hermit who collects dried yak poop for fun and profit. But for your own serenity, you need to accept the fact that they will most likely stay on this plane of existence. And eventually, date someone else.

Step 387: Someday, try to be friends

This can only happen when both of you are really and truly okay with it being over, hence the need for separation, at least initially.

But this is someone who meant a great deal to you and vice versa, and some of the most wonderful friendships can come from exes, as long as you're honest, with yourself and each other. And never ever share details of your current sex lives.

Step 388: Be on each other's team

This doesn't have to do with breakups, but it's critical and therefore a good chapter-ender. When you are dating someone, you should be on their team and they should be on yours. Take their side, even if they're maybe wrong. If you find yourself unable to be on their team, that's a good sign that it's not meant to be, but at least give a good-faith effort.

Believe genuinely in them, and let them know it. Be the drum major leading the Him Parade, or Her Parade. Life is often dark and cruel, so give each other the warm, portable ember of knowing that someone is always in your corner. That alone can serve as proof that life is not that dark, or that cruel.

DISCUSSION QUESTIONS

1. What is the most ridiculous place that you've gone by yourself in the hope that someone cute would come talk to you?
2. Which do you, personally, feel is worse: heartbreak or colon cancer?
3. What was the most pointless reason you ever broke up with someone? Were you right or wrong? You were probably right.

10. Times Were Tough

There's not a funny way to say this, because it isn't funny, but it's true: Sometimes sad, inexplicable things happen. These are the big ugly surprises lurking in the shadows of an otherwise normal Friday afternoon or Wednesday morning, waiting to jump out and change everything.

Sometimes these unexpected things will be small, short-term pains in the ass, like your car breaking down on the freeway when you are en route to a friend's wedding, or spilling coffee on your shirt before a job interview. Sometimes they will be enormous, long-term sorrows, like ongoing illness or the death of someone you love. But no matter what it is, you can handle it... or, at least, act adult in the face of it.

Like heartbreak, these unpredictable crises are not something you should live in fear of. Perpetual fear won't protect you. Fear is not a citronella candle; scary life happenings are not mosquitoes. They happen in ways we can't predict, control, or understand. The only guaranteed outcome of feeling scared all the time is that you will *feel scared all the time.*

These events are the true litmus tests of adulthood, and when you pass through to the other side of one, you will find yourself changed. As my mother would put it, these experiences are an AFGO (another fucking growth opportunity, pronounced *aff-go*).

If nothing else, and if it's not too terribly sad, someday this rough patch might be a great Times Were Tough story. Times Were Tough stories are a beloved tradition among my friends. You share a particularly unbearable experience—a middle school head-lice inspection or a bicycle trip home in an ice storm, perhaps—then you finish the story by saying, in a solemn voice, "Times were tough." And then everyone listening says, in equally solemn unison, "Times were tough."

Legal disclaimer

Before we begin—and this may come as a shock—this chapter is not intended to serve as binding medical or legal advice, okay? It's just rough, general guidelines, which is why there will be no step 469: Master a defibrillator with these simple moves! If you're wondering what to do in a real defibrillator situation, call a doctor. Don't consult a book written by a twenty-seven-year-old journalist.

Step 389: Keep your cool, and don't fall apart (at least until afterward)

An emergency can pretty much be defined as a time when it feels impossible to be cool, but it's also when you need that calm exterior most. Whatever is going on, pause a second, take a deep breath, and remind yourself that you can handle it.

Turning off the "HOLY SHIT WHAT AM I GOING TO DO?!" air-raid siren in your brain will make it much, much more likely that you'll move forward in the right direction. Unless someone is actively having a heart attack, you have more time to think and deliberate than it seems. The decisions you make rashly are usually the bad ones.

It's easy to look at something enormous, or even something middle-size, and feel that there is just no way you can possibly face it. Luckily, you are capable of handling many, many, many things that seem impossible. You have no idea how good you are at, say, holding it together during a medical emergency, or packing up to move cross-country, until you actually do it.

Step 390: Most things that feel like an emergency or a disaster at age twenty-one are not, actually, an emergency or a disaster

There's nothing wrong with feeling overwhelmed when facing something you've never had to before. The good news is that for 100 percent of the problems you will ever experience in your life, at least one other person has already experienced and lived through it.

Maintaining perspective is crucial. Whatever is happening is a temporary state of being. Time will keep moving forward, and eventually you will be on the other side. So before freaking the F out, take a deep breath, do a little research if possible, and remember that most things just don't matter in six months' time.

Things that are not, technically speaking, disasters:

- Car breakdowns
- Anything having to do with clothing, unless some of yours actually catches on fire, in which case, maybe
- Cat vomit
- Person vomit
- Any kind of vomit, usually
- Being broke in a temporary way, even if you did overdraw your bank account
- Anything involving your fingernails or hair (again, unless they're on fire)

Step 391: Keep a few items always available for wardrobe malfunctions

The best offense here is a good defense. Having these three things in your car or purse can salvage many clothing "emergencies":

- A stain-removing pen
- Clothing tape (tape your bra straps in place, say, or use if a button has popped off)
- A couple of safety pins

DISASTER PREVENTION

Remember a few paragraphs ago where I said not to live in fear, because it wouldn't do any good? While that's still the case all these paragraphs later, there are simple steps you can take to prevent some disasters, or at least cut them off at the ankle, if you will. Just imagine how sad that disaster will look, hobbling around on stumpy ankle-feet.

Step 392: Own at least basic first-aid supplies

Here are some things that should be in your medicine cabinet:

- A couple sizes of Band-Aids
- An Ace bandage (for sprains)
- Neosporin (be sure to put on before your bandage for safer, less-infection-prone healing! If you're sensitive to Neosporin—if your cut looks angrier the next day—go for bacitracin instead)
- Hydrogen peroxide (for cleaning out wounds after they have first healed; use soap and water on a fresh wound)
- Rubbing alcohol (for sterilizing)
- Tweezers, for splinters and such
- Benadryl cream (for bug bites and other itchy things)
- Gauze and first-aid tape
- An ice pack
- Thermometer

And essential over-the-counter remedies to have around:

- Aspirin (for headaches)
- Ibuprofen (for muscle aches)
- Pepto-Bismol (for stomachaches)
- Benadryl (for allergies)

Step 393: Actually clean your cuts. Don't just suck on them or wipe them on a napkin

Cuts should be washed out with gentle soap and water, then spread with a thin layer of Neosporin or bacitracin and bandaged. Sunburns can be relieved with aloe; I like to keep one of the gels that mix aloe vera with a topical anesthetic in the fridge so it is delightfully cool when I smear it on angry red skin.

Remember that if you are bleeding, pressure is your friend. Get some gauze and apply pressure to the area, which allows the skin to start its healing process and stop the bleeding. Once bleeding has stopped, bandage it.

Step 394: Deal with little burns

This assumes small second- (blistering) or first- (just red) degree burns, not serious burns, which are known as third-degree. As my friend Elisabeth pointed out, burns and murder are not analogous in grading. First-degree murder will get you life imprisonment; first-degree burns just need aloe.

Hopefully this is obvious, but if someone is seriously burned, or the burn covers anything other than a very, very small area of their body (not counting sunburns), they need to go to the hospital immediately. If the skin is taut, white, and without feeling after a burn, it's possible that it's third-degree and needs to be looked at right away. Even second-degree burns can be serious if they're bigger than three inches.

But smaller, run-of-the-mill burns? The molten-steam-rising-out-of-a-Hot-Pocket kind? You can deal with those at home. First, and as fast as you can, run the affected part under cold water. Then Neosporin and bandage it.

Step 395: Put together a little emergency kit for your house

A kit can be prepared slowly: For the next few weeks, just pick up a gallon of water whenever you go to the grocery store. Then put that gallon in a closet, and know that if your water were to go out, well, that's one day that you wouldn't have to worry about. Repeat this until you've got a week's worth of water, figuring one gallon per person, per day. Also, put a gallon in your car.

You can slowly supplement your water supply with other useful items such as non-perishable food (but first take a moment to consider how you'd feel eating this food cold—I don't suggest clam chowder for this very reason), a flashlight, a little emergency radio, and also something to relieve the terrible boredom/anxiety that you'd likely experience in the event of an emergency. Buy a special emergencies-only board game. That way, if everything else is awful, at least you have the tiny pleasure of this new board game.

Step 396: If the opportunity arises, take a first-aid class

Yes, even if you took it in eighth-grade health class ten years ago. Note that I said "if the opportunity arises," like maybe if your workplace is offering it. I'm not going to suggest that you sign up for it at the senior center, although if you are the kind of amazing safety go-getter who seeks it out yourself, hats off to you. First-aid class is one of those opportunities that does present itself. Unlike most opportunities. So take advantage.

Step 397: Have some basic provisions in your car

Again, a gallon of water, some non-perishable snacks, a flashlight, and a warm blanket can live happily in your car, a cozy little stock-pile of things that you will probably never need but would be infinitely grateful to have if you did. Also, buy a ten-dollar first-aid kit at Target or something, then stick it in your trunk.

ADVANCED ADULTING: HAVE SOME SERIOUS PROVISIONS IN YOUR CAR

Here is an amazing list of things above and beyond those mentioned above. Mary Henderson, a former park ranger and all around badass woman, put together this list for me. Some of these things are more important for those who live in rural areas, but hey—you never know when you'll be on a road trip. And road trips attract emergencies like mobile homes attract tornadoes.

- **Fold-up shovel:** For digging out of the snow, or the mud, or the muddy snow. Outdoor supply stores have these.
- **A pocketknife or multi-tool:** So small, so useful, so happy to live in your glove box.
- **An ice scraper:** Everyone who lives somewhere cold already has one, but if not, don't be like me and use CD jewel cases.

• **Windex wipes:** When your window is all fogged up, you *will* smear the inside with your hand and leave big hand grease marks everywhere. Windex wipes protect you against yourself.

• **Jumper cables:** "Oh, do you need a jump? I have cables," is such a grown-ass man or woman thing to say.

• **Tire gauge:** Know it. Love it.

• **Commercial window breaker,** also known as the Lifehammer, as popularized by *Mythbusters.* You will probably never, ever use this. But fifteen dollars is a worthwhile price to pay for something that could save your life. Not only does it allow you to shatter windows, but it also has a seat-belt cutter. Put it where you can grab it fast.

• **Paper goods:** Paper towels and toilet paper are cheap. But when you need them and don't have them, you would pay a lot for them. A roll of each goes in the trunk.

• **Cell phone car charger:** Self-explanatory.

Step 398: Do not roll around with less than a quarter tank of gas

My little gas light is on so often that I worry about whether the bulb can burn out. I do not know why it is so difficult for me to just go ahead and fill up the tank. This is the same principle as toilet paper—my car will need that gas eventually, so why not just put it in there now?

But the fact is people who always have at least a quarter tank of gas and refill the tank as soon as it dips below that line will never run out of gas on a backwoods mountain road and have to be rescued by a kindhearted trucker. Or murdered by a non-kindhearted trucker.

Also, on the subject of emergencies: Remember to fill up your tank at the first hint of an emergency, otherwise you will wait for hours at a gas station.

Step 399: Get AAA, or some sort of roadside assistance

Knock knock.

Who's there?

An eighty-dollar towing job on top of the many hundreds of dollars it will take to repair your car.

Knock knock.

Who's there?

Walking three miles down the interstate to the gas station.

I could continue with these chilling knock-knock jokes for seven or eight more pages, but the point has been made. AAA, or roadside assistance from your cell phone or car insurance company, will cost perhaps five or seven bucks per month that you will not miss and will be so terrifically worth it.

Step 400: Get renter's insurance

Again, this is relatively very cheap—I pay maybe fifteen dollars per month to be covered for twenty thousand dollars' worth of damage in the event of a fire, flood, or earthquake. Be sure to read the fine print here—many policies don't cover for floods, and some will require specific information about the construction of your apartment.

Step 401: Take pictures of your nice things

You can opt to have extra coverage for certain categories of things—computers, for example, or jewelry, or musical instruments—but you need to be able to prove that, at one time, you owned them. Take thirty minutes and wander around your apartment with a camera phone, documenting all the nice things you have that hopefully nothing bad will ever happen to...but if something did happen, you would want replaced.

Then send these pictures to yourself, or put them in the cloud—just make sure they don't exist solely on your computer, because what if your computer burns up?

Step 402: Keep your cool in a car accident

This is a hard situation to be cool in, but you must be. Otherwise, things could go terribly, terribly further awry for you.

If you get in a car accident, your first step should be to get out of traffic if the cars can still drive. Pull over to a safe place.

Assuming no one is seriously hurt, make this as cool and business-like as possible. Do *not* say it was your fault. Do *not* apologize in a way that implies you are at fault. Ask people if they're okay. Be kind and decent, but get their information. That means name, address, cell phone number, driver's license number, insurance info and policy number, license plate, and description (make, model, color) of each car; give all of yours, too. Call the police. If there are witnesses who weren't involved, get their numbers as well.

As soon as you can, write down all the details you remember, because the insurance companies will have about a billion questions. Even shit that seems completely irrelevant should be noted because insurance companies are completely insane. Before you go, take pictures of all the cars and the road itself.

You need to call the police, even if they don't come out in person, because many states require you to file an accident report. Don't call 911 unless someone is seriously injured or traffic is blocked; Google "police [city name] non-emergency number" and call that one. Then call your insurance company and let them know what happened.

Also, go to the doctor even if you feel okay. You never know when things will surface down the road, and it's best to get checked out.

Numbers to program into your phone

Spend the fifteen minutes on Google that it takes to get all these in your phone, because generally speaking, the times you'll call them are the times you least want to lose any time:

- The non-emergency number for the police department in your town
- Your insurance company's phone number (if you have more than one kind of insurance, put all of them in)
- Someone labeled IN CASE OF EMERGENCY
- Poison control
- A number to a local animal hospital, if you have a pet
- Your doctor's phone number
- Your pharmacy's phone number

Step 403: Understand your health insurance, and what you are covered for

Pop quiz, hotshots: What's your deductible? What is a deductible, anyway? Do you have an HMO or PPO? What's your coinsurance? What is coinsurance?

Health insurance is a wretched institution and you will probably get angry just by reading the fine print. But this righteous anger is not helpful; you will strike zero blows against the health care monolith by remaining ignorant as to what, exactly, you are covered for. Look at your policy, then Google any words you don't understand.

Step 404: Know what some serious medical warning signs are

This is by no means a comprehensive list, but there are some things that indicate you need to seek help immediately. This means the emergency room or, at the very least, an urgent care clinic. Such symptoms include but are not limited to:

- Any seizure, unexplained loss of consciousness, or serious trouble with your normal mental processes
- Ongoing bleeding; blood coming out of any orifice
- Serious shortness of breath
- A sharp, stabbing pain in your lower-right abdomen (this could be appendicitis)
- Paralysis
- A high (over 101-degree) fever that persists for twenty-four hours or more

Again, this is not a complete list and there are many, many situations when you will need to go to the hospital for other reasons. But these things are nearly always big red flags.

Step 405: Know when to call an ambulance

Severe bleeding, serious trauma, shortness of breath, unconsciousness, and people who need more than minimal help to get to the hospital all warrant calls to 911. If you are wondering, *Should I call an ambulance?* the answer is probably yes, because that would be a terrible thing to be wrong about. Remember that in most places, there is no charge to call an ambulance, only for transportation (which is, indeed, very expensive). So when in doubt, call them and when they get there, ask. They won't lie to you.

Step 406: Keep perspective when you get injured

Whenever I get hurt, I sort of subconsciously assume that this is how it will be forever, that my toe will always remain stubbed and that now there is nothing to do but stoically accept this new life of pulsating toe pain. *Why me, Lord? Why me?!*

But here is the interesting thing about pain: It usually evaporates. You can't necessarily sense that evaporation, but the next minute, or day, or month, or year, you go looking for that feeling or sensation and it isn't there anymore.

Note: If the pain doesn't leave, then you should absolutely seek medical treatment. That also goes for emotional pain. You must feel it, but if you feel it and feel it and can't stop feeling it, that's the time when you need to care about yourself enough to seek professional help.

Step 407: If you need counseling but can't afford traditional methods, there are other resources available

You can, completely anonymously, call a crisis line and say, "Hey, I'm really depressed but I don't have health insurance or a lot of cash. Is there anywhere you can point me toward?"

You don't have to give this person your life story if you don't feel comfortable, but know that there is low-cost or free counseling nearly everywhere, everyone from psychiatrists doing pro-bono work to community mental health centers to spiritual counseling (which, p.s., you do not necessarily need to be a part of that religion or church to take advantage of). If this is something you need, then don't let money dissuade you from it.

OTHER PEOPLE'S DISASTERS

We all need each other all the time, but there are certain make-or-break times when you really need to step up and give a person you care about as much help and decency as you can muster. Often, these will be the times when you feel least comfortable around them and least able to provide help in a meaningful way. But don't underestimate your helpfulness. Think about the last time something hard happened. Think about the people who really showed up and supported you, or were at least present, versus people who disappeared into the woodwork. Which kind of person do you want to be?

Every single one of us will have someone close to us die. Not to be a downer, but it's true. I once interviewed a funeral director who said that, on average, people are "touched by [his] industry" three times in their life. If you stop and do this nightmarish calculation, it seems right.

But more often, we're on the periphery of grief—a friend's mom dies, say. And then we don't know what to say to that friend, how to be around them.

Whatever you do, don't let fear of saying the wrong thing prevent you from saying anything at all. You don't have to re-invent the wheel, or try to talk this person out of feeling bad. You mentioning it won't remind them, because chances are really good they hadn't forgotten until you brought it up again.

People who are grieving such a loss can feel very alienated because no one quite knows what to say and gives them their space . . . and then everyone is giving space when maybe that's not quite what's needed.

Step 408: Say the right things when someone has suffered a loss

Let's start with the DON'Ts:

• Don't tell them you know how they feel, unless you have experienced something *very* similar. If this person's parent or sibling has died, don't mention the time your great-aunt passed away.

- Don't try to minimize their loss, or feel like you need to cheer them up, or say anything along the lines of "This is for the best."
- Don't avoid them because you feel uncomfortable. Your discomfort is very small compared with theirs.

See? That's not too many things to remember. Let's go on to the DOs:

- Do tell them that you're so very, very sorry for their loss.
- Do create space for this person to talk about their loss, to say the same thing over and over if needed. Listen and don't feel a need to fix their problems, because in this case, you can't.
- If this person lives far away, do call *and* send a condolence note. In fact, send one if they're close by, too. It's not hard.

Step 409: Write a decent condolence note

It's simple, and not a communiqué that requires creativity, innovation, or personal flair. It's a note that conveys a few things: I love you, I am so sorry, I am thinking about you. They can be short and sweet, and sharing a memory you have of the person who has died can be particularly moving.

> Dear So-and-So,
>
> I am so very, very sorry to hear about your mom. She was always so kind, gracious, and charming, and an all-around wonderful human being—I'll never forget the time she counseled me until three in the morning about why I should dump the jerk I was dating, and she was so right. I love you and am thinking about you. Please call anytime, day or night, if you want to talk.
>
> *Love,*
> *You*

Step 410: When someone is in grief, let them be in their grief

Unfortunately, when someone close to you is in deep grief, you can't do much to help, but you can do things to hurt. When someone close to you is going through this, you have to let them go through it. Sometimes, providing a distraction—a stupid Will Ferrell movie, a trip to the beach, whatever it may be—can be welcome. But for the most part, this person is inside something so large in scope that they can't see anything else.

They may be full of things they want to say but keep inside because they're worried about dragging you down. Let them say whatever they need to say; be quiet while they say it. Read between the lines as to whether they want to talk about something but aren't saying it, and if so, encourage them. Let them say it for a fourth, fifth, sixth time in a row, because sometimes when we face something big, we have to repeat it, out loud, a few times before we believe it.

Extroverts want to process and process aloud, then circle back and process another seventeen times. Introverts may want to be by themselves, and find the expectation to talk to others exhausting.

Don't be afraid to ask them what they need, and how you can help. The things you need in grief may be completely different than what I need. Do they want a distraction? A hug? Someone to hold them while they cry? Some space to themselves? Whatever it is, do your best to give it to them even if it's not what you would want.

Step 411: If someone invites you to a funeral, you need to have a really compelling reason to skip it

Funerals aren't for the dead, they're for the people left behind. If someone asks you to be there, even if you didn't know the person who has died, it is a good-person move to go. Imagine how you would feel if someone you loved very much died and there was almost no one around to mourn them. This would be a special new shade of pain added to the miserable rainbow you are already looking at.

Step 412: A miscarriage should be treated like a death

A miscarriage is one of the deep pains that people carry around with them. It's not as public or obvious as a death, but you should treat it the same way: Your friend is in anguish, and they have lost something very significant. The same principles apply. Write them a letter to let them know you are thinking of them, that you love them and that you want to be there. Then create spaces for them to talk about it, if they want to, or enjoy a distraction if that's what they need. Do not tell them it's for the best. Do not undersell, to them or yourself, what they have gone through.

Step 413: Be cool when your friends are in the hospital

A hospital stay is not nearly as bad as a death, but it's a similar dynamic:

- Something bad that no one wants has happened;
- This is not a day-to-day situation, and so you probably feel uncomfortable and freaked out in addition to the regular sadness; but
- The emotional needs of the person who is sick or injured take precedence over your own.

Don't excuse yourself with an "I don't like hospitals." This is like "I hate funerals." Oh, really? Do you? Most people just adore being in the hospital, they'll be thrilled to take up the slack you create. No, no, no. You need to harden up and be a good friend.

First, try to ascertain if they want visitors or not. The best way to do this is just to call and ask. For some reason, people always sort of assume that anyone in the hospital has regressed to very early childhood and is no longer capable of holding conversations or deciding things for themselves.

Before you visit, call the hospital to find out what the visiting hours are, and if there are any restrictions on what gifts you can bring. For example, lots of times flowers aren't allowed in burn units because they may have bacteria, and someone who has recently undergone surgery may be on a restricted diet.

Step 414: When a doctor or nurse comes in, leave immediately

You don't need to *go* go, but you do need to step out into the hallway. It is quite possible that this person has been waiting to talk to the doctor all day about something specific or embarrassing, and really doesn't want to discuss something like their bowel movements in front of you. Spare them the humiliation and also the anxiety that could come if they don't say anything and then lose their chance to get to the bottom of their pooping issues.

Step 415: Be actually helpful to your friends, rather than vaguely helpful

Rather than saying, "What can I do?," anticipate a specific need and offer to fill it. People usually feel a little uncomfortable saying what they actually need because they don't want to be a burden, so they'll say, "Oh, nothing." Whereas "Can I watch your pet?" is much easier to say yes to.

Step 416: If it's you who's having a hard time, accept that love and help graciously and gratefully

Just like the proper response to a compliment is not to try to tell the person why they're wrong about you, the proper response to offers of help that you need is not to say you're fine.

You can sense the difference between a sincere offer and someone saying it because they have to. Let the latter off the hook, and take the former up on it. People who love you sense so clearly your pain. It hurts them, too, and they want to alleviate their own pain, at least, by trying to do what they can for you. Let them.

THE LAW

Hopefully this goes without saying, but committing felonies is a decidedly non-adult move. Yes, even white-collar ones. Do your best to keep your nose clean, and if you do regularly flout the law then be subtle and quiet about it. Don't be dumb or obvious about any recreational activities that the law might frown upon.

Step 417: Don't drink and drive, and yes, tipsiness counts

Duh. If the horrific potential safety consequences don't convince you, think about a suspended license, losing your job, having your name published in the crime blotter in your local paper, and spending thousands of dollars on a DUI attorney who—newsflash—may be able to alleviate some of the punishment, but can't get you off entirely.

Step 418: If you need legal help, ask around for a good recommendation

Usually lawyers are willing to give just a tiny, tiny bit of their time for free, but they are more likely to do this if you come as a referral. "Hi, I'm John, I'm actually Susan Calabridi's son, and I had a quick question I was hoping to ask you."

Some lawyers, if they're really decent, will just answer your question then let you know if you need further counsel.

Step 419: Know that there is often legal aid available

Many states have a lawyer referral service through their bar organization, and can help recommend a lawyer who may be able to lend help for a minimal fee. Others have legal aid societies set up for issues of justice—say, for victims of domestic violence, or people experiencing civil rights violations.

Another good option to find affordable law help is to call law schools in the area, and see if they have a clinic in the type of law you need assistance with. If they say no, ask if they know any schools that do.

Step 420: Pick your battles with the police

You never need to admit anything to a police officer—no, you have no inkling of how fast you were going—and if you truly feel like your rights have been violated or the charge is unfair then you should pursue it in court.

But if it's just a speeding ticket, chances are good that you were indeed speeding. Call the court, and say, "Hey, I have this speeding ticket and I'd like to plead no contest and I was wondering if you could reduce the charge if I just paid it in full now."

Other times, there may be the option of either doing community service or taking driver safety classes in order to have the charge dropped. Depending on how tight money is, this is always worth looking into.

Step 421: Know how to share bad news

It's an awful position to be in, but sometimes you will need to inform people about bad news. It's best to do this in person if you can, but don't keep people in suspense, because they will imagine the very worst thing possible.

Be direct, be clear, give as much information as specifically as you can, and tell if and when you'll have more. Be sympathetic, and also be prepared for a variety of reactions. Some people will dissolve, others will appear unmoved, and this is in no way an indication of how they actually feel.

"Hi Megan, this is Kelly. I'm so sorry to say this, but I have some terrible news." Brief pause to allow this to sink in. "Amanda died in a car accident last night."

If the person in question is not dead then you need to say that immediately, ideally before you state what bad thing has happened.

"I'm so sorry to let you know this, but I have some bad news. Amanda is in the intensive care unit at such-and-such hospital because she was in a serious car accident last night."

Then fill in the details as well as you can.

Step 422: Discuss will and estate issues with your parents

No one wants to talk about this. A conversation that hinges on the premise, "What will life be like when you're dead?" is awkward and painful and generally the opposite of the things human beings enjoy in a conversation.

But not discussing death doesn't change reality, which is that chances are good that your parents will, at some point, no longer be alive. Figuring this stuff out in advance is infinitely easier than trying to muddle through after the fact. If they don't have a will, ask them to make one. This does not make you a cold person who won't care when their parents die. It makes you someone who will not have legal issues to grapple with on top of all the other mountainous awfulness that is losing a parent.

Step 423: If there are serious complications or squabbles within the family, you may want to hire an attorney

No one wants to fight about money issues with family, but an attorney can help defend your interests, and can also provide a buffer against anger in the future. ("That wasn't me, that was the attorney.")

Step 424: Make a will

Yes, it seems unnecessary, and chances are it is. But if you're asking your parents to make one, it's only fair.

DISCUSSION QUESTIONS

1. Does this chapter make you feel more or less depressed about life? Explain.
2. What is the ratio of kindly logging truckers to murderous logging truckers, do you think?
3. What is your worst Times Were Tough story?

11. Families

Some of you reading this have super-happy, super-close families who gather each Sunday to eat, sing, laugh, love, and play everyone's favorite board game, during which no one fights and everyone wins. Some of you have chosen never to speak to your mother again. Most of us are somewhere in between, veering at various times closer to one side or the other of that continuum.

You can't change your family, but you can change how you deal with them. You can choose to emulate their good behaviors while rejecting any chaos or dysfunction that may come along with it.

As a grown-up, it's your job to establish new adult relationships with your family members. It's your job to draw boundaries with them. It's your job to figure out how to be a good family member, and how to love them the best you can. These, as you can imagine, are all sizable tasks, far more difficult than remembering that sweaters get folded, not hung up. But the payoff is much, much larger.

A brief note: A lot of this chapter is about the tough parts of being in a family. That's because no one has to tell you how to have a blast drinking with your cousins, or how to enjoy eating the kind of birthday cake your mom's made every year since you were little. Part of the beauty of family is that great things are so natural, so easy, and so self-evident. But because it's such a big and important part of our lives, the challenges are much larger and trickier.

A short list of things your parents are not

- An ATM machine
- Caretakers of the place they think of as their house but is actually your pied-à-terre, where you drop in with no notice and behave however you want
- Gods
- Monsters (most of them, anyway)
- Responsible for picking up after your mistakes
- What stand in the way of you being a whole human being

Step 425: Bring as much grace to bear as you can when you interact with them

Before I get into this—which isn't just for families, but also for friends, significant others, co-workers, and the world at large—I will pause to introduce Laney Kibel, a licensed clinical social worker who has more than twenty-five years' experience with individual, family, and couples therapy.

"I like the word *grace*—in terms of being graceful in your interactions, being graceful in your interpretations, expecting the best, and assuming there's no malice in what people are doing to you," she said. "When in doubt or when your feelings have been hurt, ask for an explanation and an apology."

Give people who love you the benefit of the doubt. Chances are good they're not doing whatever it is to spite you. Chances are good they're doing it because they're just sort of pains in the ass. But they still love you.

Okay. On with the chapter. First things first: proving to your parents that you are, in fact, an adult, and deserve to be treated as such. This does not happen via a big hissy fit that culminates with you screaming, "YOU ARE NOT THE BOSS OF ME ANYMORE!"

Step 426: Remember that you're the one who's changed, not them, and the burden of proving that growth is on you

Your parents have been adults who more or less take care of themselves as long as you've been alive. You are the one who is now different, and you're the one who has to demonstrate that to them.

If you've been off at college, you've continued growing but they haven't been there to witness it. They were there when you started walking, but they weren't there on the first day of your real, grown-up job.

To me, I'm a grown-ass woman with a 401(k) and a regular fitness routine. Usually, that's how my parents see me, too. But they can still see me as an infant who, without their divine intervention, would've quickly suffocated under the weight and volume of her own poop.

And that's okay. The alternative to having people who view you that way is, I imagine, an undignified poop-smothered end. It's okay for them to see me that way, sometimes, and it's okay for me to push gently and respectfully back.

Step 427: Understand that as much as they want it for you, they also may need to mourn your independence a little bit

You being a grown-up means you are no longer the child they nurtured from infancy. They love you as an adult, too, but it is painful to see something you made and love more than anything spiral away from you. Those feelings are theirs to sort out, not yours. But accept that they probably have them.

Step 428: Be aware of what it means to them to be an adult, then highlight those elements of your life as proof you are a grown-up

If your dad always hammered at the importance of having a regular job, next time you're feeling the need to assert your adulthood, mention the fact that not only do you hold down a regular job, but you just got a promotion. If your mom is obsessed with healthy living, let her know that not only are you eating well but you've even been working out recently. Reassure them that the lessons they tried so hard to pass on to you have indeed been learned.

"Sometimes it's difficult for parents to see adult children as adults if they're not doing the things [the parents] value as adults," said Sheila Walty, a licensed clinical social worker. "One of the things you can do is...find out what they value, then connect it with whatever part of that adult value you agree with."

Step 429: Do not accept money regularly from them

It's hard to prove you are independent if you depend on your parents for things, since that is in fact the opposite of what independent means. This happens especially with money. Accepting your parents' money makes them shareholders in your life. And they probably see themselves as the kind of shareholder that gets a vote when big decisions are made.

Do your very, very best to find a job (chapter 5) and get your finances in order (chapter 6) to live within your means and only very rarely request a withdrawal from Parental Interstate Bank.

"Taking handouts from your folks shouldn't be routine," my friend Nancy quite wisely said. "You should be able to conduct a reasonable life without their financial assistance."

This is especially important if your parents are the type who give money with strings attached.

Crystal Mattox, a licensed marriage and family therapist, told me one of her clients was getting married, and the bride's mother refused to help pay for the wedding unless the couple agreed to get married at a specific location. The bride, quite reasonably, refused the money and got married where the couple wanted.

This kind of controlling behavior, Crystal said, is a slippery slope.

"If they help with the house, do they get to pick the color of curtains?" she said.

Step 430: There is a difference between turning to your parents and relying on your parents

Your parents will always wish to feel like they are a part of your life, and they will always wish to feel wanted and valued. That's the key: want them, don't need them. Asking your mom for her thoughts is different from not being able to make a decision without her weigh-in.

"It doesn't mean that you should start viewing your parents as useless; it's just a transition from benevolent dictator to trusted adviser," Nancy said.

Step 431: Pick up the tab sometimes at restaurants

NO BIG DEAL!

Once you can afford it, of course. This is undeniably grown-up, and makes two statements: One, you're doing well enough to buy dinner, which in and of itself is a great sign. Two, you are aware that this parent-child relationship is no longer one where all the obligation lies with one party.

BE GOOD TO THEM

You can't ever repay what your older relatives have given to you, and you're not obligated to. It's not a debt that you have to spend the rest of your life repaying. But all parents, except in rare and abusive cases, deserve your gratitude and appreciation. They gave their life to you, willingly. The least you can do is call on their birthday.

It's not just that they deserve it, but that you should want to give it.

It's depressing but true that you will only ever have less time with your grandparents and parents, never more. They will, someday, be gone, and you will go on without them. So be good to them and love them now. Tell them that you love them.

Being good means different things to different people, but here are some general strategies for coming to appreciate and demonstrate your love for them.

Step 432: Your parents have first names. They have secrets you will never know. They do not just exist as an extension of you

"Imagining my mother as a child was unfathomable," Laney said. "I could see pictures and see she actually was once a child. But it was impossible to imagine what my mother was like as a teen or in the workplace."

But as we grow, she said, we should see our parents as whole people. I asked why that was important.

"I'll put the question back to you: Why is it important to you for them to see you as a whole person and not just a daughter?"

Step 433: Get to know them as people

What did your dad want to be when he was a kid? Who was your mom's first crush? What do they look for in a friend? What is the saddest they've ever been?

When you get to be an adult, you can actually be friends with your parents, and it's so, so satisfying. Get to know them not just as your parents but as actual people, and in time they will come to regard you as someone they can confide in, someone with whom they can share details beyond the "Aunt Susan is coming to visit next week" sort. One of the proudest days of my life came when my mom called me to ask my opinion on a problem she was having at work.

Step 434: Remember, when you talk to them, that you are not the only person with a life

Obviously, you should call on their birthdays and respective Hallmark holidays, but ask—and listen to—how their day was. Write them a note wishing them many years of love on their anniversary (and, even better, put a couple of lines in there about what they've taught you about love, by their example). Learn of their triumphs, and congratulate them. When possible, go celebrate their milestones in person, rather than expecting they'll always come to visit you.

Step 435: Call as much as you can

Okay, maybe not as much as you can, but there is no reason you can't call every week or so. They love you and they miss you and chances are good that when you left, you took a big old chunk of them with you. If you don't live in the same town, then phone calls are all they have to sustain them between the occasional visits.

It doesn't have to be an hour-long conversation. If your mom or dad tends toward long-windedness, let them know at the beginning of the conversation that you're on your way somewhere, or someone is about to stop by. A ten-minute call is way better than none.

Step 436: While you can and should assert your independence, let them know their input and opinion still matter to you

"I am learning that letting them be part of important decisions and asking their advice helps maintain the intimacy of the parental relationship, and lets them know I still need them, just maybe in a different sort of way," was my friend Rachel's great response to the question of how to involve your parents in your life.

Step 437: Send them cards, maybe with a recent photo of you and your friends inside

This costs maybe three bucks total (fifty-cent stamp + fifty-cent photo + two-dollar card) and will give your mom or dad twenty-five dollars' worth of pleasure. Write a pen-pal-style note inside, maybe explaining the photo ("Molly and I went to see Boyz II Men at the casino!") and let them know you love them and miss them.

Step 438: Let them live vicariously through you, and share your triumphs freely

Basically, there are two people in the world who will almost never, ever tire of the subject of How Great You Are. Your friends are happy for good things that happen to you, but no one else cares about the blow-by-blow of how great you did on your work presentation.

"Include them, so they get to see the fruits of what they've done," said counselor Sheila. "Their pride is often based in how their kids are doing."

Remember: You are their life's work (although, as we established above, you're not the only thing in their life). They spent more time trying to make you into a decent, functional human being than they probably spent on anything else. It's nice to let them know when their efforts have paid off.

BOUNDARIES

Boundaries is one of those words that you shouldn't use too often around casual acquaintances. Frequently referencing your boundaries implies you're the intense oversharing type who talks a lot about your dreams and unexpectedly drops raw details about your sex life.

But boundaries are everything when it comes to families. There is a Venn diagram at play here: things your family wants from you, and things you can provide. Hopefully these circles very nearly overlap, but the farther apart they are, the more extensive the boundaries to set will be.

Step 439: No one, ever, will set your boundaries for you. So learn to set them yourself

This isn't even an issue of other people not wanting to. They are simply not capable of it. No one in the world, except you, is inside your head. No one in the world can take your emotional temperature with the perfect accuracy that you can. No one knows what's fine with you versus what feels like a nail file grating your stomach.

Step 440: With a given relative, figure out what you can and can't do

This, Laney said, is the first step: Figure out what your boundaries are.

"The first thing you need to do in setting a boundary is checking in with yourself," she said. If you decide you do not want to do something, then you can offer an alternative, though you don't have to. If

Things your family wants:

- daily phone calls
- Veto power over significant others
- regular church attendance
- presence at all holidays
- docility
- instant agreement in all topics

- weekly phone calls
- presence at some holidays
- going to church on Christmas and Easter
- Diplomacy

Things you can provide:

- No phone calls
- Going to Las Vegas instead of Grandma and Grandpa's 60th wedding anniversary
- Sullenness, crabbiness, apathy

boundaries go here

a relative who stresses you out wants to go on a trip together, you can decline but also figure out a way to spend less time together with an easier escape route, should things go south.

Yes: You should do things you don't feel like doing for your family. Sometimes, I don't feel like calling my grandmother as much as I feel like lying in bed watching episodes of *Mad Men*. If you don't feel like something but know it would make a relative of yours more happy than it makes you sad/bored/neither sad nor bored but also not getting to do something you'd slightly prefer, just do it. It's good karma. Seriously, call your grandmother right now.

But there is a fine line between not feeling like something, and not wanting or being able to do something. The things that you truly can't or won't do, for your own sake: Those are the boundaries.

Step 441: Graciously deflect them when they're overstepping their bounds

Crystal said that it's important to remember that chances are very good the reason they want to give so much input is that they care about you and just want you to make (what they are certain is) the right decision. You can and should say, "I know you want to help me, and I know you are trying to support me." But you can shut the conversation down when overstep happens.

"You can say, 'I hope you hear that I can figure this out myself. I appreciate your concern.'"

If they won't drop it, then let them know there will be a consequence.

"Dad, if we can't let this topic go, I'm going to have to hang up and we can talk later."

Step 442: Your family does not get veto power over your life decisions

Sometimes, you just have to say, "I'm sorry you feel that way. This is what I'm doing." Then do it. This, of course, is much easier to say if you're not dependent on them for money.

Step 443: Use "and" instead of "but"

The problem with saying something like, "I love you, but..." is that the *but* sort of invalidates the first part of the sentence, and sets up whatever you are about to say as being in direct opposition with your love for them.

It feels off at first, but you can use *and* instead.

"I love you and I need you to respect that this is the decision I've made" sounds very different from "I love you but I need you to respect that this is the decision I've made." Yet they're saying the same thing.

Step 444: You don't always have to pick up the phone and deal with things right then. You can take a little bit of time to figure things out for yourself

Sometimes, you're equipped to deal with shit that your family needs you to talk about, and sometimes you're not.

VISITS AND HOLIDAYS

Holidays are so fucking *fraught*. There are so many moving parts, so many things that have to happen, so many things that must not, under any circumstances, happen, so many opportunities to hurt so many feelings. Holidays, in short, are a time to summon every bit of adulthood you can bring to bear. Holidays are a time when you can screw up spectacularly, or—*or!*—you can come out, in the immortal words of Britney Spears, stronger than yesterday.

Step 445: Take everyone's wishes into account, then set your own schedule

Particularly if you live far away, this may be the only part of the year your parents get to spend quality time with you. If you live far away, this also is probably your only chance to see your really old friends.

Ask in advance when it's really important for you to be with the family, then decide how much time you should/want to spend with them and let them know when you'll be around and when you won't. Maybe you'll be with the family in the earlier evening, but leave at 9 PM to meet your old friends...and maybe make out with that guy you thought was so cute in high school. There is nothing like a boozy December 23 impromptu high school reunion.

Step 446: If you are a child of divorce, do not twist yourself into knots to make everyone happy

If you can make it to both Thanksgiving dinners, great! If you don't want to, that is your right. You can go to both, or one, or neither. You're a grown-up. Grown-ups get to set their schedule and make decisions for themselves. The paradigm for decision making does not have to be, "What will leave everyone feeling least hurt?"

Step 447: Figure out how to make yourself an adult part of the celebration

Bring something for Thanksgiving dinner, something you make a killer version of, something that people will happily anticipate in the years to come. Arrive for Christmas with all your presents already wrapped, so you don't have to hit your mom up for wrapping paper. Don't pick fights with ornery relatives (see step 464). Go with the flow, and make people happy you're there.

Step 448: Be a good houseguest when staying with relatives

This is especially important when staying at your parents'. It's so easy to regress to your teenage self. You're back in your bed, they're making food for you, you're having muted versions of the fights you had in high school—you may as well leave your dishes on the coffee table and disappear into the bathroom for ninety minutes.

But acting like a good houseguest goes a long way toward establishing that you are not, in fact, your time-traveling high school self.

Pick up after yourself. Offer to help with dishes. Go get some groceries, then cook breakfast. Be mindful of not interrupting routines. Don't hog the shower, don't leave wet towels on the bed. Before you leave, go buy some fresh flowers for the kitchen table. These are actions that implicitly acknowledge that you are not permanently entitled to a bedroom in your parents' house—which, in turn, implies that they should not treat you like the teenager who was.

Step 449: If they drive you nuts, get a hotel room or stay with a friend

In both cases, you can plead convenience—"There are so many people staying there right now, it'd probably be easier for me to just stay with Steve. He's got a guest bedroom." If you're traveling with a significant other, say they're allergic to the pet.

You could even, controversial though this may be, tell a gentle version of the truth: "You know, Dad, I feel like every time I come stay with you, we end up fighting. I really want to see you, and I think this is a good way for us to spend time together while still having our own space."

This can go a long, long way toward restoring your sanity. It also subtly reminds your relatives that you are not just there to visit them; you are there to visit lots of people.

MOVING BACK IN

If you live with your parents, you need to be working hard to move out. You just do. If you are living with your parents, moving out is priority one in embracing your adulthood. It is nearly impossible to feel like you are standing on your own two feet when your mom grocery shops for you.

But it happens. People lose jobs, people get out of bad relationships, people graduate and take nine months to find work. View this as a temporary, non-ideal situation, but one in which you can still act maturely and conscientiously. Much of that mature conscientiousness should be dedicated to figuring out and working on whatever your next move will be.

Step 450: Before you move in, have a long, difficult conversation about what you expect, and what they expect

Ideally, you'll start this discussion with an end date—"I will have figured out another living situation by [month]." Six months is a good upper end to things; three's even better. This tells them—and yourself—that this isn't a permanent state of being. You're there because you're in a hard spot, and hard spots don't evaporate overnight. But inertia is so easy to come by, and having a solid deadline keeps you on track to get out.

You also want to discuss money—can you contribute any?—and chores, and expectations. The problem here, of course, is that as my friend's smart dad Alan put it, if you're accepting someone's help, you also have to accept their advice. But the more you understand what is expected of you, and the more you can articulate your (inherently restricted) boundaries, the happier both you and they will be.

Step 451: If you are living with your parents, they control what happens under their roof. They do not control you

Being in your childhood home does not mean you are a child again. You must stick to the expectations they've set out for how you conduct yourself in the house. They might be unreasonable. They might be unpleasant. All the more incentive for you to get your life together and go.

However, you should remember that you are still an autonomous human being. You still get to make decisions for yourself.

Say your parents hate your boyfriend. While they are within their rights to say they don't want him in the house, they are out of line in insisting you break up with him. Every time you step out the door, you regain the autonomy you give up when you step inside. Use it.

Step 452: Do non-monetary things to help out

Showing your parents that you appreciate what they're doing for you goes a long way, and a great way to do that is to figure out things that they can't or don't really want to do around the house, then do them.

"It's not that you owe it to them, but that you want to do something to show your appreciation," Sheila said. "Everyone is way more willing to give when they feel appreciated."

Step 453: Get out

Really. Find roommates, find a job, find a way to make it on your own. You can. Seriously.

NEW RELATIVES

Family is not a static thing. Yes, you're born with some, but all along the way you gain and lose people. Happily, there are more gains than losses. People marry each other, babies are born, and graying black sheep return to the fold.

While people always enter into a family due to love, it's not necessarily *your* love for that person that brings them. But while you may not adore them right off the bat, you will probably grow to. In the meantime, you can be decent.

Step 454: When someone is in the process of becoming family, make them feel especially welcome

Even if you've never become part of a family by marriage, you've surely spent a holiday at a friend's house. Some families are just *delighted* that you're there and for the day, you are family. Some don't include you in anything because they don't notice you. You are an afterthought.

Get to know this new person. Welcome them, let them know that anyone who Cousin Sarah loves is all right by you. Tell them a little bit about the family itself—not deep dark stuff, but the inside jokes, the traditions, who maybe will get a little bit too tipsy, who to avoid sitting next to unless you want to hear the latest Limbaugh talking points.

Step 455: Trust the judgment of the person who is bringing them into the family

Here I will introduce Molly, a particularly insightful friend of mine who grew up in a family that blended, unblended, and reblended several times over. She maintains great relationships with father figures from her childhood but also has recently gained a new stepfamily.

So let's say one of your parents is getting married.

"Your job is to be supportive of your parent, to try to trust them and trust their judgment," she said.

But what if you don't like the spouse-to-be?

"I felt that way about some of my mom's boyfriends at first, but they've all grown on me over time," she said, adding that there's a difference between someone you just don't super care for versus someone whom you actively think is bad for your loved one. "The thing that's really important is that this person makes [my mom] happy, and is kind to me. Everything else is secondary."

Step 456: It's okay to feel apprehensive, but try to be enthusiastic about new people, at least on the surface

Having grown up as an only child, Molly said, it was weird for her to gain three step-siblings at age twenty-seven.

"I'm lucky in that both my two stepsisters and my stepbrother are really enthusiastic—they're excited about me, and having me be a part of their family," she said. "I was a little caught off guard by their enthusiasm, partially because I'm an only child, but I was so touched by the warmth with which they received me. It comes back to having an open mind and giving myself a chance to appreciate this as a good thing, and not more complication."

Step 457: You don't have to be Best Friends Forever with someone else's new significant other

There is no need to make them a friendship anklet, or go on a one-on-one road trip, or anything. They're not marrying you, after all. You just have to be cordial and kind.

Step 458: If you do have serious concerns about the person, voice them to your relative

You have to do this kindly and respectfully, but this is the same as telling a friend when they're fucking up their life (see step 310). Remaining silent is not the loving thing to do.

Step 459: You can and should remain in touch with former step-relatives, if you want

If you consider someone a relative, even if it's by marriage, they remain your relative when the marriage is over. Just because your dad divorces his wife doesn't mean you do.

Molly keeps in close touch with her former stepdad.

"I think, coming from a kind of non-traditional, blended family, I have recognized that if you've got a dad, even if he's not your 'real dad,' you shouldn't take that for granted," she said. "If they want to be a part of your life, and you want them to be a part of your life, then just keep working on it."

Step 460: When you are the new guy or girl of the family, do some chores

That is a gross simplification for step-title-writing purposes. But you could take a page from one especially clever aunt I know.

When she started coming to family celebrations, she would always find a chore to do—washing dishes, say, or setting the table. Not only does this demonstrate that you're a helpful, thoughtful sort of person, but it will also goad other people into coming and helping you, and then you can just chat happily away.

Step 461: Suspend judgment on the family you're entering into

A good 60 percent of families are an acquired taste. When you first show up, there is so much backstory, so many traditions, so much invisible social matter that you can't see and then accidentally bump into. It's easy to feel lonely and lost in the mix.

Maybe this is the kind of family that loves to holler at one another. Maybe they sit quietly, and that's their togetherness. Whatever it is, chances are decent that it's not what your family does.

But this is how it will go: The first few times, everything will be sort of confusing. Visits four through ten will still feel a little probationary. But sooner rather than later, you will understand the physics of this family, and feel welcome. If you don't feel welcome, summon your maturity and slog through it. Every family visit comes to an end.

TOXIC RELATIVES

You know if you have a relative who is a toxic presence in your life.

When I was a reporter in Mississippi, I covered several towns that had maybe eight hundred people in them, the sort of place where people neither left nor arrived. And if two dudes in their seventies were fighting during a town hall meeting, you knew this was not the first problem they'd had. Their differences likely went back to a girl problem that happened in the 1930s. There is a similar dynamic at play with unreasonable family members. Whatever you're fighting about this moment isn't the fight you're having. It's just the latest skirmish in a long war.

As Molly put it, "Part of being an adult is knowing the difference between the relationships that you can grow from, and the ones that are going to hurt you."

There is, of course, the nuclear option. You can write someone off. You do not owe them your presence in their life. Sometimes, you have to do that. But more often, you need to figure out a way to limit their presence in your life while hopefully improving the relationship.

Step 462: Decide, consciously, that their dysfunction and their chaos are not yours

There are some things that aren't your fault, but are your problem. Relatives who make your head and heart hurt are high on that list.

You can't control them. You cannot cure their substance abuse issues, or their deep-seated anger. All you can control is yourself, and your reaction to their behavior. When you internalize their self-destruction, when you allow yourself to be manipulated and abused and squished to fit around their issues, you do yourself a great disservice.

You can—and should—say to yourself, *I don't have anything to do with this. This is not my deal. This is her problem, and I can't solve it, and I'm going to detach with love.*

These are hard, hard things to do. These are things that likely require therapy, or Al-Anon, or similarly extensive work on yourself. You need to do that work on yourself. That is the other side of the "can't control them, can control me" equation.

Step 463: If someone is constantly passive-aggressive, act dumb and take them at their word

This was a brilliant strategy from Sheila.

"Even if someone's lying to you, act like they're telling the truth," she said. "If they say, 'I want to do this for you, and it's a gift from me, and I don't want anything in return,' even if you don't think that's true, act like it is and hold them accountable."

This, she said, gives you a watertight alibi if they try to guilt you later. "Then, if they say, 'I did this for you, why won't you do that for me?' you can say, 'That was a wonderful gift you gave me.' If we hold them accountable, it puts them in a position of being uncomfortable because they didn't speak their truth, rather than us being uncomfortable because they didn't speak their truth."

Step 464: When a family member hurts your feelings, do not strike back with the same

You all know this already, but it's the kind of thing we know but never remember when it counts. The solution to someone hurting your feelings is not to hurt them back. That does not unhurt your feelings, it just makes it so unlikely that anything useful will be accomplished.

How responsive and open are you to what someone has to say immediately after they hurt you? There you go. You cannot control what that person has done or said; you can only control your response.

"Rather than fly off the handle and assume there was intention, be graceful and think, *Okay, would they really want to be hurting me? Maybe a conversation could help clear this up,*" Laney said.

Step 465: If they won't have a conversation, disengage

Sometimes, people are willing to have a conversation. Sometimes they're not. It may or may not be a permanent thing. But for whatever reason, right now they don't or can't hear what you're saying, especially if they're really angry.

"When you finally have established, *Okay, we're not going anyplace,* then it becomes a matter of self-protection," Laney said. "You're not going to convince your mother to be different than who she is, so on your behalf, you have to come to the point of, *I'm not going to expose myself to hurt anymore.*"

Step 466: Before you write someone off completely, make sure you've had a serious talk first

I asked Laney how to make an exit when you just could not deal with someone anymore, be it friend or family member. What should you say?

"Why didn't you say something to them earlier?" she asked. "Half of people out there come from divorced families . . . and what you don't learn is how to resolve conflict. Resolution never comes, because we go away from each other and that's the resolution. We leave families, we leave friends. But it is so much more valuable when we are willing to fight the good fight to save the relationship."

Step 467: You do not owe them your presence

"I don't think, because someone has brought you into the world, or is related to you by blood, that it entitles them to mistreat you, or fail to operate under the standard that you want people in your life to live by," Crystal said.

If you have given a good-faith effort to make it work—if you have clearly outlined what it will take for them to repair the relationship with you, if you have offered to go to counseling together, if at the end of the day you both look at the same situation and see vastly different things, then your life may be better without them, at least for now.

You don't have to write them off forever. You can say, "You know, I think we both need some time to ourselves. I'm still willing to do X, Y, and Z. Until those things are done, I can't be in your life."

Step 468: Recognize that family is like love—a huge pain in the ass that's worth it a million times over

The concept of family isn't even about what it means to be a human. It's about what it means to be a mammal. It is a deep and powerful and primal thing. It connects us to one another, to the past, and to the future in ways that cannot be replicated elsewhere. So when you feel the stress of obligations, or frustration with this or that person, remind yourself that whatever is bothering you is a small facet of something very large and valuable. You are, in the eyes of the world, small and insignificant. But to a select few people, you are big, and important, as they are to you. So seriously. Call your grandmother.

DISCUSSION QUESTIONS

1. What's the most powerful guilt trip your mom has ever laid on you? On a scale of one to crying, how guilty did you feel?

2. Who is the black sheep of your family? What, precisely, makes them the black sheep? Can someone please, please organize a Black Sheep of the World conference, complete with Creepy Uncle Muscle Car Show and Crazy Aunt Spirit Healing Seminars? Please, someone, do that.

3. Have you called your grandmother yet?

12. Conclusion

You are already way more of an adult than you think you are. Truly. Be good, be decent, be responsible, be kind. And don't forget to send thank-you notes.

Acknowledgments

Without the incredible advice, support, and feedback from the following people, this book would be maybe fourteen pages long, and no one would ever have seen it for self-evident reasons.

Thank you first and foremost to Meredith "Editor" Haggerty, for brilliant edits and kindly phrased suggestions and a *lot* of glorious .bmps, and Brandi Bowles, a literary agent who is fearsome in the very best way, and the second most talented editor ever, after Meredith.

Thank you to Bill Church and Michelle Maxwell, who were so very, very, endlessly patient with me, and Dana Borowitz and Adam Biren, for similar reasons.

Thank you, Ruth Liao, for the idea that became this book. Thank you to Jessica Maxwell, David McRaney, and Dana Haynes, for sage advice born of experience with this terrifying process.

Thanks to Will Bragg for so many super photos, and thank you to everyone at Grand Central Publishing, including but not limited to Carolyn Kurek in managing editorial, Giraud Lorber in production, flawless copy editor and ruthless mistake-finder Laura Jorstad, and Brigid Pearson in art.

Thank you Nancy Kaffer and Rachel Norman, for setting such wonderfully adult examples for me and for generous, near-constant feedback. Thank you to those willing to weigh in with edits, including Sarah Moore, Joce DeWitt, Megan Crandall, Andrew Ghetia, Shadra Beesley, Erin Sarin, and Elisabeth Frei.

Thank you to everyone who took the time to explain to me how to be an adult, including Bonnie Trumbull, Alan and Carol Kaplan, Jillian Kramer, Charles Price, Conrad Venti, Ron Kelemen, David Rosales, Carol Currie, Marissa Van Dyke, Karen Cristobal, Bharat Sharma, Susan Owre Gelberg, Jason Seibert, Shantrell Austin, Chris and Steve Hightower, Molly Woon, Stacey Dycus, Shane Rosenblatt, Brittni Lipscomb, Christine Lipscomb, Christina Olson, Tina Earhart, Sam Hart, Cindy Jackson, Sarah Von Bargen, Mary Henderson, Ben Lundin, Jared Mason-Gere, Laney Kibel, Crystal Mattox, Sheila Walty, Kyle Sexton, and Dana Michaels.

Thank you to the wise, if occasionally inebriated, patrons of *f*/Stop, plus Mark and Tiffany Bulgin at IKE Box and pretty much everyone in Salem. Thank you to all the wonderful and smart blog readers, who provided so many clever tips and suggestions that ended up in here. Thank you to my friends (most of whom were named above) for not only understanding why I was being a neurotic hermit but also for loving me anyway when I emerged.

Finally, thank you most of all to Mom, Dad, Olivia, Elizabeth, and Dave.

Index

About the Author

KELLY WILLIAMS BROWN is an award-winning features reporter and columnist. She is originally from Louisiana, now lives in Oregon, and is sometimes, but not always, an adult.